NEW OLD WAY

Also by Frank Forencich:

Exuberant Animal
Beautiful Practice
The Art is Long

NEW OLD WAY

ANCESTRAL HEALTH AND SAPIENCE FOR THE MODERN WORLD

FRANK FORENCICH

EXUBERANT ANIMAL®

New Old Way is a work of creative nonfiction, philosophy
and commentary. References, links, reading list and more
are available at www.newoldway.earth

To Mom.

How I wish we could dig into this together.

CONTENTS

The most pervasive fallacy of philosophic thinking is the neglect of context.

—John Dewey (1859-1952)

When your life support system is threatened, all other problems fit inside that problem.

—Naomi Klein

PREFACE

They told me to just get over it. They told me I was being too idealistic and that I should just move on. It was time to sober up, knuckle under, and get with the program.

But no matter how hard I tried, I just couldn't shrug it off. In my lifetime, my home, the Santa Clara Valley of central California, went from being a rural paradise and one of the most productive agricultural regions on Earth to a hyperactive, unaffordable spasm of concrete, noise, development, and technological capitalism. Historians have written that prior to the nineteenth century, central California was the "Serengeti of North America," a lush, wild land packed with animals. Wild salmon swam in the rivers, birds filled the sky, and grizzly bears prowled the hills. It was a precious, glorious habitat.

But in the span of just a few decades, the plants and animals of my youth were obliterated by miles of freeways, condos, shopping malls, and technological fortresses. Farms and orchards disappeared, their bounty replaced by trucks and aircraft that would bring our food from the farthest corners of the world. But it was all for the best, they said. It meant jobs and money and investment and real estate profit. Pave paradise, put up a parking lot, and get rich.

Well, I never did get over it. The experience traumatized my body and my spirit, gnawing on my life like a chronic illness. Later, I discovered it wasn't just the valley of my childhood that was under assault. Everywhere I went, I saw the same disrespect for the natural world and the same tired excuses of why it had to be this way.

Destruction of habitat was simply a side effect of doing what had to be done, they said. It was basic economics; the invisible hand was going to make everything better—just wait and see. The land and animals are there for our use, our pleasure, and our profit, nothing else. And if something went wrong, well, we could just go somewhere else. So get over it.

But my body and my brain remained unconvinced. In the years that followed, I became an outdoor athlete and developed a powerful interest in health, but even in that world the conventional explanations didn't ring true. Doctors told me my body was just a stand-alone organism, a hairy bag of water that wasn't connected to the world in any significant way. I was just a biochemical machine, a collection of molecules, organized by DNA. Health was nothing more than a set of numbers and lab results. If something went wrong, my only option was to visit a medical technologist who would repair my broken mechanism.

But I never got over that explanation either. By the time I was an adult, I was a man without a functional story, lost in an alien world I just couldn't accept. And to make matters worse, I felt completely alone.

Driven by equal measures curiosity, discontent, and rebellion, I went on an educational binge. I ignored advanced degrees and sensible career moves in favor of learning for its own sake. Better answers had to be out there. I camped out in the library for weeks at a time, drinking in ideas like water in the desert. I feasted in bookstores and traveled to distant cities for workshops and trainings for no other reason than to advance my interest.

By conventional measures, my effort was an utter waste of time, and I was counseled once again to get over it. But in the process, I discovered that I wasn't alone after all. I found that there were a lot of other people out there who couldn't get over the conventional explanations either: people who loved the natural world and feared its destruction, people who saw unity between their bodies and habitat, people who were willing to risk their time and their lives to create new forms of culture based on something more honorable than profit. I discovered writers, teachers, professors, and trainers who lived by the belief that there had to be a better way. These people pulled me out of my loneliness and into a world of action and resolve.

This book is dedicated to all those people who just couldn't get over it. I hope they never do.

INTRODUCTION

You can cut all the flowers but you cannot keep spring from coming.

—Pablo Neruda

Most of us like to think we're smart. We like to think we're highly intelligent people and, even better, members of a highly intelligent species, *Homo sapiens,* "the wise animal." We celebrate our cleverness at every opportunity and speculate about even more audacious acts of intelligence yet to come. We look down on the other animals and pity them for their limited cognitive capacity. Surely they must long to be like us, the greatest species in the history of life on Earth.

But we're wrong about all of this. In fact, we are deeply irrational animals. Research in cognitive science and behavioral economics consistently shows we're easily swayed by suggestion, hormones, culture, placebos, and nocebos. We like to think we make well-reasoned, calculated decisions about what to do in our lives, but mostly we act on impulse and out of habit. We delude ourselves in things both great and small.

Our ancient, aboriginal bodies are running the show, but from their Paleolithic perspective, the world remains a wild and dangerous place. Carnivores lurk in the shadows, and safety is illusive. Life is mysterious and wonderful, but it's also unpredictable and insecure. We do what we can to survive, but we're always on alert for omens that will tell us about the future. And when times get really hard, we turn to hope to get us through.

In modern conversations about the state of the planet, hope has become a surprisingly controversial topic, especially in the circle some now call the "doomosphere." A small but growing community of environmental realists is urging us to see the future for what it is, without illusion or distortion. These authors decry our widespread addiction to "hopium," a psychological crutch that leads us into delusion, denial, and passivity.[1]

As the doomsters see it, the problem with hope is that it's often used as a substitute for action. Hopium seduces us and lets us get away with life and business as usual. When we're under its influence, our sense of urgency fades and we lapse into habit, convention, and reliance on the status quo. As they see it, the solution is to give up hope entirely and get to work creating a functional future. Hope is for dreamers, not for people who are intent on making a difference.

The doomists make a good point, but I fear they go too far. The call for realism is vital and welcome, but to suggest that people give up hope is a gigantic, almost unimaginable ask. For most of us, hope is essential to survival and even sanity. As far as we know, the drive for hope is a human universal, common to every people that has ever lived. And not surprisingly, a substantial body of research shows that hope is a powerful force in health and recovery from illness. Asking people to give up hope is tantamount to asking them to give up on life itself.

But the doomists are right about one thing. For many, especially those of us under the influence of mass marketing and consumer culture, hopium is a narcotic that sets us up for denial and inaction. Hoping, after all, is so much easier than doing. And in this sense, hope actually diminishes our prospects for a functional future. Most notably, hope enables our inaction on climate change, a cultural passivity that writer Kim Stanley Robinson has described as "the great dithering." We aren't actually doing anything to remedy our situation, but we're hopeful that things will be better, so we relax. In this sense, wishing is worse than nothing. If all we do is hope, there isn't going to be much hope for any of us.

This is not to say we should simply give up. Without question, hard times are ahead. Our environmental and social future looks dark, and we're going to need every tool, skill, and orientation we can lay our hands on. The trick is to make our hope relevant and meaningful. That means coupling it with action, engagement, and courage. Instead of using hope as a substitute for action, we can use it to make our efforts stronger. Act first, redouble our efforts, and then at the end of the day, hope for success and a better tomorrow.

This book won't give you hope in the conventional sense. It's not written to bolster your confidence in a utopian future or to put a glossy layer on a looming planetary catastrophe. Rather, it's a call for a more sophisticated, sapient kind of hope, a hope based on seeing clearly and acting with resolve. The idea is to look for hope in the most vital and powerful places, especially the incredible adaptability of our bodies, the resilience of the biosphere, and our endless capacity for cultural creativity. When we couple this kind of hope with radical realism and the courage to face what we're doing to this beautiful planet, we put ourselves in a position to lead healthier, more meaningful lives. Couple hope with action, and we've got a fighting chance to do some good.

PREDICAMENT

> The greater the degree of match between an organism's constitution and its environment, the more likely the organism is to thrive... The greater the degree of mismatch between environment and design, the greater the cost.

—Peter Gluckman and Mark Hanson
Mismatch: Why Our World No Longer Fits Our Bodies

Imagine you're traveling through space on some fantastic starship, hurtling across the galaxy at warp speed. The adventure is thrilling, but you're a long way from your home planet, and you miss it almost every day. In your spare moments, you gaze at the stars and daydream about the summer days of your childhood. You long for the carefree afternoons in the outdoors, playing in the grass, swimming in the lake, climbing trees, and digging in the dirt. You loved your world, and it loved you back.

But suddenly, your daydreams are interrupted as the navigator calls for a stop and your captain pulls the ship into orbit around an unfamiliar blue–green planet. According to the ship's database, it's a technologically advanced world, powered by fossil fuels and managed by vast networks of computers. The dominant lifestyle is based largely on corporate capitalism and commerce. The inhabitants are reportedly highly stressed, and many are suffering from a wide range of debilitating lifestyle diseases. Social, political, and environmental systems are reported to be stretched to the limit, and some are on the verge of collapse.

The captain barks his orders. You and a small team are instructed to visit the planet's surface and do an assessment. The transporter beam hums into action, and suddenly you're standing on a street corner in a major city, surrounded by strangers. The noise is overwhelming, the air is hot and noxious, and the streets are packed with cars, trucks, and buses. People scurry about, heads down, looking at phones, oblivious to their surroundings. Taking in the scene, your body rebels and withdraws. You've been briefed on conditions, but nothing can prepare you for the feeling of being so completely out of sync with this world. The conditions strike you as frantic, exhausting, and distinctly unhealthy. Your body longs for home.

WELCOME TO OUR ALIEN ENVIRONMENT

This is not sci-fi. This is our predicament, our here-and-now reality. We haven't traveled across the vast reaches of space to get here, but the effect is the same. Our ancient bodies are struggling to adapt—in an evolutionary blink of an eye—to some radically novel conditions. In historical terms, our collision with the modern world has been almost instantaneous. If our ancestors had traveled forward in time to today's world, they'd be mystified and shocked by the magnitude of the change.

This is the problem of mismatch, sometimes called "the evolutionary discordance hypothesis." Far more than a scientific curiosity, it's one of the most pressing problems of our age. All of us are struggling to align our bodies, minds, and spirits with a world that looks and feels increasingly alien.

WIRED FOR ANOTHER WORLD

The story begins deep in prehistory. Over the course of thousands of generations, every detail of our anatomy, physiology, and psychology has been sculpted for survival and reproductive success in wild, natural, outdoor environments. Our skeletal, muscular, circulatory, nervous, and hormonal systems are the way they are because they enhanced our survival prospects in natural, ancestral habitats. Every cell, organ, feedback loop, and mental inclination has been shaped by our vast experience as hunters, gatherers, and scavengers. You are here today because your body is good at surviving in ancestral conditions.

In contrast, our bodies are almost entirely unprepared for a world of cars, couches, computers, and concrete. We're just not suited for a life of sedentary work, chronic stress, technological acceleration, and looming planetary catastrophe. Our normal, evolutionary impulses clash with modern reality, setting us up for stress, addictions, and other dysfunctions. In essence, we are animals attempting to live outside our normal ecological range. We're primates incarcerated in zoos, wild orcas in concrete swimming pools, dogs left indoors for days and weeks on end. We're round, hunter–gatherer pegs trying to fit into square, industrial–technological holes. If we try really hard, we can force the pegs to fit, but damage is inevitable. This is the paradox of our time: we are misfits in a world of our own creation.

CONTEXT MATTERS

In the modern, Western world, we attempt to solve our problems by studying things in isolation. We put objects, animals, and people on the exam table and look for defective mechanisms and flawed components. But when dealing with living organisms, context is vital, a fact vividly illustrated in Bruce Alexander's legendary "rat park" studies. As a young researcher in the 1970s, Alexander was struck by the fact that most studies of addiction were carried out on isolated rodents in cages. Cocaine and other substances were introduced, and in fact, many animals became addicted.

But Alexander objected that the rats were living in an abnormal environment and the results could not be trusted. To test his idea, he built an enriched environment in his laboratory, complete with everything a rodent might desire: natural features, room to move and companions to play with. When he later introduced the "addictive substances," few of the animals became addicted. It turns out they had better things to do with their time.

As every biologist knows, there's a big difference between results obtained by studying organisms *in vitro* (Latin for "within the glass") and those obtained *in vivo* (Latin for "within the living"). Just because an organism behaves a certain way in a cage, flask, or Petri dish doesn't mean those results will be borne out in the real world. That's why biologists say *in vivo veritas* ("in a living thing there is truth"), a play on *in vino veritas* ("in wine there is truth").

Alexander's work is highly suggestive and consistent with our own experience. Of course our bodies behave differently in various environments. Of course there are health and behavior consequences when we're forced to live outside our normal evolutionary range. Just ask any zoo keeper. Or even closer to home, ask any dog owner. Force your pet to live in isolation for a few weeks and you'll see some serious health and behavioral problems. There's nothing wrong with your dog–the problem is with his world. The same principle holds true for all creatures, including us.

WE ARE THE 99

Modern people do have some awareness of our predicament. People sometimes joke about our ancestral heritage and it's not unusual to hear people talk about "cavemen with cell phones" and "hunter-gatherers in the shopping mall." But few of us really grasp the depth of the contrast and the radical speed with which we've entered this new reality. Specifically, we fail to comprehend the time scales of human evolution and what they tell us about who we really are.

The details are complex, but the big picture is clear. Our hominid history stretches back several million years, and during the vast, overwhelming majority of that time, we've lived as hunters, gatherers, and scavengers in wild, outdoor environments. In comparison, civilization is only a few thousand years old at best. In other words, 99 percent of our history is premodern.

This brings the true nature of our predicament into sharp focus. For 99 percent of human history, we lived in intimate contact with wild, outdoor nature. We occasionally found crude shelter, but even then, we were exposed to the forces of heat, cold, wind, rain, and sun. We lived in small tribal bands and walked long distances almost every day, occasionally running or sprinting. During this time, human experience was mediated entirely by our bodily senses, supplemented by story and song. Every touch of skin, hand, or bare feet put us in direct contact with the natural world. We ate local foods, and hunted or gathered by hand. We lived a participatory consciousness and saw ourselves as part of a larger whole, an animated, living cosmos.

THE NEW ABNORMAL

In short, the premodern period of human life is the norm, our vital touchstone for the human experience. But today this state has been eclipsed by a new, abnormal 1 percent. To put it another way, abnormality has become the new normal. It's no wonder our bodies and minds are so confused.

In his book *Tribe: On Homecoming and Belonging*, Sebastian Junger sums up our predicament perfectly:

> …humans have dragged a body with a long hominid history into an overfed, malnourished, sedentary, sunlight-deficient, sleep-deprived, competitive, inequitable, and socially-isolating environment with dire consequences.

Compounding our problem is our collective amnesia. We've

forgotten how to be normal, which is to say we've forgotten how to be true to our bodies and our evolutionary heritage. We're so consumed with the urgencies of the modern world that we're in grave danger of losing contact with the experiences, skills and ideas that make us human, whole and healthy. As some observers have put it, we're suffering from a "Paleo-deficit disorder."[2]

This calls for a review of what's truly normal for the human species:

Nature is normal. Wild is normal. Vagility, the ability to roam freely over the land, is normal. Hunting, gathering, and scavenging in natural habitat is normal. Real food, derived directly from the earth and eaten with others, is normal. Robust physicality is normal.

An integrated, participatory world view is normal. Biophilia—the innate tendency to affiliate with life—is normal. Small tribal bands with personal, face-to-face contact are normal. Social equality is normal. Poetry, song, and dance are normal.

Coherent sensory experience based on actual, on-the-ground reality is normal. Circadian and seasonal rhythm, experienced in the body, is normal. Identification with habitat and tribe is normal. Continuity between generations is normal.

Experiential, place-based education is normal. Temporal affluence—the sense of having plenty of time to live—is normal. And, with the exception of occasional infections or physical injury, robust health is normal.

In contrast, today's world exposes us to an onslaught of abnormality:

Sedentary occupations and indoor living are abnormal. Agriculture, especially its intensive modern form, is abnormal. Food products and edible, food-like substances are abnormal. Artificial light and noise are abnormal.

The relentless quest for social status is abnormal. Extreme social inequality and hierarchy are abnormal. Ambition and selfishness are abnormal. Anthropocentrism and the belief in human supremacy are abnormal.

Neck-up, cognitive education is abnormal. Literacy, reading, and measurement are abnormal. Linear, mechanical time is abnormal. Work and busyness are abnormal. Objective, nonparticipatory consciousness is abnormal.

Money-based relationships, finance, and economics are abnormal. Wealth, affluence, and poverty are abnormal. Consumer goods, advertising, and mass media are abnormal.

Temporal poverty and stress are abnormal. Computer technology, artificial intelligence, robotics, and big data are abnormal. Movies, videos, and social media are abnormal. Cars, air travel, and chairs are abnormal.

In short, almost nothing we do in a typical day is historically normal. Your house, your car, your phone, your job, your workplace, most of your social relationships, your food, your clothing, your education, your city, your favorite restaurant, and your medical care are all outside the range of original human experience. In fact, it's becoming increasingly difficult to find *any* experience, environment, or circumstance in the modern world that's consistent with our ancestral heritage. We've forgotten how to be physical, how to inhabit our habitat, and how to talk to one another. Unless you live a life of vigorous outdoor physicality or are somehow educated in the details of human history, you simply don't know normal. It's no wonder so many of us are feeling disintegrated.

We're challenged from two directions simultaneously. In *The Secret Life of Your Microbiome*, Susan Prescott and Alan Logan describe the challenge of the alien environment as a "dual burden." That is, we're suffering from increased adverse exposures, coupled with the loss of health-promoting experiences and relationships. In other words, too much pollution, noise, toxins, artificial food, stress, and cognitive overload, combined with the absence of vigorous outdoor movement, contact with natural habitat, coherent tribal experience, and quiet time for reflection. Too much of the bad stuff and not enough of the good.

To make matters worse, we even go so far as to educate ourselves in abnormality. We train our children and employees to sit still for hours at a time, to live indoors, to master entire bodies of abstract, symbolic thought, and now, to master the digital devices of our age. Today, most of our schools and universities function as little more than academies for abnormality. Then, once we reach adult-hood, we're expected to thrive under these alien conditions. Our workdays and weeks have no relationship to our ancestral heritage, natural light, seasons, our need for sleep, or the state of our bodies. We expect one another to work almost constantly and above all, to produce. But instead of fighting back—as any healthy, wild animal would—we double down on modern life. Abnormality, many of us have come to believe, is what sustains us.

Of course, it's important to remember that abnormality doesn't necessarily make something bad, dangerous, or unhealthy. In fact, many abnormal features of our modern world inspire us to curiosity and creativity. Used wisely and modestly, some of these things can extend our health, our happiness, and our engagement with life. Scientific instruments extend the range of human senses and give us a sense of awe, modern medicine saves us from infection, and literacy gives us incredible new insights into our world and one another. But when the abnormality becomes extreme, we lose contact with our original nature and suffer stress, illness, and disintegration. No amount of medical care, pharmaceuticals, or therapy can make up for the fact that we're no longer in touch with our ancestral heritage.

FROGS IN HOT WATER

If we had suddenly beamed our ancestral bodies into the modern world, the sheer abnormality of our predicament would be glaringly obvious to all of us. We'd be variously delighted and repulsed by what we'd see each day, but we'd be completely aware of the mismatch; the contrast between our physical nature and the new environment would be absolutely clear. But for most of us living in the modern world, the full extent of our predicament is largely invisible. The problem, ironically enough, is that we're really good at adapting.

This is the paradox of neuroplasticity. Our flexible, dynamic nervous systems give us the ability to adjust to almost any environment on Earth, and in every moment of every day, the synapses and circuits of our brains are rearranging and remodeling themselves to fit conditions. Neuroplasticity is constantly at work, sculpting our bodies and our behavior to whatever reality we inhabit, whether it be a grassland in East Africa or an office tower in Hong Kong.

It's an astonishing and immensely valuable process, but it's essential to understand that a plastic nervous system is both a blessing *and* a curse. It facilitates adaptation and helps us survive, but it also allows us to adjust to conditions that are suboptimal for health and happiness. Like frogs in rapidly warming water, we can get used to almost anything, including the body and spirit-hostile features of the modern world. Over time, even highly alien environments begin to feel familiar and normal. Children who grow up in a world of cars, couches, computers, and concrete may even find it hard to imagine any other reality.

In the real world, frogs are smart enough to jump out of water that gets uncomfortably warm, but it remains to be seen if we will do likewise. The problem is that we adapt by small, barely perceptible increments. First we get used to wearing clothes and shoes. Then we adapt to sitting for long hours at a desk, driving around in cars, then flying in airplanes. We adjust to noise and electronics. We adapt to a market economy that is constantly nagging us to buy things. We get used to eating food products, worrying about money, working almost constantly, and getting by without much sleep. And next thing you know, we're feeling anxious, depressed, and maybe even diseased, wondering how we got to be in such a state.

This is the shadow side of neuroplasticity. Over time, the abnormal begins to feel normal, and even worse, the normal begins to feel abnormal. As modern people adapt to a world of indoor climate control, easy food, mechanical transport, and electronic communication, our historically normal world of wild, outdoor living begins to feel increasingly alien. As our adaptation deepens, we're less likely to engage in the vigorous, outdoor behaviors that would promote our health and keep us sane. This is a recipe for disaster.

A WORLD OF WOUNDS

It may well be that more and more of what people bring before doctors and therapists for treatment—agonies of body and spirit—are symptoms of the biospheric emergency registering at the most intimate levels of life. The Earth hurts, and we hurt with it.

—Theodore Roszak
The Voice of the Earth

Given our almost instantaneous transition from ancestral to modern conditions, it comes as little surprise to find that we've inflicted some serious damage to the world and each other. Evolution simply hasn't prepared us for a world of fossil-fueled transport, powerful machinery, global commerce, computers, fragmented cultures, and social media. Our brains and nervous systems are made for hunting and gathering in wild habitats, not for managing hyper-complex environmental and social systems on a planetary scale. As misfits, it's no wonder we often behave in ways that are clumsy, inept, greedy, and sometimes violent. We are, as the saying goes, "just smart enough to be dangerous." We're chimps in Earth's china shop, wreaking havoc at almost every turn.

THE EARTH HURTS

The facts of environmental destruction are beyond dispute. Species are going extinct in record numbers and habitat is disappearing around the world. Climate change is not only real; it's far more urgent than scientists first realized. Wildfires are breaking out in Greenland, giant icebergs are calving off Antarctica,[3] permafrost is melting in Alaska, and the Himalayas are literally turning black. Major cities, including Sao Paulo, Cairo, Beijing, and London are running out of water, and according to some projections, global demand for fresh water will exceed supply by 40 percent in 2030.[4]

As Naomi Klein put it, "all the alarms in the house are going off." In 1992, an influential group of scientists signed the "World Scientists' Warning to Humanity," advising that "human beings and the natural world are on a collision course." In 2017, the call was updated, warning that "a great change in our stewardship of the Earth and the life on it is required, if vast human misery is to be avoided."

One particularly dire assessment appeared in New York Magazine in July 2017. In "The Uninhabitable Earth," author David Wallace-Wells delivered a vivid, apocalyptic prognosis:

> …absent a significant adjustment to how billions of humans conduct their lives, parts of the Earth will likely become close to uninhabitable, and other parts horrifically inhospitable, as soon as the end of this century.

He concluded with this grim warning: "no matter how well-informed you are, you are surely not alarmed enough."

Also in July 2017, the New York Times warned that the "Era of 'Biological Annihilation' Is Underway." The report called the current decline in animal populations a "global epidemic" and part of the "ongoing sixth mass extinction." According to the authors, "the problems we have with biodiversity are much greater than commonly thought" and "an irreversible era of mass extinction is underway." They went on to describe "a massive anthropogenic erosion of biodiversity and of the ecosystem services essential to civilization." Lead author Dr. Paul Ehrlich put it bluntly: "We're toxifying the entire planet."

While much of the damage is obvious, some of the most grievous wounds are invisible to the naked eye. For example, we are now in the process of drastically altering the microbial world on a planetary scale, a condition sometimes described as *dysbiosis*. Both inside and outside the human body, beneficial bacterial species are being displaced by other, less-friendly forms. Modern practices of chemically intensive agriculture and the widespread use of antibiotics are obvious contributors, but individual behaviors also play a role. As people alter their personal bacterial profiles with artificial foods, pharmaceuticals, antibiotics, antibacterial cleaning products, and stress, the effects inevitably ripple throughout the microbial sphere. In turn, these changes drive the planetary burden of disease. Individual microbiomes do not exist in isolation; what happens inside the body doesn't stay inside the body.

OUR BODIES HURT

Not surprisingly, our ecological crisis is reflected in the state of our bodies. In fact, we might well consider the human body to be the canary in the coal mine of the modern world. To be sure, many affluent people now enjoy long, productive lives of robust health, but at the same time, many of us have fallen into a quagmire of illness and lifestyle disease, the so-called "diseases of civilization." The list is familiar: obesity, diabetes, heart disease, chronic respiratory diseases, some cancers, and nervous system and mental health disorders.

The World Health Organization reports that these noncommunicable diseases kill forty million people each year, equivalent to 70 percent of all deaths globally. At the same time, a substantial number of us are in pain, either physical or spiritual, or more likely both. According to a 2011 report from the Institute of Medicine, "about 100 million adult Americans experience chronic pain..." The abuse of painkillers now claims the lives of more Americans than heroin and cocaine combined. Since 2000, more than three hundred thousand Americans have lost their lives to opioid overdoses. [5,6,7]

OUR COMMUNITIES HURT

Our communities are also hurting. Some of us are lucky enough to have a coherent home life and work setting, but for many, social relationships are tenuous at best. Families break apart, companies are in constant flux, and many of us are struggling for economic survival. At the same time, social discrimination and inequality add to the stress. Most of us have heard some variation on the statistic that "the top 1 percent own as much wealth as the bottom 99 percent." This kind of inequality is bad enough on its face, but it also has a powerful effect on the state of our health. Epidemiologist Michael Marmot has compiled thirty years of evidence on the effect of social rank and concluded that "health follows a social gradient." That is, social inequalities are powerful determinants of human health: the greater the wealth gap, the greater the health gap.

When our communities fail to function, we fall out of contact with one another and into one of the great paradoxes of our age: in a world of more than seven billion people, many of us report feeling isolated and lonely. Many social scientists now consider loneliness to be a genuine threat to public health, and some have declared it to be "the new smoking." [8]

At the same time, modern society is becoming increasingly polarized. Our political rhetoric is inflamed, and everyone seems to be choosing up sides and spoiling for a fight. Trust is eroding, fear is widespread, and security firms are going good business. Wealthy survivalists, determined to ride out the chaos, are building bunkers in remote areas.

In the US, polling data from the marketing firm Edelman suggests that public trust in government, media, and businesses has collapsed to crisis point.[9] "The public's confidence in the traditional structures of American leadership is now fully undermined and has been replaced with a strong sense of fear, uncertainty and disillusionment." Taken together, this all adds up to what *New York Times* columnist David Brooks calls the "social trust apocalypse." If people can't trust one another, how is a community supposed to function?[10]

OUR SPIRITS HURT

Naturally, our physical and social angst is reflected in a crisis of the human spirit. We see it in rising rates of addiction, not just to drugs and alcohol but also to food, work, exercise, sex, gambling, outrage, and interpersonal drama. In *The Globalization of Addiction: A Study in the Poverty of the Spirit*, Bruce Alexander writes that "the prevalence of addiction is increasing around the world." As he sees it, the root cause is *dislocation*, the loss of contact with traditional anchors such as body, habitat, and tribe. Alexander believes that "addictions are the unavoidable by-products of modernity itself."

Not surprisingly, depression is epidemic. According to 2017 estimates from the World Health Organization, depression is *the* leading cause of ill health and disability worldwide. More than three hundred million people are now living with depression, an increase of more than 18 percent between 2005 and 2015.[11] Antidepressants are among the most-prescribed types of medications in the United States.[12, 13, 14] A 2018 report from the Centers for Disease Control and Prevention found that suicide rates have increased in nearly every state over the last two decades.[15] Taken together, this is nothing less than a crisis of the human spirit.

The demands of the present are overwhelming enough, but we're also stressed by the prospect of a hugely uncertain future. Our minds and spirits reel at the prospect of radical acceleration, a dynamic reflected in the ubiquitous "hockey stick" graph of climate change, population growth, and environmental disruption. Every system we depend on is undergoing an explosion of change, and technological innovation is growing faster than we can control or comprehend. In essence, we're suffering from "future shock," a term coined in the 1970 book by futurists Alvin and Heidi Toffler. Defined as "too much change in too short a period of time," it's a spot-on description of our predicament. Many of us suspect that our modern world in its current form isn't even close to being sustainable. Something has to give.

IDENTITY CRISIS

It would be one thing if we had a map or a guidebook to help us through this predicament, but no such thing exists. We've arrived in the modern world in the blink of an eye, and we're groping to find our way. As a consequence, we're experiencing a widespread ambivalence about who we are and where we're going. We love the obvious benefits of modernity: the cheap food, hot showers, books, fantastic tools, and for some, good medical care. But we're also becoming extremely doubtful that our system is even viable. And what good is it to have amazing technology and possessions if you have to destroy your future to get them?

We're also hearing a new kind of misanthropy, a distinctly negative judgment not of people, but of our very species. Many of us are starting to wonder if humans are even capable of crafting a sustainable, harmonious relationship with the planet. We see ourselves as a deeply flawed animal, maybe even an evolutionary dead end. We hear the self-loathing in whispered conversations: "We're a planetary pathogen"; "We are the asteroid" and "a cancer on the Earth." Some of us have even begun shifting our allegiances over to the biosphere. As fans of the underdog Earth, we root for her survival, even if it means the demise of us. Even our self-declared name, *Homo sapiens*, begins to sound like a bad joke.

REALITY CHECK

So the time has come for an honest accounting of where we are and where we're going. In conventional green writing, the call to action usually goes like this: "Unless we step up right now and take serious action, the climate/biosphere/social world is going to take a big hit, and everyone is going to suffer." Catastrophe is imminent, but can be averted with the right legislation, better candidates, technological improvements, and education. So let's start organizing and keep disaster at bay.

We try to be hopeful. We want to be optimistic about the future, so we defend ourselves against the bad news. We resist "gloom and doom" predictions and insist that things will ultimately turn out for the best. But we're fooling ourselves. In fact, the catastrophe is here, now.[16] Sea levels are rising, now. Permafrost is melting, now. Habitat is disappearing, now.[17] These are not projections; they are accurate descriptions of the state of our world.

Sadly, denial is widespread, and movement toward a functional future is excruciatingly slow. Even more challenging, the trends that are making our planet uninhabitable have been building over the course of hundreds, even thousands of years. The ship of ecological destruction is driven by powerful inertia and will not be easily turned in the time required. Ecological consciousness is growing in some quarters but remains politically weak. Climate change, the biggest threat to human welfare on the planet, barely even registers on our cultural radar. As Al Gore put it some twenty years ago: "The maximum that is politically feasible, even the maximum that is politically imaginable, still falls short of the minimum that is scientifically and ecologically necessary." And this was *before* Donald Trump, Scott Pruitt, and Ryan Zinke.

Over the next several decades, the following events will almost certainly come to pass:

Human population will continue to increase and along with it, destructive impacts to land, atmosphere, and fresh water. Urban development, deforestation, and intensive agriculture will continue.

Climate will continue to warm, and sea level will rise will be measured not in inches, but in feet.[18] Extreme weather, catastrophic storms, and wildfires will become increasingly common. Coastal aquifers will be poisoned by salt water, and major cities will have to be abandoned. Hundreds of millions of people will be displaced and mass migration will become a fact of life. Entire nation–states may become destabilized.[19]

Biodiversity will continue to decline, leading to weaker, less robust ecosystems that are susceptible to crashes. Micro-plastics, endocrine disruptors, and pesticides will continue to infect our land, our water, and our bodies.

Corporate giants will continue to tyrannize society and suck the life out of the public sector. The gap between rich and poor will probably grow, and health will remain unequal. Social and economic stress will continue to wreak havoc on the human body and spirit. Depression, anxiety, and loneliness will remain serious concerns as people struggle to adapt to a polarized and socially disconnected world.

And yet, in spite of it all, public interest in environmental preservation and social justice will remain modest. Opinion polls consistently show that voters are primarily concerned about the economy and health care, with climate change and habitat destruction far down the list. Barring a truly cataclysmic event, this is unlikely to change. As the saying goes, "the climate is changing faster than we are."

This accounting may well sound bleak, but this is not defeatism. It's a sober reading of current events and trajectories that will shape our lives for generations. Our problems are deeply systemic, and it would be foolish to pin our hopes on a quick fix. The pain, destruction, dilemmas, and frustrations of our age are what we have to work with. As artists and activists, this is our raw material. We can choose to wish it away, or we can get to work.

UNEXPLORED TERRITORY

Throughout history, humans have looked to culture to guide them through the ambiguities of life. For hunter–gatherers and early agriculturalists alike, culture was a vital map for survival and meaning. It told us how to find and prepare food, manage our relationships, and feel at home in the universe. Mother Culture held the oral tradition—the essential, practical knowledge that kept people alive. She told people where to hunt, how to navigate, and what kind of plants to use for cooking, medicine, and clothing. Tribes with a strong, coherent culture were more likely to succeed, so it's no surprise to see our deep-seated and generally unquestioned inclination: when times are hard, stay close to the familiar customs, ideas, and rituals of Mother Culture.

This reflex worked well enough for tens of thousands of years, but what happens when a culture itself presents a threat to our survival? What happens when the values embedded in Mother Culture contribute to the destruction of the Earth and divisions among people? What happens when an aggressive, imperialist, profit-driven culture wreaks havoc on the entire planet? Suddenly, we're faced with a profoundly troubling paradox: In today's world, Mother Culture is both a provider *and* a threat to our future. She gives us much of what we need, but many of her ideas, values, and institutions facilitate the destruction of our world.

Of course, many of us look the other way. Despite the evidence of a culture-driven catastrophe, we persist in adhering to the familiar and the comfortable. Yes, the biological and social systems that sustain us are collapsing, but surely Mother Culture will fix everything, as she always has. So we retreat to familiar havens of the shopping mall, the sporting venue, the TV, and the digital device. Likewise, many of us reflexively vote for candidates who promise to return us to the familiar world of Mother Culture. Mom, we believe, will surely save us in the end.

But we're wrong. Culture-as-usual isn't going to save our lifeboat. Today's crisis demands a radical shift in the very fabric of our relationship with the world and life itself. Obviously, we need research, tools, data and targeted responses to the problems of our day. We need engineering solutions, policy solutions and regulatory solutions. But our challenge is deeply systemic, relational, cultural and yes, spiritual. Technical solutions and greater efficiencies, no matter how perfectly executed, are not enough. Big data, artificial intelligence, biohacking, and geoengineering aren't going to save us. Scientific research will always be valuable and welcome, but it is nowhere near sufficient to transform our lives or our future.

At the core, our problem is one of attitude, values, and relationship. There's something fundamentally wrong with our stance in the world. As the *Adbusters Field Guide* put it, "The crisis of our age is not just about depleted resources and the buildup of pollutants in the biosphere. It's also a matter of depleted imaginations and the buildup of dysfunctional ideas in the collective consciousness of our time." Or, as the medical journal The Lancet put it in their flagship issue on planetary health: "Achieving planetary health will require a renaissance in how we define our place in the world."

Our consciousness and our culture need to change at a fundamental level. Even if we somehow managed to stop dumping carbon into the atmosphere this instant, our problem would remain. Even if we stopped population growth and habitat destruction, and went all in on green energy and sustainable agriculture, our problem would still be with us. The details of policy and legislation are obviously important, but they also distract us from the real matter at hand: our values and beliefs about our place in the world.

At first glance, it might seem strange to propose relational and spiritual solutions to biological and ecological problems. After all, climate change and habitat destruction have physical causes and must have physical, policy, and legislative solutions. But human impact, physical as it is, has roots in behavior, which in turn has roots in the human mind, values, and spirit. We act upon the world by and through our relationship to it. If our spirit is adversarial, controlling, selfish, and ignorant, we get one result. If our spirit is attentive, humble, respectful, and sapient, we get another.

Call it what you will—spirit, attitude, perspective, mind—it's our relationship to life that will ultimately make the difference. If we get this wrong, we'll be looking at a future that's nasty, brutish, and short. But if we get it right, we may have a fighting chance.

HOW TO LIVE?

Historically, our problems with mismatch and planetary-scale catastrophe are unprecedented, so it comes as no surprise that Mother Culture provides very little guidance on how to navigate our predicament. We simply have no curriculum for adapting our ancient bodies to the realities of the modern, alien environment. We have no curriculum for planetary activism or social transformation. We teach the fundamentals of government and civics, but these courses are mostly informational. Likewise, we have no curriculum for exploring the human–habitat relationship. We teach courses in natural history and the basic facts about plant and animal life, but rarely do we explore the fundamental relationship between people and the natural world. Almost never do we teach the participatory world-view of native cultures or alternatives to human supremacy. In short, most of what we call "education" is not particularly relevant to the most pressing problems of our day.

It's no wonder so many of us are stressed, anxious, and confused. With no curriculum to guide us, we are unprepared to deal with the most basic questions about our place and path in the world: How do we balance the demands of daily life with the urgencies of a world in crisis? What philosophies and attitudes should we adopt? Should we adapt and get along, or should we fight like hell? What's the appropriate emotional response to our predicament? Anger and hostility? Grief, despair, and depression? Radicalism or acceptance?

And practically speaking, what are our professions and careers all about? Are they making the world a better place, or are they throwing gasoline on the fire of a burning planet? Should we quit our day jobs? Sell the car? Have kids? Go vegan? Retreat to the mountains? Go to law school? Fight from within or from the outside? Suddenly, everything is up for grabs.

WELCOME TO THE NEW OLD WAY

Given the sheer depth and wickedness of our predicament, you might suppose that we'd be having some serious conversation about wisdom right now. After all, it's right there in our name, *Homo sapiens.* But sadly, no such thing is happening. Wisdom seems to have fallen off our cultural radar in recent decades and has almost entirely disappeared from casual conversation. For the ancient Greeks, philosophy was literally the love of wisdom (philo-sophia), and the most revered of all the disciplines, but today a look through Google's Ngram viewer (which tracks the use of various words and phrases in print over time) shows a declining incidence of the word *sapience.* From a peak in 1830, we see a steady decline to a low point around

1990—and there's a similar trend in the use of the word *wisdom*.

We see a similar void in the world of politics. Given the obvious importance of good judgment in the conduct of human affairs, we might expect that our major political platforms would refer to wisdom or sapience in some explicit way, but a look at the 2016 party platforms reveals no such thing. The Republican platform made no mention of sapience and only two very narrow references to wisdom. The Democratic platform made no mention of wisdom or sapience. The Green Party platform included many references to ecology and ecological restoration, but no mention of wisdom or sapience.

In traditional cultures, the quest for wisdom was held as an integral part of human life, but today it's disappeared from the radar of popular consciousness. We don't teach it in any explicit way, nor do we honor it as an essential aspiration. Do we simply assume that it's an outdated artifact of a bygone era? Something for monks and sages, but not for busy modern people? Wouldn't this be a perfect time to refresh our memory of this vital, ancient perspective? Wouldn't this be a good time to wise up?

Just as wisdom has fallen out of favor in the modern world, the word *health* has also failed to live up to its potential. To be sure, some of us have access to incredible medical resources, and arguably, many are of us more health-conscious now than ever before. But much of that attention is fragmented, piecemeal and disconnected. Every day we're exposed to a glut of health-related information, but we lack an understanding of how to put it together into a coherent whole.

The problem is that we have yet to connect our understanding of human history with what it means to be whole and healthy. Our biomedical approach provides us with gobs of information about the fundamentals of anatomy and physiology, but we continue to view the body in isolation from environment, culture, society, and history. New research gives us tantalizing evidence of the body's interdependence with the wider world, but we have yet to absorb this understanding into popular practice or culture. And because we treat and think of ourselves as stand-alone organisms, we find it almost impossible to become truly whole.

If we're ever going to be truly healthy, we need an evolutionary perspective and a sense of "ancestral health." If you haven't heard this term before, you might be inclined to think it's some kind of specialty, but when we look at the deep history of the human body and the extent of our adaptations in the course of evolution, it becomes obvious that *all* health is "ancestral." This understanding gives us context and tells us something vital about the source and the scope of health. In turn, it puts us back into contact with the forces, qualities, and experiences that give us life.

This book explores the common threads that unite our quest for health, sapience, and relevance. The goal is to help you navigate the mismatch between your aboriginal body and the modern world and in the process, find a sense of peace, relevance, and equanimity in the face of unfolding chaos. It won't ask you to live out in the bush, nor will it offer easy solutions for everything that ails us. Instead, this book offers a historical perspective about how to be normal, healthy, and sapient. It's about being true to our evolutionary heritage and our bodies, while still being effective and functional in the modern world. It's remedial education for the confused human animal.

As you'll see, this book is a call to action, engagement, and relevance. It will challenge you to become a physical activist, a lifestyle activist, a narrative activist, and a relational activist. It will ask you to think differently about your role in this world and to make good on your insights. Along the way, we'll take inspiration from both the old and new. The modern, New Way is obviously powerful and brings us vital tools and knowledge, but it also threatens to make our planet uninhabitable. In contrast, the Old Way offers essential perspectives and a proven path to relationship, participation, and sapience. As you'll see, these two visions of the world are complementary; each makes the other stronger. Our goal, therefore, will be integration and a "best of both worlds" approach.

New Old Way explores the highly interconnected themes of biological mismatch, health, environmental destruction, activism, philosophy, and the creation of an engaged, meaningful life. In the spirit of simplicity, each chapter is built around a single word, an element that teaches us something vital about navigating the challenge of the modern world: ancestry, body, habitat, tribe, action, medicine, life, stress, story, and if all goes well, sapience. Ultimately, this book aims to give you tools, orientations, and strategies that can help you navigate our highly inconvenient world. It's a path to building a long-term relationship with our planet and each other. This is a book about how to be whole.

MEET YOUR AUTHOR

As a curious reader, you'd surely like to know something about your author and his qualifications. Like you, I'm a mismatched animal and I'm often confused about how to make my way in the world. Like you, I aspire to sapience, but often find myself struggling with the fundamentals. My aboriginal body feels out of place, and I'm plagued with doubt about the best path forward. On some days, it seems that direct, militant action against bad actors is the only sensible response to the assault on the biosphere, while on other days, equanimity and adaptation seem the wisest course.

Like the writer E.B. White, I too "arise in the morning torn between a desire to save the world and a desire to savor the world. This makes it hard to plan the day." It also makes it hard to offer sound opinions on what readers ought to be doing with their lives. Savoring the world is good for the body and the spirit, but fighting for the future is essential too. You can make a case for either path, or both.

In any case, I've had some valuable experience in my sixty-plus years. I've traveled to Africa to study our ancestral environment, spent several decades practicing the physical arts, and read my way through a small mountain of books about health, medicine, and ecology. I've climbed some big mountains, learned the art of bodywork, and practiced my share of meditation.

As an undergrad at Stanford, I studied human biology in a unique, multi-disciplinary program that integrated the "hard" and "soft" sciences that relate to the human body and health. My professors didn't put it quite this way at the time, but the curriculum was a beautiful yin–yang. The "yin" sciences of psychology and sociology were a perfect complement to the "yang" sciences of biochemistry and evolutionary biology. Together, they formed a unified whole and provided a model that will resonate through the pages of this book: yin–yang, soft–hard, East–West, new–old. As you'll see, this synergistic approach feeds our understanding of both health and sapience. In fact, as you'll also see, health and sapience may even be names for the same thing.

ANCESTRY

If you don't understand the past, you won't have a future.

—Cherokee saying

Before we can make sense of mismatch and the human predicament, it's essential to consider the story of how we got here. In our frenzied rush through the modern world, we rarely pause to reflect on the past, but our minds, bodies, and cultures are in fact creations of history. Understanding the story of our origins gives us a sense of identity and trajectory; it tells us who we are and what we might become.

Without an appreciation for history, the events and processes in our lives will feel random and arbitrary and we'll inhabit a strange and sometimes frightening world of *non sequiturs* (Latin for "it does not follow"). In such a world, shit just happens, and none of it makes much sense. Sensations and experiences come and go with no apparent relationship to one another. We concoct wild explanations for events that would be much better understood as historical processes. And to make matters worse, our decisions will be shortsighted and disconnected. To paraphrase George Santayana, we might say, "Those who don't appreciate the past are condemned to live in a world of nonsense."

THE HISTORY OF HISTORY

The fascinating thing about our history is that until quite recently, we didn't really know for certain that we had one. Our tools and methods just weren't up to the task. Historians did most of their work by studying written documents, but prehistory is, by definition, undocumented. This limitation has given us a highly distorted view of the past and continues to drive our tendency to focus on recent events. We can still see it in the way our history textbooks give a wildly disproportionate share of attention to events of the past few thousand years. Prehistory is often dismissed as a distant and irrelevant curiosity.

This reminds us of the story of the drunk on a dark street corner who looks for his car keys under the street light. The keys may or may not be there, but that's where the light is, so that's where he looks. But as it turns out, the light provided by written documents represents only a tiny fraction of human experience. The really important story has always been out there in the dark, waiting to be discovered.

Starting in the mid-nineteenth century, scientists began to probe the darkness with scientific instruments. A breathtaking series of discoveries in geology, biology, and cosmology broadened and illuminated our sense of the distant past and gave rise to the story we now call "Big History." In a very real sense, the greatest discovery of the modern age was not antibiotics, DNA, or the expanding universe, but the discovery of history itself. For the first time in history, we know the true dimensions of our time on Earth.

Today, Big History is readily accepted by the scientific community, but popular culture has yet to catch up and many of us remain mired in small history perspectives. And even for those who accept the scientific reality of Big History, the past still feels like an abstraction, not a powerful presence in our daily lives. The paradox is striking: Our brains and minds—sculpted by deep history itself—are inclined toward short-term survival and attention to the present moment. Even when we understand the reality of history, most of us find it difficult to feel its immensity and its power.

But the effort is essential. If you don't understand the full scope of our past, you can't possibly understand the true nature of the human body, health, or the human mind. Likewise, the reality of mismatch will remain invisible. Your angst, alienation, and suffering will feel random and inexplicable. Frustrated, you'll blame yourself for your anxiety and depression. You'll come to the conclusion that your unhappiness is a character flaw, a personality disorder, or a neurotransmitter deficiency. In turn, you'll reach out for any fix that offers relief, no matter how arbitrary.

The good news is that science has given us a powerful, factual sense of history and our place in it. By the late twentieth century, we pieced together the story of Big History and the temporal scales that go with it. Sometime around thirteen billion years ago, an unimaginably powerful event set the universe in motion and set the stage for star formation, solar systems, planets, and life as we know it. We now know that all the elements in the universe, including the very matter of our tissue and organs, came from the bodies of exploding supernova stars. As Carl Sagan famously put it,

> All of the rocky and metallic material we stand on, the iron
> in our blood, the calcium in our teeth, the carbon in our
> genes were produced billions of years ago in the interior of a
> red giant star. We are made of star-stuff.

Every plant, animal, and microbe on this planet shares this same primordial origin. All living beings, from viruses to blue whales, are made of the same raw material. The stars are our ancestors.

MEET LUCA

This is all plenty incredible in its own right, but what's really astonishing is the fact that all of us—humans and every other life form on Earth—have descended from a single common ancestor, known as LUCA, the last universal common ancestor.[20] In all likelihood, she was a simple microbial cell, similar to a modern bacterium. Her remains did not fossilize, but her existence has been inferred by comparing the genomes of her descendants, organisms living today. If we could play the movie of life backward, we would find LUCA at the starting point for a story that's been unfolding for almost four billion years. All living creatures are linked to this single-celled creature, the root of the tree of life.

LUCA is astonishing, but in another sense, her existence shouldn't come as a complete surprise. In 1859, Charles Darwin proposed the idea that there was only one progenitor for all forms of life. In the *Origin of Species* he wrote, "Therefore I should infer from analogy that probably all the organic beings which have ever lived on this earth have descended from one primordial form, into which life was first breathed."

The significance of LUCA is immense—scientifically, culturally, and even spiritually. In short, LUCA unites us. She tells a story of shared origin and history. We may well behave otherwise, but we— all the plants, animals and humans of the biosphere— are truly, literally one. We may look like singular, isolated individuals, but we are intimately related to everything that moves, breathes, and grows. The history of life on earth is coursing through our veins every minute of every day. Rachel Carson put it perfectly:

> To understand biology is to understand that all life is linked to the Earth from which it came; it is to understand that the stream of life, flowing out of the dim past into the uncertain future, is in reality a unified force, though composed of an infinite number and variety of separate lives.[21]

LUCA puts everything, including our politics, in a new light.

When all life is kin, we come to a fresh understanding of "family values." In this light, the conversation is no longer just about the welfare of Mom, Dad, and the kids. It's about the welfare of the entire biosphere, our extended family. And of course, the small family cannot stand apart. Whatever happens to the big family inevitably affects everything within the circle. From this perspective, our continuing assault on the natural world begins to look very much like a case of domestic violence writ large. Habitat destruction is nothing less than violence against the family, the self, and the future.

In the world of politics, this broader sense of family values would make for a powerful reframe. This new (old) definition implies a radically inclusive approach that suggests a new (old) sensibility, an ethic, and even a practical vision for the future. Even better, the conventional small family values still apply: love, honor, respect, communication, sharing, and wisdom. Big family values are pro-social, pro-habitat, and pro-future. So where are the political leaders who will stand up and speak out for this vision? And who could possibly vote against family values?

As a people, we have yet to fully appreciate the meaning and significance of LUCA, and it may be a long time before we fully integrate it into our culture. Nevertheless, a sense of wonder is inescapable. Your body is not an arbitrary, isolated object that simply appeared on Earth. It's a leaf on an immense tree, a continuation of a process that is vast beyond our ability to comprehend. Your body is not decades old, but hundreds of millions of years old. Every cell in your body contains a story of continuity and connection. It's an amazing, awe-inspiring story. As Darwin himself put it, "There is grandeur in this view of life." Believe it or not, act like it or not, we are all children of LUCA.

OLD WAY

You're gonna need us.

—Popular Native American refrain

No matter how you measure it, human ancestry is vast. *Homo sapiens* first arrived on the scene some three hundred thousand years ago, but our physical, genetic, and psycho-spiritual roots are far deeper. We can point to any number of chronological markers to tell our story, but one of the most important is our divergence from the chimpanzee and bonobo line, some six or seven million years ago. Starting from that modest beginning, our earliest ancestors were small-bodied, small-brained vegetarian scavengers and opportunists. Contrary to the popular cartoon vision of burly caveman hunters, we were actually hunt*ed*–gatherers, stalked and occasionally eaten by predators. We were wild animals.

Around three million years ago, our ancestors crafted the first stone tools and then, perhaps a million years ago, we began the opportunistic use of fire. Not only did cooked food taste good, it also made for better nutrition and in turn, bigger brains, better hunting and more free time to explore and wonder. By seventy thousand years ago, humans began to develop early forms of art and culture and a remarkably consistent worldview, a culture that's been described by writers like Elizabeth Marshall Thomas as the "Old Way."[22] This proved to be a powerful formula that sustained humanity for tens of thousands of years, and in fact, the aboriginal societies of Australia and Africa have been the most successful and enduring cultures on the planet. Seen through the lens of Big History, this is who we are.

Unfortunately, many modern people have no idea that an older, more holistic way even exists, and it rarely crosses our minds that the indigenous worldview might actually be superior to our own. In the West, we believe in progress and continuous improvement. If it's old, it must be primitive, crude, simplistic, and irrelevant. And in this respect, we are often blind to the power of indigenous ways that still flourish in many human hearts, minds, and bodies.

In the mid twentieth century, C.S. Lewis and Owen Barfield described this dismissal of the past as "chronological snobbery," the belief that "intellectually, humanity languished for countless generations in the most childish errors on all sorts of crucial subjects, until it was redeemed by some simple scientific dictum of the last century." A typical example comes from the philosopher Joseph Priestley, writing in 1771: "The human species is capable of unbounded improvement…mankind in a later age are greatly superior to mankind in a former age." Popular insults of our day include "medieval," "primitive," "backward," "knuckle dragger," "troglodyte," and of course, "animal."

Richard Dawkins describes this perspective as "the vanity of the present, of seeing the past as aimed at our own time, as though the characters in history's play had nothing better to do with their lives than foreshadow us." Even in the face of substantial evidence to the contrary, many of us persist in the belief that indigenous knowledge and worldviews are extinct and therefore irrelevant. But in fact, the old ways still live, and in some ways, they are more sophisticated and sapient than our own. Our deep ancestors may have been uneducated in the modern sense, but they were highly intelligent and fully capable of crafting sophisticated solutions to the challenges of life.

IS BACK THE WAY FORWARD?

Naturally, caution is in order. As our world edges ever closer to the abyss, some of us fantasize about returning to a simpler time and have come to the conclusion that the ways of our ancestors are an ideal solution for health and sustainability. We adopt the myth of the "noble savage" and assume that all native people were paragons of virtue and moral perfection. If we could simply go back to a native lifestyle, our problems might be solved.

But we must take care. Given the level of angst we're experiencing at the moment, it's easy to fall into the romantic trap and imagine that life in prehistory was a golden age of health, fulfillment, and cosmic integration. It's a common human tendency to romanticize other times, people, and cultures; when life is hard, we look elsewhere for comfort and coherence.

But in fact, there was plenty of hardship in the Paleo. People suffered physical adversity, injury, illness, and occasional starvation. The Old Way provided a sense of unity with the world, but people surely experienced their share of distress and conflict. It's probably the case that ancestral bodies were strong and athletic, but the wild life was physically demanding, dangerous, and often short. The Paleo was not a utopia.

Likewise, it's easy to paint all native and indigenous cultures with the same broad brush. But there was plenty of diversity in our past, and not every native culture has been a paragon of ecological and social virtue. Some native people abused their habitats, set wildfires, and over hunted.[23] We hear a good deal about egalitarian tribal behavior, but violence was probably not unusual either. No culture is perfect.

Nevertheless, there's a lot to be learned from the Old Way. For all its diversity and variation over time and across the planet, it remains a proven formula that might well give us practical, psychological, and spiritual guidance. The Old Way contains the original wisdom of our species, the sapience that we so desperately need. It is definitely worth a closer look.

MEET THE OLD WAY

The Old Way is not a single philosophy, but rather a system of belief, a culture, and a vision of the world and our place in it. It's a path and a way to live. There's plenty of diversity in Old Way rituals and practices, but the common thread is interdependence, interrelation-ship, and what Zen teachers call "interbeing." In this view, nothing is autonomous; nothing stands alone. The words of Chief Seattle are typical: "Humankind has not woven the web of life. We are but one thread within it. Whatever we do to the web, we do to ourselves. All things are bound together. All things connect."

At its core, the Old Way is built on a unitary cosmology. When everything is interconnected and interdependent, the focus is on re-lations, not on static objects. Boundaries can be fuzzy and dynam-ic, and because everything connects, the geometry of the Old Way is circular. Everything returns. A typical passage from the Native American Black Elk:

> Everything an Indian does is in a circle, and that is because the power of the world always works in circles, and every-thing tries to be round. In the old days when we were a strong and happy people, all our power came to us from the sacred hoop of the nation, and so long as the hoop was un-broken the people flourished.[24]

In Old Way cultures, the world is literally alive, a view that to-day we call *animistic* (from *anima*, "soul" or "spirit" in Latin). Every place, animal, plant, and natural phenomenon has awareness and feelings, and can communicate with humans. Objects, places, and creatures possess a spiritual essence. Soul and spirit exist not only in humans, but in animals, plants, rocks, mountains, rivers, and other entities in the natural environment, including thunder, wind, and shadows. Religious studies scholar Graham Harvey defined animism as the belief "that the world is full of persons, only some of whom are human, and that life is always lived in relationship with others."

In this kind of culture, human beings live in deep engagement with the world. Mind and spirit are always relational and interacting with the flux and flow of plants, animals, weather, and other people.

There is no attempt to stand apart from nature or to be objective. In fact, precisely the opposite. The goal of life is to form an intimate, integrated relationship with the world and to penetrate deeper into its mysteries.

In this culture, people assume a continuity between their bodies, habitat, tribe, and cosmos. In the Iroquois tradition, this sense of extended physicality is sometimes called "the long body."[25] An eleventh-century official in China expressed it this way:

> Heaven is my father and earth is my mother and even such a small creature as I finds an intimate place in its midst. That which extends throughout the universe, I regard as my body and that which directs the universe I regard as my nature. All people are my brothers and sisters and all things are my companions.

Likewise, a Zen parable: "To your way of thinking, your skin is a thing which separates and protects you from the outside world. To my way of thinking, my skin is a thing which connects me and opens me to the outside world, which in any case is not the outside world." With its emphasis on interdependence and continuity, it's no surprise that the Old Way embraces what we might call a "big health" orientation. That is, health is a matter not just of individual physical welfare, but of the whole. Health is shared across communities of people and habitat. An early Buddhist teacher put it this way: "If the people are sick, I too am sick; only when everyone is healthy will I too be healthy."[26] In ancient Greece, Socrates offered a typically indigenous view: "This is the reason why the cure of many diseases is unknown to the physicians of Hellas (Greece), because they are ignorant of the whole, which ought to be studied also; for the part can never be well unless the whole is well." Likewise, we find a typical Native American maxim: "The hurt of one is the hurt of all. The honor of one is the honor of all." And, by extension, "the health of one is the health of all. The disease of one is the disease of all."

Native people saw interdependence with one another and tribe was considered fundamental, not just to survival, but to identity. This pro-social worldview shows up in many indigenous and Eastern cultures but is most conspicuous in the African philosophy of *ubuntu* (pronounced uu-boon-too) According to ubuntu, there exists a common bond between all human beings, and it is through this bond that we discover our own human qualities; we affirm our humanity when we acknowledge the humanity of others. Our identity is not independent; it is interdependent, intimately connected to the life and welfare of the tribe, the family, the community. We define ourselves not as individuals but as participants in something larger. As the Bushmen of the Kalahari put it, "We are people through other people" and "I am what I am because of who we are."

Not surprisingly, the Old Way has its own ethics and moral code. As participants in a highly interdependent world, there is no thought of domination or imperialism. In fact, the Old Way is the archetypal "leaver" culture of Daniel Quinn's *Ishmael.* Take what you need, but leave the rest. Behave like a good guest on the land. Habitat provides, but you've got to live lightly and respect your home. Modern people might call it an ethic, but this was also a form of practical sapience. It's folly to destroy the thing that keeps you alive. To abuse the world is to abuse yourself.

OLD IN THE NEW

Looking at these features of the Old Way, it's tempting to assume a sharp divide between indigenous and modern perspectives or to conclude that the interdependent worldview has died out. But the distinction is not always so clear cut, and in fact, there have been plenty of modern, nonindigenous people who have seen—and continue to see—the world through the traditional lens of continuity, participation, and relationship.

Zen philosopher Alan Watts put it this way in his book *Does it Matter?*:

> …civilized human beings are alarmingly ignorant of the fact that they are continuous with their natural surroundings. It is as necessary to have air, water, plants, insects, birds, fish and mammals as it is to have brains, hearts, lungs and stomachs. The former are our external organs in the same way the latter are our internal organs.

Likewise, psychologist Carl Jung saw continuity all around him: "My self is not confined to my body. It extends into all the things I have made and all the things around me…Everything surrounding me is part of me."[27]

John Muir held a famously Old Way vision of human relationship to the natural world: "We are now in the mountains and they are in us, kindling enthusiasm, making every nerve quiver, filling every pore and cell of us." And his legendary declaration of interdependence: "When we try to pick out anything by itself, we find it hitched to everything else in the universe.

Dr. Martin Luther King Jr. preached an Old Way orientation when he called for a "world perspective" and a vision for the entire planet. "We are all caught in an inescapable network of mutuality, tied into a single garment of destiny. Whatever affects one directly affects all indirectly. We are made to live together because of the interrelated structure of reality."

So too the Prussian naturalist Alexander von Humboldt, sometimes called "the father of environmentalism." Humboldt described nature as a web of life and Earth as a living organism. "In this great chain of causes and effects, no single fact can be considered in isolation… Everything is interaction and reciprocal."

Jonas Salk, the inventor of the polio vaccine, also saw interdependence throughout the living world: "The time has arrived in which we have to realize that we are all parts of a single organism." Like-wise, the ecotheologian Thomas Berry showed profound Old Way sensibilities: "The universe is a communion of subjects, not a collection of objects… the health of the earth is indivisible."[28]

Dave Foreman, the founder of the Earth First! movement, put his Old Way perspective this way: "Damn it, I am an animal! A living being of flesh and blood, storm and fury. The oceans of the Earth course through my veins, the winds of the sky fill my lungs, the very bedrock of the planet makes my bones…I am the land, the land is me."[29]

Similarly, we also see echoes of the Old Way in the art, writing, and poetry of the Romantic era of the late eighteenth century. Distrustful of the scientific rationalization of the world, romantic artists believed that a close connection with nature was mentally and morally healthy. Key figures included William Wordsworth, John Keats, William Blake, Henry David Thoreau, Ralph Waldo Emerson, and Walt Whitman. Romantic era poets saw the imagination as a spiritual force, and believed that literature, especially poetry, could improve the world. Blake's poem "Auguries of Innocence" spoke for the spirit of the age:

To see a world in a grain of sand,
And heaven in a wild flower,
Hold infinity in the palm of your hand,
And eternity in an hour.

We can be sure that this kind of philosophy would resonate with native and indigenous peoples around the world; this is the language of the Old Way.

NEW WAY

For fifteen hundred centuries, we kept the Old Rules, then broke them all and erased the Old Way from our lives.

—Elizabeth Marshall Thomas
The Old Way: A Story of the First People

Old Way culture held sway with a coherent worldview through the vast majority of our history on Earth. For thousands of generations, it told us who we are and how to relate to the world around us. It didn't give us much in the way of power or wealth, but it did provide us with a powerful story of inclusion and a place in the cosmos.

But over the course of the last ten thousand years, a New Way began to eclipse the Old. As the domestication of plants and animals took hold, humans began to develop new ideas about their relationship to habitat and the world at large. For the first time, the land could be manipulated. If you put enough labor into it, habitat would support you and even give a surplus in good years. This was the beginning of a completely new way of seeing and living in the world, the first division between man and environment, between wild and tame. For the first time in history, we began to dream of mastery.

Domestication and agriculture set the stage for a radical transition in human consciousness. According to some historians, the shift began some five thousand years ago as climate shifted and a vast swath of northern Africa and central Asia began turning to desert. In *The Fall: The Insanity of The Ego in Human History and The Dawning of a New Era*, Steve Taylor suggests that prior to that point, indigenous cultures were largely free from war, hierarchy, patriarchy, and ecocide. People lived in relative harmony with the natural world and one another, but as food became increasingly scarce, tribes began to challenge one another for territory. In turn, violence, domination, and patriarchy began to overwhelm traditional, indigenous values. The egalitarian norm began to collapse and was replaced by the rise of ego, hierarchy, exploitation, and imperialism.

The advent of the written word accelerated the process. Symbols began to take on a powerful, independent significance, and human consciousness became increasingly abstracted from the world. Especially in the West, imagination began to follow the linear sequences of written language. The written word gave power to the literate class and in turn, a sense of social hierarchy, while numbers gave rise to accounting and paved the way for trade, commerce, and a merchant class. The circle of human and natural life was soon eclipsed by rows, columns, straight lines, boxes, and pyramids.

The ancient Greeks were instrumental in the transition. As philosophy took written form, philosophers developed a powerful interest in taxonomy, categories and "laws" of thought. Within these systems of logic and rationality, contradiction was something to be avoided, not relished. As Aristotle put it, a thing must be either "A" or "not A." This "law of the excluded middle" made sense to the Greeks, but to practitioners of Old, native ways, it must have seemed crazy. To indigenous people and many modern people as well, it makes perfect sense to say that a thing can be both "A" and "not A." In fact, the both–and qualities of our world often ring both beautiful and true.

The erosion of the Old Way further accelerated in the fifteenth century with Gutenberg's invention of the printing press. Suddenly, language could be chopped up into bits, rearranged at will, and delivered to large numbers of people. In turn, this paved the way for an explosion of literacy, science, and the modern age of cognition. Looking through his telescope, Galileo discovered flaws in the supposedly perfect heavenly realm, and Copernicus demonstrated the fact that the sun, not the earth, is at the center of the solar system. Young anatomists and physicians began to see errors in medical texts and in turn, to reject arguments that flowed from authority.

Newton discovered laws of motion that held true in both the heavens and on Earth, while Descartes declared that the universe and the body were nothing more than sophisticated machines. Francis Bacon championed the scientific method and experimentation. In turn, these discoveries set the stage for an explosion of knowledge in the modern era: the discovery of evolution, germ theory, DNA, the expanding universe, and Big History. By the mid-twentieth century, the New Way became firmly established as the dominant paradigm of the modern world.

By some accounts, the ascendance of the New Way was driven by actual changes in the human brain. In *The Master and His Emissary*, Iain McGilchrist makes a powerful case that the increasing use of a symbolic alphabet led to dominance of the left hemisphere. As we now know, the left and right hemispheres have distinctly different ways of attending to the world. In general, the left side specializes in linear thought, language, and logic, while the right side traffics in metaphor, myth, holistic imagination, and the experience of the body. The hemispheres communicate and share many functions, but they can also inhibit one another. And when the left side begins to dominate, the result is an increasingly rigid, linear culture, a world in which hierarchy, logic, and efficiency begin to tyrannize ancient human experiences and perspectives. Naturally, the process feeds back on itself: the more we use the left hemisphere to create linear and rational systems, the more we see the world in precisely these terms. In turn, we become lopsided, unbalanced, and disintegrated.

NEW WAY THEMES: LOST IN THE HOMOSPHERE

As civilization developed and left brain attention came to dominate the human experience, the New Way coalesced into an estranged, alienated worldview. Nature became Other, and something called "the environment" came into view. Rocks, animals, trees, bodies, and habitat were no longer part of us; they were things to be

studied or exploited. The universe became a vast billiard table, popu-
lated by inanimate objects that operate on mechanical principles. In
the Old Way, the universe is throbbing with life, but in the New Way,
all is mechanism.

In this worldview, we stand apart, or try to. Distance is considered
essential in the creation of knowledge, and researchers are taught
to maintain rigorous separation from whatever they're studying. In
scientific and academic circles, identification with objects, animals,
or processes is considered a grievous error. The "Man from Mars"
perspective is the standard for objectivity; our consciousness is nonparticipatory. Historically speaking, this is a profoundly abnormal
way to relate to the world.

In this view, the entire cosmos can be dissected, nothing is sacred, and nothing is off limits. Trees, rivers, mountains, and animals
are objects to be used as desired. Even people are treated as objects
to be hired, exploited, and discarded. The disconnect even extends
to the world of medicine, where patients are often treated as medical objects, faulty mechanisms to be repaired, processed, and dis-
charged from the system. In this culture of objectification, everything's a thing.

At the same time, New Way culture is strongly atheistic, which is
to say, it has no room for spirit, supernatural powers, or mystical influences, only mechanical causality. This perspective "works" in the
sense that it gives us power, control, knowledge, and highly sophisticated tools, but we lose a sense of meaning and participation in
the process. We become masters and possessors of nature, but we're
left wondering, "What's the point?" This is precisely why so many us
have mixed feelings about the scientific enterprise. We're in awe of
what it reveals, but feel stranded without a story.

The New Way also features some disturbing perspectives on the
body. As Descartes saw it, the mind is an independent entity, not under the influence of habitat, bodily states, society, or culture—nothing

more or less than a biological calculator. In the modern world, we enshrine this perspective in our cultural heroes. As Sherlock Holmes put it, "I am a brain, Watson. The rest of me is a mere appendage." Likewise Thomas Edison: "The chief function of the body is to carry the brain around." Intelligence, we like to think, is a free-floating aptitude. It's really good at solving puzzles, but it's completely detached from the body and the world around it.

Fundamentally, the distinction between Old and New worldviews is a matter of connection and relationship to the world at large. Anthropologist Edward Hall once made a distinction between low-context and high-context societies. The Old Way is high context; everything in life depends on everything else. In contrast, the New Way is low context, or maybe even *no* context. In the Old Way, native people, hippies, and ecologists believe "It's all connected," but in the New Way, we might well say "It's all disconnected."

In the process, the circular, relational view of the Old Way is replaced by hierarchy. Beginning with Aristotle's biology and History of Animals, we've committed ourselves to the idea there's a great chain of being (Latin: *scala naturae*, "ladder of being"). As popularized in the Middle Ages, the chain starts with God and progresses downward to angels, demons, stars, moon, kings, princes, nobles, commoners, wild animals, domesticated animals, trees, other plants, precious stones, precious metals, and other minerals. Earth (rock) is at the bottom of the chain.

Obviously, our modern social world is structured with a similar geometry, with the pyramid growing higher and steeper with each passing year. In essence, the New Way is built upon an unspoken caste system, with humans (mostly rich, white male humans) at the top and nature at the bottom. In the 1970s, ecopsychologist Theodore Roszak observed that dominant industrial cultures hold the same oppressive stance toward minority peoples and nature as a whole–if you can exploit one, you can just as well exploit the other.

In this sense, there's very little difference between slavery and the domination of ecosystems by clear cutting, strip mining, and relentless construction. It's all the same diseased relationship and attitude. Nature is the ultimate underclass.

Even the modern concept of environmental "stewardship" reeks of hierarchy and presumed human supremacy. After hundreds of years of abusing the world, we now declare that we're going to manage Mother Nature in a "sustainable," eco-friendly manner. But this is simply the same old story of hierarchy. As self-declared masters and possessors of nature, we cling desperately to our alpha status. We've got the best knowledge, the best science, the best technology, and the best corporations, and now we're going to manage the entire biosphere as well as the atmosphere. For a culture poised on the brink of destroying its own future, this is a pretty outrageous claim to make.

As we've seen, Old Way culture was and is built on an ethic of being a good guest on the planet. In contrast, New Way culture behaves as if it owns the place. We are the legendary "taker" culture of Daniel Quinn's *Ishmael*. The world is nothing more than a resource to be exploited; we want to have our planet and eat it too. The most breathtaking example of this attitude is the Doctrine of Discovery, a legal justification created by European monarchs to legitimize the colonization of lands outside of Europe. Beginning in the fifteenth century, this narrative gave Europeans license to seize lands inhabited by indigenous peoples. In 1792, US Secretary of State Thomas Jefferson declared that the Doctrine of Discovery would extend from Europe to the new US government.

Obviously, the Doctrine of Discovery is nothing more than cultural and ecological imperialism, dressed up in legal language. Not surprisingly, it's been condemned as socially unjust, racist, and in violation of basic and fundamental human rights. The United Nations Permanent Forum on Indigenous Issues cited the Doctrine of Discovery "as the foundation of the violation of their (Indigenous people) human rights."

Not surprisingly, freedom, independence, and individualism are held as cardinal virtues of the New Way. The emphasis is on the *ego-system*, not the ecosystem. Writing in the sixteenth century, John Donne declared that "no man is an island," but today we're more likely to say that "every man (and woman and child) is an island." New Way philosophers coin phrases such as "I think, therefore I am," but this focus on the individual would be unimaginable to indigenous people. In the broad context of human history, our individualistic orientation comes across as rare, abnormal, and deviant.

This focus on the individual is far more than a cultural quirk; it has far-reaching implications for our relationship to the world. In our conventional experience, we're accustomed to thinking of the self as a static thing that we're born with and that stays in place until the day we die, but recent research in animal behavior suggests that the sense of self can be learned, amplified, and maybe even forgotten. Using the mirror-recognition test (commonly used to test self-awareness in nonhuman animals), researchers at the Shanghai Institutes for Biological Sciences in China found that a monkey species that was previously deemed unable to recognize itself in a mirror can learn to do so.[30]

This suggests that our sense of self is plastic and is almost certainly influenced by culture. In Old Way cultures, with their emphasis on unity and interdependence, our sense of self would have been relatively weak and dynamic; native people would have experienced occasional moments of self-consciousness against a background of integrated, participatory life experience. But in the New Way, our insistent and even militant declarations of independence serve to reinforce and strengthen the sense of self and in turn, our feelings of isolation. More awareness of the self means less contact with the whole and in turn, more anxiety, stress, and eventually, depression.

As the New Way worldview came to dominate modern

consciousness, it paved the way for the growth of capitalism, consumerism, materialism, and the commercialization of human life. Once reality was broken up into lifeless, autonomous objects, it became progressively easier to monetize the world around us. Anything could have a price.

Steam and coal gave us power for our machines, and Adam Smith gave us the narrative of an invisible hand that magically turns individual self interest into the common good. For the first time in history, self-centered behavior became acceptable and even admired. Normal tribal values were eclipsed by a transactional economy, and people came to be valued exclusively for their productivity and financial worth.

In the process, corporations gained the legal status of persons and began to outstrip governments in power and influence. This was the rise of neoliberalism and the corporate takeover of the public sector. Insulated from liability, corporations became free to do what they do best: internalize profit and externalize cost. Maximize your rewards and get the public to pay for the consequences.

Today, corporate power has become the most overwhelming social force on the planet, eclipsing even entire governments. In the 1970s, there were some seven thousand corporations operating internationally, but by 2008 the number had increased to about eighty-two thousand, with eight hundred ten thousand foreign affiliates. Corporations now account for fifty-one of the largest one hundred economic entities in the world. (The others are countries.) Today, corporate messaging has radically transformed human consciousness and turned society into a bottom-line culture in which every decision hinges almost exclusively on economic and financial consequences. The driving question for modern behavior is not "Is it healthy?" or "Is it sapient?" but "Will it pay?"

The New Way has brought wealth and power to some, but it has broken the circle of interdependence. Seduced by our material success, many of us have come to view human affairs in isolation from the rest of the living world. In effect, we've created an exclusive club of human interest called the "homosphere," a very narrow and destructive sense of "us."

The homosphere is built on the belief that human beings are the only truly significant entity in the universe. In the Old, indigenous ways, people participated in an intimate dialogue with the world, but today we've stopped listening. As theologian Thomas Berry put it, "We are talking only to ourselves. We are not talking to the rivers, we are not listening to the wind and stars. We have broken the great conversation."

Our homocentric view is most conspicuous in our legal system. That is, modern jurisprudence deals exclusively with human–human relationships and has little, if anything, to say about the natural world. In other words, nature has no standing and no voice. It can be exploited with minor restrictions, but it has no rights. Animals, plants, soils, oceans, and aquifers don't get a vote in our proceedings. Their interests are considered irrelevant.[31]

In essence, we behave as if the rest of the living world is only there to serve us. The vast majority of our conversations about health, medicine, economics, education, law, and government are about human-to-human interactions. Attempts to bring nonhuman elements into the conversation are rejected out of hand as inconvenient, impractical, and even crazy. Corporations have a voice, but forests, rivers, and oceans do not. Nature is not invited to our party.

This is the fundamental delusion of the New Way: if we just get everything right inside the homosphere, all will be well. But man does not live by humanity alone. We need nature, not just to survive, but to remain sane, creative, and whole. A homosphere without a biosphere is a recipe for disaster.

NEW OLD WAY

> The challenge facing us is to bring together the primitive
> and the highly sophisticated. We need to discover a har-
> monizing integration between the sacred energies we bring
> with us from our Source and the indispensable tools we
> have developed upon our journey.
>
> —Andrew Bard Schmookler
> *The Parable of the Tribes*

When we look at the New Way and its historically abnormal, alienated relationship with the world, it's tempting to reject the entire perspective out of hand. It's given us tremendous power, but it's also put us on the brink of a planetary catastrophe. In 1977, at the UN Conference on Indigenous Peoples, the Hau de no sau nee (Iroquois) people put it in the starkest possible terms: "The way of life known as Western Civilization is on a death path on which their culture has no viable answers." Other native voices have characterized the Western way of life as a DIE culture, built on the values of Domination, Individualism, and Exclusion.[32] Many indigenous people would agree with this assessment, and so would a lot of nonnative people.

At this point, some of us will be inclined to abandon the New Way entirely and retreat to the mountains, but it would be a mistake to make rigid, black-and-white distinctions or to classify the Old as "good" and the New as "bad." In fact, it's precisely this kind of dualistic thinking that makes us blind to vital commonalities and nuance. The New Way offer some powerful benefits, just as the Old Way has weaknesses of its own. We need to have some sophistication in our thinking and our living.

And speaking practically, we simply can't return to the lifestyle of the Paleo. Romantics talk about rewilding and living in the bush, but it's just not a realistic option for most of us. There's simply not enough land on this planet for millions of people to hunt and gather in anything resembling a true ancestral lifestyle. And even if you could convince your family and friends to join you for life in the bush, you wouldn't have an oral tradition or a habitat-based culture to guide you. It took many thousands of years for indigenous people to work out the details of survival in a harsh environment; we're simply not going to reproduce it from scratch in our lifetime.

Even going back to an agrarian, Amish-style life—arguably one of the most sustainable, healthy models of human life—seems impossible. Even if we were to disregard the obvious challenge of moving millions of people from cities to the country, most of us have no idea how to farm, manage animals, do carpentry, or carry out any of the thousand other tasks of rural self-sufficiency that would be required. At the same time, going forward with our economically obsessed, technologically driven, future-hostile model seems equally untenable, if not insane. So where do we go for health and sanity?

The good news is that there's a powerful emerging trend that unites the Old and the New. Paradoxically perhaps, modern science is beginning to verify and even expand on the old wisdoms, especially the lessons of interdependence and continuity. New understandings in the fields of biology, microbiology, and systems theory verify the understandings of traditional ecological knowledge, sometimes known as TEK. As climate activist Bill McKibben put it: "The wisdom of the sweat lodge is beginning to find common ground with the findings of the ecologist."

It's almost as if the scientific adventure of the last four hundred years has been a hero's journey, the archetypical myth famously described by Joseph Campbell. Our scientific protagonist leaves home—the Old Way—and travels to strange and unexplored lands, learning many exciting things along the way. He journeys into the deepest reaches of space and time, the inner depths of the cell and the atom, the mysteries of the brain, and the organization of biological systems. The journey is exciting and fruitful, but it all leads back round in a circle as our scientific protagonist returns home to the unitary, interconnected worldview of the Old Way.

This is precisely what we're seeing in a flurry of new research and interdisciplinary hybrids. Life scientists are showing an increased willingness to cross categories and embrace new evidence of interdependence. There's fresh interest in integrative, biophilic studies, disciplines that connect human health to the larger world: conservation medicine, ecological medicine, environmental medicine, evolutionary medicine, and social medicine all have their own journals, conferences, and curriculums.[33] Science, it seems, is going holistic.

Around the world, scientists are emphasizing the need for a multidisciplinary, relational perspective. In "Down to Earth: Planetary Health and Biophilosophy in the Symbiocene Epoch"[34] Susan Prescott and Alan Logan make a powerful case for this point of view. As they see it,

> The crisis of noncommunicable disease does not sit in isolation from other global concerns; rather, it is intertwined with growing socioeconomic disparities, disconnection from the natural environment, climate change, biodiversity losses, and environmental degradation. It is becoming increasingly clear that health at all levels—person, place, and planet—is interdependent.

This rediscovery of interdependence is particularly evident in recent discoveries in the microbial world, especially the microbiome. The vast microbial populations in and on our bodies participate in a wide range of metabolic functions, including digestion and the production of neurotransmitters and vitamins. We now know that the microbiome is incredibly powerful in shaping human health and life experience, even our cognition and emotions.

It's a hot new area of research with great potential for curing disease and improving health, but the bigger message is actually philosophical and existential. The two million unique bacterial genes found in the microbiome dwarf the twenty-three thousand genes in our own cells, which raises the question of who exactly is in control of our bodies and our lives. As Tom Insel, the director of the National Institute of Mental Health, put it, this outnumbering "has enormous implications for the sense of self… We are, at least from the standpoint of DNA, more microbial than human." To put it in the simplest possible terms, "I" is actually a "we."

As revealed by modern science, the human body is, quite literally, a community, a superorganism. Some 90 percent of the protein-encoding cells in our body are microbes, which raises the question of just who is occupying whom. "We are massively outnumbered," says Jeremy K. Nicholson, chairman of biological chemistry and head of the department of surgery and cancer at Imperial College London. Another researcher put it this way: "Don't look now, but the pronoun 'I' is becoming obsolete… Thinking of plants and animals, including humans, as autonomous individuals is a serious over-simplification."

And it's not just humans. As it turns out, *every* species is a composite of microbial and nonmicrobial life. Plants, and animals too, are made of relationships. In a 2017 NPR commentary, biologist David George Haskell marveled at the intricacy of a single leaf on a sugar maple tree, and the fact that each leaf is a community of fungus, bacteria, protist, alga, nematode, and plant:

> A 'maple' is not an individual made of plant cells, but a community of cells from many domains and kingdoms of life. Microbe-free plants likely do not exist in nature and, if they could be constructed, would quickly die for want of the vital connections that sustain life.

For Haskell, "the fundamental unit of biology is not the 'self,' but the network. A maple tree is a plurality, its individuality a temporary manifestation of relationship." He calls us to expand our biological imagination. "When we gaze at a maple leaf, we now see not an individual made of plant cells, but a thrumming conversation, an embodied network. The "self" is a society."[35]

Entire forests show similar characteristics. In 2016, NPR's Radio Lab told the story of Suzanne Simard, a forestry professor at the University of British Columbia.[36] One day, while digging a hole in the forest floor, she discovered a vast network of roots, completely invisible from above. This "forest underneath the forest" turned out to form a literal "underground economy" of nutrient exchange. By injecting radioactive gases into tree trunks, Simard was able to track the movement of substances between individual trees. Much to her astonishment, she discovered that different species of trees actually shared food and information underground.

Simard mapped the underground network and discovered that the biggest and oldest trees were the most highly connected, networked by fungi that trade minerals for sugar. Using this network, trees send nutrients to one another. Weak or injured trees pass carbon to neighboring trees, especially young trees of any species. Trees can also send chemical warning signals to one another. As Simard puts it, "the forest acts as an organism or superorganism."

As the science of interdependence takes root, we're even seeing expanded awareness and appreciation at the institutional level. In 2016, the University of Sydney appointed the world's first professor of planetary health and launched a planetary health platform "founded on the interconnectedness of human and natural systems." At Harvard, the Planetary Health Alliance, a consortium of over 95 universities, NGOs, government entities, and research institutes, is dedicated to "deciphering the links between accelerating global environmental change and human health." Sounding very indigenous, the mission statement declares: "Everything is connected. What we do to the world comes back to affect us."

In 2017, the prestigious medical journal The Lancet launched a new journal devoted to planetary health. The editors issued a call for "a new global health ethic" with a focus on the "ecological foundations of health" and offered a simple, holistic definition that echoes the wisdom of the Old Way: "Traditionally, medical science is based on systems within the human body. Planetary health broadens health research to include the external systems that sustain or threaten human health."

This emerging New–Old confluence is also taking place in the world of activism. Beginning with the protests at Standing Rock in 2016, environmentalists and native people have joined forces to resist fossil fuel development, dams, and other destructive projects. This alliance is particularly active in the climate change movement, where organizers are coming together with an inclusive, big-tent approach. An increasing number of nonnative people aspire to become "indigenized," and many now think of themselves, like their native compatriots, as "water protectors." Big environmental organizations—historically white and affluent—are forming new partnerships with native activist groups, based on a shared interest in preserving habitat and a functional future. A powerful hybrid is in the making, one with the potential to reshape the worlds of politics, government, and culture.

A NEW INTEGRATION

As we've seen, the Old Way offers the promise of a normal, healthy human experience, but we can't simply go back to life on the grassland. The New Way offers powerful, practical benefits that we can be grateful for, but it's also destructive to communities, our planet, and our future. It would be madness to give up science and objective reasoning, but it would be equally insane to go forward without some sense of participatory consciousness in an animated, interdependent world.

As it stands, we're wildly out of balance. The New has tyrannized the Old for far too long and threatens to overwhelm it entirely. Doubling down on modern technologies, methods, and perspectives will only prolong our agony. Without some counterbalancing sense of traditional human understanding, the New Way is destined to wrap itself in an ever-tightening spiral of destruction, anxiety, and grief. This is where the change must begin. To put it bluntly, it's no longer acceptable or sapient to treat the Earth and one another as objects for manipulation, or to treat the mind and body as two separate, disconnected domains. It's no longer acceptable or sapient to hold the world at arm's length with alienated consciousness. To create a functional future, we have to stand *with* the world, not apart from it. In this sense, the Old is the essential antidote to the runaway excess of the New.

The solution, as with most of the dualities in our lives, lies in creating a sense of integration, a yoga of New and Old. The word yoga is from Sanskrit and is derived from the root *yuj*, "to attach, join, harness, yoke." At one level, it's a way to unify mind and body, but more generally, it's a practice that seeks to integrate the totality of the human experience, a way to become whole.

To put it another way, we need to become ambidextrous in our relationship to the world. On one hand, we must maintain a connection with our ancestral past, our animal nature, our habitat, and our interdependence. It's vital that we rediscover our wild physicality, our tribal nature and our participatory consciousness. On the other hand, we must respect the discoveries of science and master the skills required for modern living.

By itself, there's nothing wrong with the taxonomy, objectivity, and left-brain analysis of the New Way, but as always, it's a question of proportion. What we desperately need right now is balance: more Old, less New; more body, less head; more art, less analysis; more courage, less calculation. The task before us is to create a balanced, synergistic approach, an alliance of yin and yang. In this, the Old becomes the complement of the New. Each provides what the other lacks, and in this process, each can make the other stronger.

BODY

I never feel that I am inspired unless my body is also. It too spurns a tame and commonplace life. They are fatally mistaken who think, while they strive with their minds, that they may suffer their bodies to stagnate in luxury or sloth. A man thinks as well through his legs and arms as his brain. We exaggerate the importance and exclusiveness of the headquarters.

—Henry David Thoreau
Journal June 21, 1840

On the face of it, life in the modern world feels wildly complex, chaotic, and intimidating. Everywhere we look, we're confronted by the epic challenges of mismatch, environmental destruction, and social injustice. We'd like to make a difference, but few of us have the resources to bend public policy toward a functional future, and many of us feel utterly powerless.

But there's a hidden possibility that lies a lot closer than you might think. That's because your body is an essential part of the solution. Being healthy is not just important for us as individuals, it's also essential for learning the world, making good decisions and shaping the future. In other words, improving your health doesn't just make *you* better—it also makes *us* better.

The way we train and nurture our personal vitality has effects that extend well beyond the boundaries of our skin. Most obviously, our pro-health practices make our bodies more resilient and better able to withstand the rigors of mismatch and the myriad dilemmas we face each day. Being healthy also gives us a psycho-physical surplus, which means we'll have more to give to the world. But even beyond that, health is powerfully contagious and far more influential than you might think. The way we stand, move, and behave also moves the people around us. As Nicholas Christakis and James Fowler observed in their book *Connected*, our behaviors ripple widely through our social networks and impact not just our friends, but even our friends' friends' friends.[37] In other words, taking care of yourself is a profoundly pro-social and pro-future act.

KNOW THE ANIMAL

The first step is to recover our physicality and get to know our bodies. What does it mean to be a human animal? As inhabitants of our own skin, this might seem like the easiest thing in the world, and in the Old Way, this kind of knowledge is taken for granted. In the Paleo, everyone in your tribe would have been physically engaged, simply by virtue of vigorous daily movement and exposure to the elements. In this world, all of us were physically educated and athleticism was normal.

But tragically, this is not what we see in the modern world, where physical ignorance and apathy have become normalized. Labor-saving devices, mechanized transport, and climate-controlled dwellings deprive the body of essential, life-promoting physical challenge, transforming our entire world into what is essentially an assisted-living facility. It's no wonder we've lost touch with our animal nature. In a very real sense, we no longer know who we are.

This is where it helps to know the back story, especially the one about René Descartes and his demons. As you might remember,

Descartes was a dedicated skeptic who refused to believe anything that wasn't explicitly proven to him with empirical data. To be on the safe side, he proposed to doubt everything, *even the actual sensations from his own body.* After all, he reasoned, there might be some kind of evil demon pumping false information into his brain, and how would he ever know? To avoid this conundrum, he resolved to identify exclusively with his mind and leave his body out of it.

To our modern minds, this might strike us as a sensible proposition, but from an Old Way perspective, it comes across as one of the strangest, most abnormal ideas in history. Descartes was instrumental in paving the way for modern science, but he would have been laughed out of any native tribe. For indigenous people, physical sensation was (and is) absolutely essential for survival. In a hunter–gatherer setting, you don't doubt such sensations; you pay close attention to what they're telling you. This is how you stay alive. In fact, success as a hunter–gatherer hinged on developing a sense of intimacy and trust with what your body revealed about the world.

But in the West, we took Descartes at his word, and now we're living with the consequences: a nasty mind–body split that causes no end of human suffering, an education system that gives priority to cognition over physicality, and a staggering epidemic of lifestyle disease that's sapping the vitality of people around the world. Mind–body duality has given us some great power, but it has also inflicted some terrible costs.

The legacy of Descartes lives on in scientific and academic circles in the form of extreme skepticism about personal experience. Data rules the day, and the body has no voice in the process. On the contrary, hard-headed researchers caution against giving weight to individual stories or lived experience. As they often put it, "anecdotes aren't evidence." In other words, the subjective, personal experience of individuals simply doesn't count. Your body may be telling you a rich and powerful story about the nature of the world, but unless that story is confirmed by a rigorous, double-blind study with precision measurement and statistical analysis, that story is irrelevant. To be sure, this orientation is good for advancing scientific progress, but it's a catastrophe for personal power and the legitimacy of the body.

In short, we've become the talking heads of the animal world. We've fallen in love with cognition, obsessed with the brain and infatuated with our intelligence. We treat the body as an afterthought, a transport device, and an inconvenience. Above all, we think of the brain as a top-down, command-and-control system that tells the body what to do. The only time most of us pay attention to our bodies is when something goes wrong. Sadly, we've got it precisely upside down.

THE BODY IS PRIMARY

It's essential to remember that the body came first, long before our higher-order forms of cognition. In our daily lives, we're usually unaware of the flow of influence, but the body is always a major, if not *the* major driver of behavior and cognition. In other words, our thoughts and decisions are never exclusively cognitive. In fact, the body is always getting into the act: If you're holding a warm beverage in your hand, you're more likely to rate your companions as "warm." If the clipboard you're holding is heavy and solidly built, you're more likely to rate a job candidate as "substantive." If you're sitting on a chair with a hard edge, you're more likely to drive a hard bargain in a negotiation.[38]

And yet we continue to delude ourselves. As dedicated Cartesians, we believe that thought is an independent process. Cognition lives in the head and must therefore be superior to everything below it. But the top-down forces of mental control and willpower are recent, relatively weak, and notoriously unreliable. In contrast, the bottom-up forces are ancient, persistent, and incredibly powerful in driving our behavior and decisions. Survival is always the ultimate priority. If the body senses a threat in any form, it seizes control with direct, neu-ro-hormonal overrides. It's no wonder the ancient, aboriginal forces usually win out. We are, first and foremost, bodies. And in many ways, our bodies are smarter than we are.

This perspective has been championed famously by neuroscientist Antonio Damasio. In his book *Descartes' Error*, he bemoans "the abyssal separation of mind and body" and declares that "There is no such thing as a disembodied mind."[39] Damasio believes emotions play a critical role in high-level cognition and decision-making. In other words, rationality requires emotional input and cannot operate independently. Feelings motivate reason, intelligence, and creative action. Damasio is skeptical of traditional neuro-centric, brain-centric accounts of how the human organism functions. As he puts it, "The brain is a servant of the body."

EMBODIED COGNITION

The primacy of the body is reflected in the emerging concept called "embodied cognition." The idea is simple: intelligence is not concentrated in the head or in any particular region of the brain but is distributed throughout the body and even the so-called "outside world." A typical definition puts it this way:

> ...the nature of the human mind is largely determined by
> the form of the human body—that ideas, thoughts, concepts,
> categories and all other aspects of the mind are shaped by
> the body.[40]

In *Embodied Cognition: A Field Guide*, author Michael Anderson tells us that

> the nature of cognition is being re-considered. Instead of
> emphasizing formal operations on abstract symbols, the
> new approach foregrounds the fact that cognition is, rather,

a *situated* activity, and suggests that thinking beings ought therefore be considered first and foremost as acting beings.

In other words, our mental activity doesn't come out of thin air, as Descartes would have it. Rather, it's the product of physical cells, tissues, and circuits interacting with one another. The body, in partnership with the microbiome, constantly produces hormones, myokines, and other informational substances that circulate through the bloodstream and in turn, influence what we think and say. George Lakoff, the cognitive neuroscientist best known for his book *Don't Think of An Elephant*, put it perfectly: "Every thought you have is physical."

In this light, our modern educational hierarchy comes across as outdated, misinformed, and tragically flawed. By focusing exclusively on the mind and exiling the body, we're really only training a fraction of the total animal. It's no wonder so many students rebel; their bodies want to be part of the action.

In the popular press, embodied cognition is often presented as a new concept, but it's really been obvious to artists and philosophers for a long time. The philosopher William James knew it well: "Pretend what we may, the whole man within us is at work when we form our philosophical opinions." Likewise, the sculptor Auguste Rodin in describing his famous work:

> What makes my Thinker think is that he thinks not only with his brain, with his knitted brow, his distended nostrils, and compressed lips, but with every muscle of his arms, back and legs, with his clenched fist and gripping toes.

The body, in other words, is the original source for our intelligence and our behavior. One of the greatest tragedies of our time is that we've exiled and devalued our physicality, the very wellspring of our creativity and our intelligence. Medical commentators are quick to complain about sedentary living and the health consequences of inactivity, but the problem runs far deeper than most of us realize. As long as we continue to exclude the body from our attention and our cultural conversations, we'll never be able to generate the kinds of solutions we so desperately need.

To be sure, there's plenty of hand-wringing these days about lifestyle disease—obesity, diabetes, heart disease, and all the rest. But bad as these afflictions are, we're missing the real tragedy: the demise of our very physicality, our most precious heritage. Our culture has normalized physical apathy, and even worse, we seem to have come to an implicit agreement that people simply aren't going to exercise or eat right, so we'd better go all in on technological "solutions." But giving up on the body is tantamount to giving up on life itself. If an alien power has suddenly arrived on Earth in prehistory and imposed the kind of physical neglect we're experiencing today, we would have fought back with every fiber of our being, tooth and claw.

THE VOICE OF THE BODY

The body speaks to us in a language without words. In prehistory, people listened carefully to this voice and used it to help them navigate the survival challenges of the natural world. If the body spoke of danger or safety, of changes in weather or the movement of animals, people paid attention. But today, we've stopped listening. The body tries to express its passion for movement, sensation, exploration, and experience, but we close our ears and turn away. Consumed with work, cognition, distraction, and amusement, we shut ourselves off from the wellspring of our vitality. The body, we foolishly think, can wait.

This is a perilous way to live. Like any normal person, the body wants to be heard and appreciated. If we ignore the voice of physicality for long enough, the body stops talking and retreats into apathy, lethargy, and depression. We go in search of remedies, but no amount of chemical intervention can make up for the failure of our attention. If we're going to be whole, we have to give the body its voice and listen to what it's telling us.

THE CHALLENGE OF FAMILIARITY

The time has come to refresh our physicality and get back in touch with our animal selves. On the face of it, this might seem like a simple proposition, but our effort is complicated by familiarity and neuroplasticity. That is, the longer we live in our bodies, the more they fade into the background of our attention.

When we're infants, the body is utterly astonishing in its form and capability. We spend hours exploring it, playing with it, and above all, noticing it. It's an endless source of fascination. But as we become increasingly familiar with our physicality and the world, our sense of awe and astonishment begin to fade. The body—this vast, ancient, magnificent, pulsing natural system—dissolves into the background of awareness.

It's an odd and distressing process. The human body (which includes the brain) is easily the most sophisticated, complex, and awe-inspiring "thing" in our universe. By all rights, we ought to be living in a constant state of amazement at our form and function. But as our bodies become increasingly familiar, our fascination wanes and the body disappears from the radar of our attention. And the longer we live, the more invisible our bodies become.

Naturally, this process is made a thousand times worse by sedentary living and domestication. As we grow into adulthood, our physical experience becomes increasingly routine and habitual. Forced into chairs and vehicles thousands of times each year, we become increasingly divorced from our physical capability, a condition sometimes described as sensory–motor amnesia. After years and decades of chronic sitting, sensory and motor circuits stop talking to one another. In a very real way, the body goes numb and yes, dumb.

And that's just the beginning. Without regular physical experience, our very sense of identity begins to degrade, with serious mental health consequences. When we're no longer grounded in the body, our sense of self begins to drift and we become lost in space. In turn, we're more apt to become anxious, frightened, and vulnerable to minor stressors. No amount of medication or cognitive therapy can remedy this affliction. What we really need is a return to our native physicality.

THE TAO OF EXPERIENCE

So how are we to remember and know the body? Guided by modern culture, many of us turn to New Way methods. We read everything we can about training, exercise science, and diet. We read research reports and listen to experts. The information we discover is sometimes useful, but it doesn't really get to the heart of the matter. The body, after all, doesn't really care about research, data, charts, or numbers. What the body really cares about is experience.

Experience is the native language of the body. Every adaptation and adjustment comes about because the body had some kind of physical encounter with the world. For the vast, overwhelming majority of our time on this planet, experience has been the body's exclusive teacher. If you really want to know your body, you've got to put it into authentic, meaningful, physical contact with the world. There has to be a doing, a striving, and an engagement. Theory is all well and good, but without experience, there can be no adaptation.

As it stands, most of our attempts to understand and know the body fall into two distinct camps: the romantic and the classical. This distinction was famously explored by Robert Pirsig in *Zen and the Art of Motorcycle Maintenance*. As he saw it:

> The romantic mode is primarily inspirational, imaginative, creative, intuitive. Feelings rather than facts predominate…

The classic mode, by contrast, proceeds by reason and by laws—which are themselves underlying forms of thought and behavior...

We recognize the classic perspective when people talk about systems, hierarchies, sequences, units, precision, and quantity. In contrast, the romantic emphasizes experience, aesthetics, passion, wildness, sensation, and quality. This is precisely what we see in the world of human movement. When the romantic steps into the gym or the studio, he's looking to create an experience with meaning. He understands the language of feeling, expression, and inspiration. For him, quality movement is considered an end in itself. If it feels good, it probably is good.

Classicists, on the other hand, focus their attention on data, quantification, and measurable results. When the classical exerciser laces up his shoes, he's looking to achieve a certain performance result, an outcome. Practice sessions are a means to an end, ideally a record-setting performance or a trip to the Finals.

In the world of sports and movement, the romantic prefers dance, yoga, aikido, and tai chi and wouldn't be caught dead with a clipboard. The classicist prefers weight lifting, running, swimming, or other activities that can be readily quantified and analyzed. He derives a sense of satisfaction from recording his performance and comparing it to previous efforts.

To each his own, but from a historical perspective one thing is clear: For the vast majority of human history, the romantic view has been the default. Hunters and gatherers never measured any dimension of their bodies or their performance and yet they succeeded in a world that demanded robust, daily athleticism. But today, the classic mode has come to dominate our approach. The focus is on left-brain, professional knowledge, research, data, methods, and statistics. It's about optimizing sets and reps and getting all the wonky details just right.

This practice may well yield some valuable clinical benefits and training refinements, but when you get right down to it, we are still animals. And in the world of animal bodies and physicality, the romantic view has been the exclusive perspective for millions of years. The classical orientation has its uses, but if all we do is measure and track our performance, we risk obliterating the very thing we're trying to experience—a joyful and integrating sense of living in our bodies. Our bodies come into the world as robust animals, fully wired for physicality and exuberance. We have what we need to succeed. If you really want to know your physicality, go outdoors and put yourself in direct contact with weather, plants, animals, and natural terrain. Put down your phone and push yourself.

GOING WILD

From a historical perspective, being physically normal means being strong, endurant, agile, and resilient, but it also means being wild. Wildness is our default state, our natural condition. For the vast majority of our time on this planet, we've been wild animals living in outdoor settings. To be wild means to be fully alive and openly physical. It means feeling the power of Life as it courses through your bloodstream. It's the full expression of your animal nature. And it's perfectly normal.

Modern health experts sometimes tell us that *wellness* is our objective, but the word lacks power and vitality. It has no claws, no teeth, no bone, and no blood. It's sterile and lifeless. In contrast, *wildness* has a deep and powerful history that puts us back into community with all the other creatures of the Earth. And it's a powerful antidote to the domestication that pulls so many of us into sedentary living and depression.

Wellness is a bland, indoor word, but *wildness* has heart and spirit, guts and gonads. It connects deeply into human and animal history, into the very spirit of the biosphere. Wildness is exciting, risky, dangerous, exuberant, and in turn, erotic. Wellness is a low bar that demands little in the way of commitment or risk, but wildness is an aspiration to merge with the entirety of the biosphere and the spirit of every animal that has ever lived. Wellness is simply a state of being okay, but wildness is the feeling of being outrageously alive.

This suggests a practical, rarely discussed strategy for building and maintaining our health: seek out wild people, especially those with the insight, awareness, and energy to resist the seductions of domestication. Look for vitality, curiosity, and imagination. Look for people who understand the perils of modernity and are willing to consider something different. Look for people with light in their eyes and fight in their spirit. Hang out with these people, and you'll see your health improve.

MOVEMENT

That which is used develops. That which is not used wastes away.

—Hippocrates

When it comes to recovering our wildness and our native physicality, vigorous movement is the obvious place to begin. The benefits are familiar and scarcely need elaboration; it's safe to say that every aspect of the human experience is enhanced by regular movement. Not only is it good for the heart, lungs, and muscular systems, but it also has profoundly salutary effects on the brain and in turn, cognitive performance.

If vigorous physical movement were a pill, it'd be the best-selling drug in history, but physical movement is far more than medicine. It's a way to know ourselves, our bodies, and the world. It's a way to connect with the flux and flow of life itself. It's a way to express some of our deepest emotions. It's a way to communicate and to understand.

Before going further, it's essential to understand the fundamental difference between *exercise* and *movement*. To put it simply, exercise is a repetitive, stereotyped pattern of activity we practice to "get in shape." Movement is a much broader category that includes all kinds of physical activity, including a great many behaviors that lie outside the realm of exercise—things like dance, gardening, physical labor, and sex.

Once again, history tells what we need to know. Prior to the modern age, there was no such thing as exercise. Primal humans gathered, hunted, played, and danced, and got plenty of movement simply staying alive. In contrast, exercise has been part of our experience for only a tiny fraction of our time on earth. Likewise for nonhuman animals—never do we observe other creatures doing anything resembling exercise. They hunt, gather, graze, mate, play, fight, and flee, but never do they perform repetitive movements for the sake of "staying in shape." They move their bodies for pleasure, to explore, or stay alive, but otherwise, they eat, explore, or rest.

This suggests a broader view and a new appreciation for context. Instead of isolating ourselves in specialized facilities with specialized machines, we'd do better to engage in experience that's common with every primate and every mammal, a deep heritage that goes back more than a hundred million years. When we move our bodies, we celebrate our kinship with the natural world and make ourselves part of something much, much larger than ourselves.

Ultimately, it's movement, not exercise, that keeps us healthy. Across the board, research shows that *all* forms of physical movement are health-promoting and that exercise is only one possibility among many. This leads us to a powerful general principle: when it comes to maintaining health, exercise is optional, but movement is essential. No one ever died from lack of exercise, but a lack of physical movement is absolutely dangerous to our health. As long as we're getting vigorous movement during the course of our days, we can skip the exercise altogether. If we can make our lives more vigorous, our health will largely take care of itself.

There are as many ways to move as there are people on Earth, but a few general principles will go a long way:

MAKE IT FUNCTIONAL

All the movement arts are good, but no matter your particular style, a functional orientation is essential. Functional training is a concept that's emerged from the athletic training and physical therapy communities over the last several decades. In contrast to common appearance-based disciplines, the focus is on our ability to execute practical movements that are relevant to the actual challenges of our lives. It's our ability to move powerfully, gracefully, and effectively that counts.

In other words, stop obsessing about how your body looks or should look. Instead, follow the recommendation of functional coaches around the world: "Work movements, not muscles." Remember, there were no cameras or mirrors in the Paleo, and you could easily go an entire lifetime without knowing what your body looked like. So stop worrying about appearance and focus instead on competence. Work the movements that will support you in daily life: walking, squatting, reaching, lifting, and carrying.

There's no need to get overly sophisticated with any of this. Challenge your strength with body weight exercises like squats and lunges. Do some pull-ups and swing some kettle bells. Do some dead lifts with dumbbells or rocks. Bend your knees and make every exercise a core exercise. Use your whole body to move the weight. And above all, train for the way you want to live.

MAKE IT DIVERSE

In today's world of high-performance athletic training, it's tempting to suppose that the path to health lies in some perfect workout formula, administered by an expert, but from a practical and health standpoint, sporting specializations and sophisticated training programs are suspect. In moderation, they can improve our athletic performance, but over time, highly repetitive movements take their toll on joints and tissues, and probably even the nervous system.

This all makes sense in terms of human evolution. Hunting, gathering, and exploration are inherently diverse. The hunter must adapt to a variety of terrain, plants, animals, and weather. Every hunt is different, and even in gathering, people are constantly changing their postures to adjust to conditions. We can be certain that repetitive-strain injuries were rare in hunter–gatherer societies. People were smart enough to change their movement patterns when discomfort set in.

So dive into a practice you love, but don't linger too long. Try different sports and training practices. Play with your physicality. Avoid year-round training by taking a seasonal approach. If you like strength training, try endurance. If you love cardio, do some weights. If you always move in a single plane or at a single speed, try something that turns or spirals. Work diagonal patterns, arcs, circles, and figure-eights. Keep moving your movement. What you lose in specialization and elite achievement, you'll gain in pleasure and longevity.

GO OUTSIDE

Many of us are conditioned to believe that the place to move the body is the gym or studio, but if you really want to learn and understand your physicality, the place to go is outdoors. This is where your real physical education takes place. This is where you'll learn the way your body responds to natural light, temperature changes, variations in habitat, weather and terrain (uphill, downhill, sidehill, rough, smooth, sandy, muddy). This is primal, essential knowledge that can only be learned in natural habitat.

Working out in an indoor gym has value, but it's really an *in vitro* experience ("in glass"). You can learn how your body responds to exertion, and you can learn some things about movement quality, balance, and posture, but there's only so much you can do inside. In contrast, outdoor experience is *in vivo*; you're in direct contact with the ancient forces that sculpted your body in the first place. It makes sense to assume that this is the ideal environment to learn what you're made of.

Even better, put yourself in situations that demand a physical commitment. Serious outdoor exertion and adversity are powerful teachers. Climbing, backpacking, mountain biking, scrambling, and solid hiking tell us who we are. If you really want to learn your body, go further than you think you can. Stick your neck out, extend your physicality, and you'll find out what you're made of.

MOVEMENT IN CONTEXT

In our popular imagination, we like to think exercise is something called a "workout" that takes place in a specialized setting such as a gym or studio. It's separate from our regular lives, and we're quick to suppose that it's going to take us a big chunk of time, a shower, and a change of clothes to make it all work. Obviously, this presents a barrier to participation, which is why so many people shrug it off.

But what if we could integrate movement right into the fabric of our lives as they are? Instead of looking for a special facility or setting, what if we could practice our physicality right where we live and work? Instead of looking for a perfect solution, maybe could we make do with regular movement snacks, right in the midst of the daily chaos.

Imagine the setting: You've been chained to your desk for hours or stuck in a meeting, trying to hash out the excruciating details of an urgent project. Everything is taking longer than you think, and you can feel your vitality draining away. You don't have time to go to the gym, the pool, or the track, but there's a stairwell, a hallway, or a parking lot where you can escape for awhile. You've only got ten minutes, but ten minutes is a lot more than nothing.

Start with running in place and take it from there. Get up on the balls of your feet and add some variations in your steps. Wide "monster" running is fun and pumpy. If you've got room, add some skipping, lateral runs, hopping and zigzags. Add in some squats and swings. You might not have a kettle bell handy, but you can do similar movements. Squat, touch the ground with your fingertips, reach high, then repeat. Now, do some reaches overhead and some standing backstroke moves. Do some fantasy jump rope. Get your breath and blood moving, then go back to work.

Naturally, these movement snacks aren't going to raise your fitness to an elite level, but that's not the point. The idea is to work these short sessions into your life as it unfolds. Even one minute of running in place, repeated often, adds up to a real difference. Of course, you might get a little sweaty, and you might attract some attention, but this is a small price to pay. Better to be openly physical and engaged than to miss out entirely. Don't let the perfect be the enemy of the good.

TRAIN STRONG TO BE STRONG

In the popular imagination, physical exercise is mostly about muscle and adipose tissue, but in fact, the effect is always psycho-physical. The beauty of movement training is that it works across the entire mind–body continuum. If you stimulate the body with vigorous strength or endurance training, you're touching the mind and spirit too.

You've probably noticed the benefits in your life already. Think of the last time you were faced with an onerous work-related task you didn't want to deal with. You struggled at your desk for a while, then gave up in frustration and headed to the gym or the open road. You hit it hard for an hour or so and on your return, the onerous task just didn't seem so intimidating; you dove in, focused and refreshed, and got it done. Physical exertion made the difference. Boosting your physicality gave you psycho-physical power.

It's no wonder strength and resistance training have a proven anti-depression effect.[41] The specific details of the training program aren't particularly important; it's the exertion that counts. Challenge the body to become stronger, and the entire organism goes along for the ride. In this light, physical training becomes super-relevant to our modern predicament. It's about a lot more than making our bodies stronger—it's about making our lives stronger. It's about building our capacity to persist under the weight of cognitive overload, social stress, and large-scale systemic crises. In this sense, physical training is an essential antidote to the challenge of mismatch and life in this alien environment.

STAY IN TOUCH

In the end, the essential ingredient in maintaining your vitality is not the number of workouts you do or the specifics of your training, but your relationship with your body and your physical experience in the world. Just as we substitute the word *movement* for *exercise*, we can also replace *fitness* with *physicality*. The word *fitness* is confusing because it's used in entirely different ways, depending on context. In the world of biology, it means reproductive success, but in the world of health, it's all about strength, muscle and cardio. In contrast, *physicality* is primal and unambiguous. It takes us all the way back to our deep ancestral roots and our common heritage with all animal life.

This puts our focus back on what really matters. Is your physical

memory fresh, or is it fading away into the background of your awareness? When was the last time you felt the vitality coursing through
your tissue? When was the last time you felt a sense of wildness?
Obviously, it's not easy to maintain contact in our sedentary world,
but unless we make intentional efforts to close the gap, we'll drift
further and further away from what's truly important. So don't get
distracted by details. Instead, savor your physicality and the feeling
of being outrageously alive. Refresh your experience with vigorous
movement, sports, manual labor, drumming, hiking, dancing, and
sex. Keep your vitality and your wildness close.

FOOD

The human animal has to eat, and for our Paleolithic ancestors,
the enterprise was pretty simple. Food was sometimes hard to find,
catch, and kill, and some of it might even have been poisonous, but
once you learned the fundamentals, there wasn't much to be confused about. Hunt, gather, prepare, eat; your tribe consumes what
habitat provides. Even well into the age of agriculture, food remained
straightforward. People lived in coherent cultures built around food
that was grown and prepared regionally and according to tradition.

But today, the situation is a thousand times more complex and
chaotic. Food comes to us at the speed of modern transport, cultures
overlap, experts argue about the details, and in the meantime, our
confusion grows. In this respect, modern agriculture has actually
given us a bumper crop of ambiguity and doubt. We like to think that
the modern age has given us sophisticated knowledge in all things,
but incredibly, we're the first people in history that don't know what
or how to eat.

Our problems are numerous. In the first place, our modern food
environment is profoundly abnormal. For the last few centuries,
we've developed ever more intensive systems for turning habitat

into calories, and we've gotten really good at it. Every link in the chain is now streamlined and optimized. From vast, industrial-scale farms to the restaurant table, we've eliminated every possible source of friction. This has given us a huge oversupply of cheap food, and today, most of us are surrounded by food, or more precisely, food-like products.

The problem is that much of what we eat in the modern world isn't, strictly speaking, food. Chemists and food scientists have learned how to tweak formulas (not recipes) to manufacture (not cook) a vast array of highly profitable and addictive food-like products. Advertisers assault us with nonstop images of these products, stimulating our appetites around the clock. None of this is historically or physiologically normal.

To make matters worse, even our basic, real foods are changing in parallel with climate change. Rising CO_2 in the atmosphere increases the speed of photosynthesis, but it also stimulates plants to produce more carbohydrates at the expense of other nutrients we depend on—protein, iron, calcium, potassium, zinc, and iron. Over the past three decades, the overall concentration of minerals in agricultural crops has dropped by 8 percent on average. Writing in *Trends in Ecology and Evolution* in 2002, author Irakli Loladze explained it this way: "We are witnessing the greatest injection of carbohydrates into the biosphere in human history."[42]

This would all be plenty bad enough, but we're also distracted by our modern obsession with single ingredients, a trend described by Michael Pollan as "nutritionism." Ever since 1747, when the Scottish surgeon James Lind discovered that citrus foods (vitamin C) helped prevent scurvy, we've gone all in on the promise of isolated ingredients. Every day brings some new claim about the merits or dangers of some particular substance, and for many people, eating has come to resemble a laboratory experiment. No longer do we say, "I'm hungry." We say, "I need protein" or, "I need carbs."

In the process, food has now become a potent source of anxiety and a battleground of competing claims. Some people simply give up and eat whatever comes, while others become afflicted with *orthorexia*, a psychological disorder defined as "an extreme or excessive preoccupation with avoiding foods perceived to be unhealthy." Likewise, our relationship with food is often saturated with religious overtones. Advocates of various diets are often quick to moralize about what people should be eating. Zealots evangelize about food selection and even attack those who are eating "forbidden foods." Some people are considered heretics, some have been successfully converted, and some have fallen from grace.

FOOD IN TWO DIMENSIONS

One useful way to cut through the confusion is to look at food in two dimensions, *content* and *context*. Content refers to the actual ingredients of our food, the macro nutrients of protein, fat, and carbohydrates, as well as various micronutrients, hormones, antibiotics, or toxins. Context refers to the setting and environment that surround our food: the way it's grown, produced, transported, prepared, shared, and consumed. Most especially, it's about the meaning that comes along for the ride.

Without question, the lion's share of modern conversation about food and nutrition is about content. In the New Way tradition, we treat food as substance, independent from both habitat and people. But in fact, food has larger meanings that speak directly to our happiness and our health. In a normal, ancestral setting, eating was a powerful experience that brought people and habitat together. Every bite told a story of land, water, plants, animals, and the people who hunted, gathered, or farmed there. Every meal reminded people who they were and where they came from. Food was grounding.

But in the New Way, food is nothing more than fuel, a substance with a certain chemical profile. We overlook the fact that food has powerful meanings, including powerful placebo and nocebo effects. To be sure, the body needs nutrients, but it also craves story. Belief is so powerful in the human animal that it's easy to imagine that so-called "bad foods," if eaten in meaningful settings, might actually be beneficial to the body. Similarly, it's easy to imagine that so-called "good foods," if eaten in meaningless settings, might well fail to nourish us. Cartesian nutritionists like to focus on the mechanical effects of specific ingredients, but for meaning-sensitive people living *in vivo*, context might even trump content. The lesson: pay attention to not just what's in your food, but what's around it.

This suggests another useful distinction: "Earth food" has a clear connection to the land and the people who grew it, gathered it, or hunted it and prepared it. You can source it. You've got some sense of what kind of habitat it was raised in and who was involved in getting it to your table. "Space food," on the other hand, has no visible connection to the land or the people who produced it. It simply shows up in your life, ready to be consumed.

Without question, the vast majority of food in the modern world is space food: drive-through, takeout, room service, vending machines, online ordering, airline food, and soon, drone delivery. It just appears in our supermarkets, in our homes, or on our tables. Our food no longer bonds us to the land or one another. Convenience rules the day.

But food is about more than chemistry. The space food that arrives on your doorstep from an online merchant may well be technically perfect in every biochemical detail. Likewise, the space food that arrives at your restaurant table may well have an ideal nutritional profile. But if you really want to eat in a meaningful way, you need to know the history of what you're eating, the habitat it came from, and the people who made it possible. Otherwise it's just a bunch of molecules. And man does not live by molecules alone.

Unfortunately, it's hard to avoid space food in today's world. Earth food is often scarce, expensive, and time consuming, but we must do the best we can. Eat the space food as you must, but make the effort to connect your food to people and habitat. Have your friends over, and go out of your way to find foods with meaning. Don't just shop for ingredients; shop for stories that bond people to the land. Then add more meaning to the mix by preparing them by your own hand. Serve earth food to your guests in celebration.

PLANTS, ANIMALS, RESPECT

As for the debate between vegetarian versus carnivorous diets, the facts are mostly old news. Without question, plant-based diets are good for our bodies, and it's also clear that modern meat production is morally abhorrent. Plant-based diets are also a lot easier on the Earth: less deforestation, less fertilizer runoff, less fresh water use, and less methane production from livestock.

But at the same time, a lot of well-informed nutritionists believe that humans need at least some meat for basic physical health. Meat consumption has been a feature of most human cultures for most of our history, and it's safe to assume we're wired to seek it out, enjoy it, and benefit from eating it.

Unfortunately, there aren't many good workarounds for this dilemma. To be sure, we can eat less meat and source what we do eat more humanely. We can stop consuming meat that is morally compromised and shift more of our consumption to wild fish and game, if we can get it. But these are only partial solutions, and for the time being we're stuck with a system that is simply unsatisfactory. Adjustments are obviously in order, but there's only so much we can do.

What we can do is pay our food—carnivorous or vegetarian—the respect it deserves. We may not be able to access the earth food we desire, but we can pay attention to its source, its history, and its meaning. This is the real problem with our modern fast food environment. When something is fast, easy, cheap, and plentiful, we're

not inclined to pay much attention to its meaning, history, or consequences. Whatever the ingredients might happen to be, it's hard to
see much significance in something you can get with the push of a
button. Why should we respect something that just appears through
a car window?

But it's really a marvel that we can eat the way we do. The modern supermarket holds the collective bounty of a thousand square
miles of land, condensed and refined by the labor of thousands of
people, powered by thousands of gallons of fossil fuels and nitrogen
fertilizers. By all rights, we ought to be in awe of the supermarket every time we visit, but lulled to sleep by familiarity, we push the cart
and forget.

So rather than stressing over the ingredients and biochemistry of
our food, maybe we'd do better to pause before we eat and think
about all the things that had to happen to make it possible. Think
about the habitat, the people and the labor that went into the process. Then, appreciate it.

TO-DO LIST

In spite of all the noise in the system, the path to health and nutritional sanity is actually pretty clear:

Start by getting over the focus on single ingredients. Stop thinking
in terms of "diet" and start thinking about whole, minimally processed food that ties people to habitat and to one another. Humans
are flexible omnivores who can thrive on a wide variety of food-based
diets. Likewise, stop worrying so much about biochemistry and the
therapeutic effects of specific nutrients. The whole food *is* the nutrient. As Dr. David Katz of the Yale School of Preventive Medicine
puts it, "The active ingredient in broccoli is broccoli."

Next, focus on a food-based diet. Humans have co-evolved with
real food for millions of years, and our bodies are intimately, mi-
croscopically adapted to whole, natural foods. Every detail of our

digestion and biochemistry is the way it is because of our history in wild habitat. Above all, learn to distinguish between real food and "edible food-like substances." When in doubt, choose the simple options.

Focus on quality, not quantity. This may sound obvious, but it's backed up by research, specifically a 2018 study published in the *Journal of the American Medical Association.*[43] Researchers found that people who cut back on added sugar, refined grains, and highly processed foods while concentrating on eating plenty of vegetables and whole foods—without worrying about counting calories or limiting portion sizes—lost significant amounts of weight over the course of a year. In other words, it always gets back to the basics.

It's not just what we eat, but also when. For many, the last meal of the day comes late in the evening, a practice most nutritionists now consider a health negative. Late eating spikes our blood sugar just as the body is winding down into inactivity and sleep. In turn, this allows glucose to circulate in the blood and probably contributes to obesity, high blood sugar, and acid reflux.[44] By eating dinner early, we give the digestive system a chance to rest completely each night. These mini-fasts allow the system to completely metabolize the day's food and clear away byproducts and inflammation. This also allows the body to divert more of its resources away from digestion and back toward tissue healing and fighting infection. Try for a solid twelve hours between dinner and breakfast. Likewise, if you're drinking, do it early.

Above all, learn to cook. Cooking puts us into an intimate relationship with the process and the substances we consume; it turns space food into earth food. By learning to cook, you can get exactly what you want, in the quantities you feel are best for your body. While you're at it, cook big. Find something that works for you and your tribe and cook a big batch of it. Have a feast, then save the rest. That way, you won't be tempted to junk out; you'll be pleasantly surprised tomorrow when you open the fridge to find some really good stuff.

FOCUS ON THE POSITIVE

Ultimately, it's all about relationship. In the world of nutrition recommendations, we're often told to avoid a long list of "bad foods" that, according to the narrative, will destroy our health. There may well be some truth to such claims, but this focus on the negative can backfire and trigger our lust for "forbidden fruits." This is why diets usually fail; they're all about restriction, deprivation, and absence. As soon as the dieter commits, he instantly becomes aware of all the things he's not supposed to eat. In this way, prohibition inspires the very thing it's intended to prevent.

Instead, we'd do better to focus on the positive. Reject the "glow in the dark" food products, of course, but pay more attention to those foods that are rich and flavorful. Hunt down the earth foods that are really dense in color and flavor. The modern supermarket may well be stocked with an astonishing number of disease-promoting substances, but it's also bursting with real foods that will make our bodies healthier. This focus on abundance by itself is health promoting. When you see yourself living in a world of nutritional plenty, you can celebrate at every meal.

SLEEP

Even a soul submerged in sleep is hard at work and helps make something of the world.

—Heraclitus

Just as vigorous movement and real food are essential to our animal health, so too is sleep. For most of our history on Earth, sleep has been a simple pleasure, a mystery, and a fundamental part of human life. In general, people went to sleep when they felt the need, and no one seemed to fret over the details.[45] Nocturnal slumber was built into their bodies at the deepest levels.

It's impossible to say precisely how old sleep is, but we can be sure that it's truly ancient. All of our mammalian ancestors slept, and it's probable that dinosaurs slept as well. Paleontologists have recently discovered several fossilized skeletons of dinosaurs in what look like sleeping positions. Even jellyfish, some of the oldest creatures on the planet, show sleep-like behavior.[46]

Without question, sleep is an integral part of animal physiology and something we ought to honor and respect, but in the New Way, we simply don't. Today we live in an achievement culture where human value is measured by the ability to produce. People are considered worthy if they can get a lot done, and in this environment, sleep is considered a nuisance and an adversary. We idolize people who claim to get by with less sleep, and in many circles, people who do sleep are considered slackers, a point of view voiced most notably by Thomas Edison, who declared sleep to be "a criminal waste of time." It's no wonder we have trouble sleeping.

To make matters worse, our modern environment is distinctly sleep-hostile. Our homes are often plagued by noise and light pollution, and hotels are commonly located next to freeways where the rooms themselves are rarely truly dark or quiet. Even campgrounds in the mountains are no longer refuges for sleep. Late arrivals and partiers keep the noise going until the small hours. It seems there's no place left that's truly dark, quiet, and safe to rest our heads.

THE STATE OF SLEEP AND DREAMS

Our modern problems with sleep began hundreds of years ago, with the advent of artificial light, a trend documented in powerful detail by Paul Bogard in his book *The End of Night: Searching for Natural Darkness in an Age of Artificial Light*. By the end of the seventeenth century, many European cities had some form of artificial light, and darkness has been under assault ever since. As Bogard tells it, we're now suffering from a very real darkness deficit. According to the World Atlas of Artificial Night Sky Brightness,[47] two-thirds of the world's population no longer experiences a truly dark night and eight out of every ten children born today will never see the Milky Way. Most people are so awash in artificial light that their eyes never make a complete transition to night vision.

Not surprisingly, a substantial body of research concludes that most people in the modern world are substantially sleep-deprived.[48] In general, most of us go to bed too late and get up too early. A Gallup poll found that the average number of sleep hours per night dropped from almost 8 in 1942 to 6.8 in 2013. And as the world warms and nights become hotter, sleep is projected to become even shorter.

The consequences of sleep deprivation are no laughing matter: poor memory, increased impulsiveness, poor judgment, decreased creativity, weight gain, muscle atrophy, suppressed immunity, and increased stress have all been linked to inadequate or poor-quality sleep.[49] In 2005, the National Sleep Foundation found that 75 percent of American adults experienced sleep problems at least a few nights per week. According to Rubin Naiman at the Arizona Center for Integrative Medicine in Tucson, sleep disorders are arguably "the most prevalent health concern in the industrialized world."

But our problem goes even deeper. Research suggests that rapid eye movement (REM) sleep—the period of our most powerful dreaming—is vital to learning and creativity, but as sleep gets shorter, we also suffer an epidemic of REM sleep loss. "We are at least as dream-deprived as we are sleep-deprived," says Naiman.[50] In essence, we're depriving ourselves of a free, easy form of cognitive and spiritual renewal. This is no laughing matter.

Compounding the problem is the fact that alcohol, marijuana, and antidepressants are REM suppressants.[51] The popularity of these substances no doubt contributes significantly to an epidemic of dream-deprivation and in turn, our struggles in adapting to the modern world. We have no idea what the ultimate consequences of population-scale dream deprivation might be, but it's unlikely to be a pretty picture. In days to come, we may well consider dream deprivation to be a public health crisis in its own right.

WHY SLEEP IS VITAL

Contrary to popular belief, sleep is not an indulgence; it is absolutely vital for everything we want to do in our lives. Sleep is a heightened anabolic state, a time for the growth and rejuvenation of the immune, nervous, skeletal, and muscular systems. Certain restorative genes are turned on only during sleep, brain function and memory consolidation is enhanced, genes promoting myelin formation are turned on, creativity increases, and synapses are strengthened. Not surprisingly, sleep, learning, and mental well-being are tightly linked. Some researchers have even taken to describing sleep as "overnight therapy."[52] If sleep came in a bottle, it would—along with physical movement—be the most powerful medicine on earth.

Not only does sleep consolidate learning and memory, but it also serves a vital housekeeping function in the brain. In a 2014 TED-MED talk, neuroscientist Jeff Iliff proposed that sleep helps the brain rid itself of metabolic byproducts that build up during the day.[53] During sleep, brain cells contract slightly, allowing cerebrospinal fluid to flow along blood vessels through the brain. This fluid absorbs waste products, which are then emptied out into the bloodstream. Among the waste products are amyloids, insoluble misshapen proteins that form deposits and disrupt metabolic function. Excessive levels of these proteins have been implicated in Alzheimer's disease, an increasingly common form of dementia. In short, our modern, sleep-hostile lifestyle may well be a major contributing factor in the rising epidemic of neurological disorders.

THE LONG AND SHORT OF IT

Sadly, many of us are tortured by the belief that sleep must come in a single, unbroken block of roughly eight hours. If we fail to perform in this way, we conclude that we have something called a "sleep disorder," a label that mostly serves to increase our anxiety and in turn make it harder to actually sleep well. But our thinking is flawed. In fact, normal human sleep is probably not monolithic and might well depend on culture and environment. The new thinking is that humans are naturally inclined toward a segmented form of sleep with two distinct phases.

In 2001, historian Roger Ekirch published a seminal paper, drawn from sixteen years of research, revealing a wealth of historical evidence that prior to the modern era, humans slept in two distinct intervals. His book *At Day's Close: Night in Times Past* explores the sleeping behavior of people in the Middle Ages, before electric lighting. He found a common pattern: a "first sleep" from roughly 8 p.m. to midnight and a "second sleep" from 2 a.m. to sunrise, separated by a period of wakefulness that included socializing, quiet time, conversation, and sex. No one expected to sleep through the night.

This pattern probably held for much of human history, but began to disappear with the advent of electric lighting in the late nineteenth and early twentieth centuries. People began to stay up later in the evening as the night became fashionable, and as the Industrial Revolution took hold, sleep gradually morphed into the single block we know today.

Of course, few of us are willing to go to bed at 8 p.m. or adopt a segmented sleeping style, but this history suggests that being awake in the middle of the night may not be a disorder at all. More likely, it is a natural expression of our animal nature. As sleep psychologist Gregg Jacobs put it, "Waking up during the night is part of normal human physiology." The new understanding also tells us that sleep is flexible; there is probably no single right way to sleep.

In fact, we're also beginning to suspect that individual variations in sleep patterns probably served an important evolutionary purpose. This is precisely what Elizabeth Marshall Thomas described in *The Old Way*. In the wild, the Bushmen (and women) of the Kalahari didn't all go to sleep at the same time or sleep for the same duration. Rather, their sleep was staggered. At any given time of the night, someone would be up, tending the fire and minding the camp. Some went to sleep early, others late, and people napped whenever they felt the need. Most importantly, sleep was never stigmatized.

Far from being a problem, this staggered pattern was actually vital to survival. Individual variation meant someone was always up and vigilant, ready to spot predators and spread the alarm. Of course, we no longer worry about being attacked by lions in the middle of the night, but this story of individual variation does put our minds at ease. If your sleeping pattern doesn't happen to fall into line with the modern, conventional standard, maybe that's simply your personal variation at work. In another time, your sleeping style would have been a valued asset. If you happen to be awake in the middle of the night, you're simply playing out a normal evolutionary pattern; you probably would have fit right in with a tribe of ancestral hunter–gatherers.

This new–old view of sleep is liberating. We are now free to think of our insomnia, not so much as a disease or an affliction, but as a normal human variation. Above all, it is not something to be ashamed of. The fact that you're awake in the middle of the night may simply be an expression of an ancient physiological inclination. You're awake because the tribe needs you to check the fire and watch for lions. In all likelihood, there's nothing wrong with you or your brain.

It's also important to remember that most of human history took place in equatorial regions that were often pretty warm, if not outright hot. In this kind of world, people would have risen early for hunting, gathering, and exploring. Then, as temperatures warmed into the afternoon, they would have sought out shade and slept for a few hours. When things cooled off, they'd be active once again. This "biphasic" or "siesta" pattern is common in many traditional cultures.[54] In other words, napping during the day is probably a pretty normal human behavior. So don't feel bad if you're thinking about the couch in the early afternoon.

SLEEP ACTIVISM AND REFRAMES

By now we've all heard the tips and suggestions for better sleep: no caffeine after noon, make sure your room is dark and cool, and cut back on the screen time before bed. If you're drinking alcohol, do it early and in moderation. These "sleep hygiene" suggestions are sound, but our biggest problem with sleep may well be the way we frame it. If we continue to think of sleep as a selfish act of indulgence that takes us away from our work and family, sleep will continue to be an adversary and we'll feel guilty about getting the sleep we truly need.

In *The Sleep Revolution*, Arianna Huffington calls for a new sleep ethic and declares that "sleep is a basic human right." This is a step in the right direction, but it's also essential to recognize that sleep is actually a pro-social act. It's a gift to everyone around you and our world as a whole. When you're rested, you're simply easier to get along with. You're more stress tolerant and resilient and you're probably more sensitive to big-picture views of the world. In this sense, sleep is not only pro-health; it's also pro-future. When you head for the couch or off to bed, you're not being lazy and selfish; you're being smart and altruistic. So do us all a favor and give sleep the respect it deserves.

Likewise, we might do well to reframe our insomnia. In spite of our best efforts and our new understanding of historical sleep patterns, many of us feel cursed to wake up in the middle of the night.

We're craving sleep, but our minds race and the anxiety comes in waves. Vicious spirals of mental energy feed on themselves, making the night a special kind of torture.

It might seem like we're stuck, but all is not lost. From a Buddhist perspective, we might say that insomnia is one thing, and our resistance is another. The formula is simple: insomnia + resistance = suffering. It's one thing to be awake in the middle of the night, but it's another thing to curse the fact that you're awake. You may not have any choice about the fact that you've woken up, but you do have a choice as to whether to resist the experience. You may well prefer to be asleep, but your body has chosen wakefulness, so make something of it. Treat your wakefulness as raw material for something pleasant or creative. And above all, trust your body. Give it the time it needs, and it'll go to sleep when the time is right.

And remember, you're not alone in your effort. When your head hits the pillow, pay attention to your breath and think about all the people and animals on the planet who are sleeping at this very moment. Billions of creatures, fully absorbed by the sweet comfort of darkness and immersed in the world of dreaming. Taken together, this amounts to a vast, incredibly powerful state of experience that's sweeping across the planet every twenty-four hours. Think deeply about this and allow yourself to participate. Feel their sleep; feel their bodies and their breath. Sink in and join the sleepers. You are not alone.

PALEO DREAMS

As for what goes on when we're asleep, we might want to reconsider our thoughts about dreaming as well. In the New Way, we tend to think of dreams as nothing more than ghostly byproducts of neural activity, chemicals and neurons sorting out their circuitry and consolidating memories. In other words, dreams are considered random and mostly meaningless—nothing more than secondary epiphenomena.

But we can be sure that things were far different in the Old Way. In the Paleo, dreams were considered vital to the success of the hunt and the very survival of the tribe. People believed in dreams and savored them whenever possible. Some cultures even believed that the dream state was the real world and that wakefulness was just an interlude between the real action at night.[55] Some tribes gathered every morning for what we would today call a "dream report."

And maybe the Old Way is better. A culture that's curious about dreams and respectful of their power simply has a more integrated experience of life. Research has little to say on this matter, but it makes sense. When we bolt awake every morning and cast our dreams aside like some kind of irrelevant neural noise, we are literally rejecting part of who we are. It's impossible to say what the health consequences might be, but we can be sure of one thing: the body knows the difference.

So try respecting your dreams. Use the night sky as a canvas for your imagination. Dream of the stars and the planets, of animals, vistas, the waters. Dream of people, your tribe. Dream of the hunt. Dream of passionate sex. Dream of your breath and your powerful animal body. Dream of the Earth.

HABITAT

Our native soil draws all of us, by I know not what
sweetness, and never allows us to forget.

—Ovid
The Poems of Exile: Tristia and the Black Sea Letters

You cannot make the land go against itself. Not for long;
the land will rebel. You must shape the vision to the land,
not the land to the vision.

—Loial the Ogier
from *The Eye of the World* by Robert Jordan

Here's another thought experiment: Imagine the moment of your
birth, deep in prehistory, somewhere on the semi-wooded mosaic grasslands of Africa. Your tribe has been hunting and gathering with some success in recent years, and your mother is healthy,
strong, and active right up until the moment of truth. The big day
comes, and from the moment you leave your mother's body, you're
exposed to a world of plants, animals, soil, and—most importantly,
perhaps—immense numbers of microorganisms. Almost instantly, they begin colonizing your body, and before long they're multi-
plying, metabolizing, and forming countless chemical and genetic

relationships with every cell in your body.

In the days to come, Mom carries you from camp to camp in her arms or wrapped in an animal skin, which exposes you to yet more microbial life. If she's busy, she sets you down in the soft grass, and before long, you're crawling around, becoming ever more intimate with your habitat. Even when you begin to walk, you're still absorbing the living earth through your bare feet. As you grow, your physiology develops in tandem with your microbiome, and barring some major illness, infection, or predator attack, you'll grow up strong and healthy. Your habitat is not only on you; it's also in you. You are literally one with the biosphere.

But microbes are just the beginning. In a natural setting, your bond with habitat is reinforced in every moment of every day. Natural light floods your eyes and even receptors in your skin, synchronizing "clock cells" throughout your body and keeping your physiology on track. The food you eat comes directly from your bioregion, and every bite brings your body into closer harmony with the physiology of the land itself. Sensation tightens the bond even further. Every touch of plants, animals, soil, and moisture is recorded directly onto your body and brain. By the time you reach adulthood, you will know your world in intimate, tissue-level detail.

Sadly, this kind of origin story is almost unknown in our modern, alien environment. Today we're born into sanitized settings that have no resemblance to our ancestral world. From the very beginning, the surfaces we touch are smooth and even sterile. The microbes we do encounter are from hospital cribs and gowns, and ecologically speaking, they're arbitrary. Later, we go home to dwellings that are also isolated from natural light, textures, sounds, and soils. We may be several years old before we have any meaningful contact with natural habitat, and for some people, the experience never occurs at all. It's no exaggeration to say many of us in the modern world are habitat- and microbe-deprived. It's no wonder our bodies and our minds are suffering. When habitat changes so radically, our intimate, billion-year-old partnership with the microbial world is broken.

At this point it's essential to step back and consider our language. In conventional green writing, there's a lot of focus on *nature* and our disconnection from the natural world. People talk about "nature deprivation," "the end of nature," and of course, our need to somehow "save nature." But the word is slippery and confounding. The question "What's natural?" could keep philosophers occupied for years, and arguably, everything in the universe is "natural," even the destructive human impulses and technologies that are wreaking havoc across the planet. The words *nature* and *natural* are seductive, but they can also obscure our quest for understanding and action. Even worse, they're often abused by advertisers who attach them to all manner of products and services, many of which have no meaningful relationship to health or the Earth.

A better approach is to focus the lion's share of our attention on habitat. This is something we can have a productive conversation about. Habitat—to choose a very unfortunate metaphor—is concrete. We can see it, touch it, hear it, smell it, and learn it. This brings our conversation down to earth and gives us a better sense of what's possible. The idea of "saving nature" looms as an insurmountable challenge, but saving habitat is something we might actually be able to do. We can save forests, wetlands, lakes, and rivers. And most importantly, we can save critical corridors between healthy ecosystems so that plants and animals can maintain their range and genetic viability. This approach also saves us from a lot of unnecessary complexity. Instead of attempting to write policies to save every threatened species, we can accomplish the same objective by simply preserving their habitat. If animals have a viable place to live, they're more likely to survive.

OLD WAY

For those of us who've grown up in the modern world, habitat may well sound like something remote and maybe even imaginary. We've seen some pictures and heard some stories, but if we want to experience the real thing in person, we've got drive for hours or fly long distances. We take a few pictures, maybe even have an adventure, then travel back home to our regular lives. The experience may have been fun and even rewarding, but it was little more than an interlude in our "normal" abnormal experience.

But for Old Way cultures, the experience of habitat was immediate, immersive, and constantly engaging. Body, culture, and land were inseparable, and all human life was built on what Aldo Leopold called an "intense consciousness of land." The relationship was intimate: The human nervous system, primed by a million years of evolution, readily soaked up detailed features of the living world, mapping it to the brain, body, and spirit. In this way, we literally integrated habitat into our selves and our culture. And of course it would be this way—our very survival in ancestral environments depended on our ability to pay close attention to plants, animals, soil, and sky. In this kind of world, every nuance tells a story, and every sensation is potentially meaningful. Knowing habitat is what keeps you alive.

In this worldview, there was no "wilderness," no sense of a dark, alien world that lay outside and apart from normal human experience. All habitat was home, occasionally dangerous but perfectly knowable. In fact, the very idea of wilderness is a construct of alienated modern consciousness, a point made clear by Roderick Nash in *Wilderness and the American Mind*.

Until quite recently, the Old Way identification with habitat has been a universal human experience, common to every culture and people on Earth. As the Yanomami of Brazil put it, "The environment is not separate from ourselves; we are inside it and it is inside us; we make it and it makes us." Likewise, the Maori people of New Zealand: "I am the river, and the river is me." So too Nez Percé leader Chief Joseph: "The Earth and myself are of one mind." These people make no *self/other* distinction with habitat. They don't even imagine something called "the environment" that is "out there." Bodies and land are continuous. Whatever happens to the land also happens to the body. As an Australian aboriginal elder put it: "To wound the earth is to wound yourself, and if others are wounding the earth, they are wounding you." The land is us.

At its core, the Old Way was animated by a deep sense of biophilia, an idea made popular by the scientist E.O. Wilson, who described it as the "innate tendency to affiliate with life and life-like processes." Unfortunately, modern people tend to misunderstand the concept. We think of biophilia in squishy, romantic terms, as in "I love nature." We think nature is inhabited mostly by soft, furry animals, majestic mountains, and glorious sunsets. We love the glossy calendars and the photographic genre sometimes described as "ecoporn."[56] Nature is comforting, soothing and will heal whatever ails us.

But for aboriginal peoples, biophilia was far more elemental. Native people did not romanticize nature; they identified with it. They knew full well the dangers and hardships of their surroundings. Leaving camp in the morning was always a risky proposition; physical adversity, insect bites, exposure, poisonous plants, thunderstorms, and predation were daily events. It's almost impossible to imagine our hunting and gathering ancestors sitting around a campfire in the evening saying "I love nature." What they really felt was a deep sense of affiliation and kinship with the animals and habitat around them. Nature was never "other."

In the Old Way, culture was the glue that united people with place. Westerners like to think that songs and stories can be taken anywhere for amusement, but for native people, songs and stories are meant to be used at specific places and at certain times. For example, native Australians developed a language of song that united particular locations in habitat with people and the cosmos. For these people, the "songlines" are the furthest thing from entertainment; they are vital bonds that connect people to the land. They are literally matters of life and death.

We even see the human–habitat bond in the "geo-orientation" of some native peoples. When giving directions or learning dance steps, indigenous people are less likely to use terms like "left" and "right" and more likely to orient their bodies in relationship to the compass points of north, south, east, and west. Reportedly, this even extends to setting tables for meals. (The fork doesn't go on the left side of the plate, they might say, but on the north side.) This contrasts sharply with our modern, egocentric orientation, in which directions and dance steps are almost always given in reference to the self. Indeed, many modern people would be hard pressed to refer to the points of the compass at all.[57]

Given their intimate knowledge and identification with the land, native people trusted their habitat to provide. Consider the Bushmen of the Kalahari.[58] Long intergenerational experience, coupled with a highly sophisticated knowledge of their habitat, led to an unyielding confidence in the land to sustain their lives. Occasional drought and shortage were to be expected, but for the Bushmen, life was like living in the middle of a vast, sparsely stocked grocery store where all the food is free. You might have to walk long distances, and you might come up empty handed on occasion, but the food is there. Apply your knowledge, skill, and persistence and habitat will provide. Low stress, no worries. If the Bushmen were ever to meet with a branding professional, they might well choose this slogan to describe their worldview: "In habitat we trust."

As we look at the intimacy and power of the human–habitat bond in native culture, it comes as no surprise to find that when this bond is severed, the outcome is uniformly catastrophic. In every case, from North America to Africa to Australia, indigenous people who are driven off their land suffer incredible hardship that goes far beyond the practical challenges of adapting to some new place. When people are displaced from their ancestral land, their primary reference point is lost, and along with it, the grounding for their bodies, lives, and spirits. When the long body is severed, so too is contact with the source of life. Some Native Americans call this trauma "the ancient grief."

In the modern world, an increasing number of people are beginning to understand the magnitude of the trauma that's been inflicted on native people, and it's not an exaggeration to describe our imperialism as a form of cultural genocide. What we're less likely to appreciate is the fact that imperialist peoples also suffer the consequences of their own self-inflicted habitat dislocation. White Europeans left their homelands and conquered indigenous people around the world, but they displaced themselves in the process, and today, many are suffering similar psychic consequences.

Of course, it would be obscene to equate the predicament of habitat-deprived white people with that of displaced native people around the world, but the parallels are undeniable. Western culture now enjoys the spoils of its domination, but we're also paying a heavy spiritual toll. Our lives may be comfortable with plentiful food, heat in the winter, and other conveniences, but we are just as isolated from the Earth as any displaced Australian, African, or Native American. Modern, first-world afflictions of lifestyle disease, anxiety, depression, substance abuse, and suicide are not so different from the sufferings of indigenous people. We can dampen the symptoms with affluence and modern medicine, but there can be no escaping the fact that we too are adrift. We all need a habitat to call home.

NEW WAY

In the Old Way, people experienced themselves as participants in habitat, but in the modern world we live like parachutists, dropping into the world more or less at random. Most of us are transients, either literally or psychically. Many of us have moved several times in our lives, and most of those transitions have been abrupt—facilitated by cars, trucks, and aircraft. The old habitat is forgotten, and we're too busy to learn the new. Instead of being grounded in place, we practice a kind of "drive-by living." Divorced from contact with the land, we follow roads and airways, not hills and valleys. Habitat is little more than scenery. Beautiful is better, but our participation is superficial at best. Mostly it's all a question of economics; we go where we can afford to go. The actual characteristics of the habitat itself are secondary. We are outsiders, foreigners in our own world.

Historically speaking, this way of life is profoundly abnormal. According to one estimate, people in industrialized countries now spend an average of 93 percent of their time indoors.[59] Modern homes, vehicles, and workplaces are tightly insulated and sealed off from the flux and flow of natural processes. Even when we do get outdoors, it's often arbitrary. High-speed transportation allows us to visit whatever habitat we choose. This year, the mountains; next year, the ocean. We look around, go for a walk, take a few pictures, and go home.

This is one of the tragic but rarely discussed downsides of fossil fuels. Climate change is bad enough, but high-speed fossil fueled transport also destroys our bond with habitat, with the Earth herself. When transport is fast, easy, and cheap, we pay less attention to our bioregion. If we need food from a remote location, we simply order it. If we need products from the other side of the world, we simply click a button. No relationship required.

It's no wonder so many of us are habitat illiterates. We live on land that we know almost nothing about. We have no experiences or rituals that bond us to habitat. We know the roads and the buildings around us, but most of us don't even know the coarsest details of species, soils, weather, and seasons. People give directions based not on natural features or terrain but on the location of business establishments: "Turn right at the McDonald's and then left at the Costco."

Even outdoor athletes miss the nuance; when your objective is simply to go fast, you're not really paying attention to details of the habitat around you. In fact, the only people in the modern world who truly know their habitat are native people, hunters, small-scale farmers, fishing guides, or dedicated naturalists. It's no wonder we feel the way we do. We're disconnected from the very thing that once sustained us. We are lost in space.

Our consciousness of habitat has not only atrophied through disuse; it's also been displaced by aggressive corporate marketing and advertising. A subversive poster by *Adbusters* magazine invites viewers to "Name these brands" alongside a column that says "Name these plants." The obvious implication is that almost every modern person would have no trouble naming the corporate brands, but few would be able to name the plants. In other words, we know our "corporate habitat" far better than we know the real, living world around us.

Modern education is also adrift. As currently structured, conventional schooling has almost no relationship to place. The standard curriculum can be delivered anywhere, even online. The Cartesian mind, believing itself to be an independent entity, likes to think it can be educated in any location. Advocates of placeless, online learning point to the advantages of convenience, low cost, and access to great professors, but the downside is the form itself. The meta-message is obvious: education has no relationship to location. Knowledge can be torn away from the Earth and delivered to anyone, anywhere, any time of day or night. The land is irrelevant.

Given our almost universal ignorance of habitat, it's no surprise we abuse it. If you don't understand something, you're not likely to value it. When people live most of their lives indoors, the life-sustaining properties of habitat fade from consciousness and the land starts to feel irrelevant. The term "habitat abuse" has yet to enter our popular lexicon, but it's a very real thing. What else are we to call our relentless dam building, clear-cutting, strip mining, and development? What else are we to call the Alberta Tar Sands project, the largest industrial destruction of habitat on the planet? If habitat were a person, this is precisely what we'd call it. Likewise, our ignorance leads to a failure of what we might call "habitat empathy." If you don't know the subtleties and powers of the natural world around you, you're far less likely to think of it as a living organism and far more likely to think of it as an exploitable object, a natural "resource." Our habitat hurts, but we don't hurt with it.

THE END OF HUMAN VAGILITY

Not only are we ignorant of habitat and out of touch with the land that gives us life, we've also lost much of our ability to physically move from place to place. As claims to private property have spread across the planet, there are fewer and fewer places where we can actually walk freely as our ancestors once did.

In recent years, scientists have begun to warn that nonhuman animals are losing their *vagility,* the ability to roam freely across their normal range and habitat.[60] A new and growing field called "movement ecology" studies the movement of wildlife and the way it's often restricted by freeways, fences, and developments. It's a serious concern, but lost in the conversation is the fact that humans have lost their vagility too.

Ask yourself: How far can you walk right now, in any direction? Chances are, not very far at all. Even if you aren't stopped short by fences or roadways, you're almost certain to be crossing into someone's property. If you live in an urban area, your vagility is measured not in miles, but in feet. The only freedom of movement we now enjoy is in selected parks or in our vehicles, which is not the same thing. In effect, we've fenced ourselves in. In the US, we like to declare that we live in a free country, but in terms of physical movement, that's simply not the case. And if you can't move your body through your habitat, how are you supposed to know it? And if you don't know it, how are you supposed to care for it?

In the Old Way, people were intimate participants in the rhythms of habitat, but today we lay claims, establish boundaries, and post "no trespassing" signs along the perimeter. We declare mineral rights, water rights, and agricultural rights. We hire security services and set up cameras to maintain digital vigilance. And it doesn't stop with solid ground. Today, multinational corporations are laying claim to vast tracts of the sea bed and polar regions, as well as the DNA code of various organisms. Some countries are even planning to stake out parts of the moon. At this rate, every last molecule of the solar system will soon be claimed by someone.

In the Old Way, this kind of behavior is considered immensely abnormal and deviant. As Chief Seattle famously put it, "How can you buy and sell the sky, the land? The idea is strange to us." Not just strange, but even a kind of cultural insanity. The idea that one person or one organization could put a stake in the ground and call it his own violates the Old Way values of participation, humility, and interdependence. It's profoundly disrespectful to the very thing that sustains us.

GEO COGNITION

Habitat is far more than just a plot of land with soil, plants, and animals. It actually has profound effects on the way we think and feel. As we've seen, a substantial percentage of our mental activity is driven by our physicality, a process known as embodied cognition.

But in fact, our whole environment is acting on our minds continuously in every moment of the day. Habitat, whether primal or modern, inevitably shapes our thoughts, our ideas, our emotions, and our creativity. We literally think with the qualities of the world around us, a process sometimes described as "extended cognition."[61]

If we took the time to reflect on our experience and cognition in various settings, this would be perfectly obvious. Some environments seem to inspire calm and creative thought, while others move us toward stress, tension, and hostility. Even simple changes in the weather are enough to change our emotions and in turn, our thoughts. A typical study confirms what we already know:

> In an experiment manipulating participants' time outdoors, pleasant weather (higher temperature or barometric pressure) was related to higher mood, better memory, and 'broadened' cognitive style during the spring as time spent outside increased.[62]

But weather cuts both ways. Research suggests that heat stress can muddle our thinking and make our brains lethargic. "There's evidence that our brains are susceptible to temperature abnormalities," says Joe Allen, co-director of the Center for Climate, Health and the Global Environment at Harvard University. A study from researchers at the Lawrence Berkeley National Lab found that when office temperatures rise above the mid-70s, workers' performance begins to drop off. A study funded by the Harvard Environmental Economics Program found that taking a standardized test on a very hot day is linked to poorer performance. All of which does not bode well for a world in the grip of climate change.[63]

A simple thought experiment is enough to tell us about the power of the habitat–cognition connection. Imagine yourself in a modern urban area, filled with concrete, cubicles, cars, and computers. Your entire city is laid out on a grid of blocks and right angles, and everything you see is square and linear. Naturally, your thought and feelings are likely to reflect this geometry. When you live and work in a quadrangle, you're more likely to think categorically, with hard taxonomies, pigeonholes, objects, linear order, and other left-brain creations.

Now imagine yourself in a thoroughly wild environment filled with trees, bushes, water, clouds, soil, and animals of all description, all of which are in motion. In all likelihood, your thoughts will be alive, diverse, moving, growing, branching, and vibrating. Your consciousness will be a reflection of your world.

Legendary architect Frank Lloyd Wright once observed, "We create our buildings and then they create us." Is it any wonder modern humans create the things they do? We're locked in a vicious cycle. We build rigid structures composed of compartments, with right angles everywhere. In turn, our thoughts become structured, linear, and regimented. Then, we turn around and use this kind of right-angle consciousness to build more of the same.

Habitat can even drive our beliefs about the nature of the cosmos. In a 2005 essay, "Are the Desert People Winning?" Robert Sapolsky speculated that forest people, inspired by the biodiversity they see around them each day, tend to favor polytheism, while desert people, struck by the stark and often brutal simplicity of their surroundings, lean toward monotheism.[64] As he put it,

> A basic dichotomy has emerged between two types of societies from very different ecosystems: societies born in rain forests and those that thrive in deserts. Think of Mbuti pygmies versus Middle Eastern Bedouin, or Amazonian Indians versus nomads of the Gobi. There turn out to be consistent and permeating differences between the two.

This is not surprising in the least. We are always under the influence of habitat. Our intelligence is continuous with the world. We don't just think with neurons and brain circuits; we think with dirt, water, clouds, plants, animals, and mountains. Given our immense, intimate history with wild outdoor environments, it could scarcely be any other way.

Habitat makes us who we are. For example, it's almost certainly the case that our cognition changes throughout the day: "morning thoughts" are surely different from "evening thoughts," and both are different from the "middle of the night thoughts" of insomnia sufferers. Likewise, it's probably the case that our thoughts differ with the kind of light we're exposed to. "Natural light thoughts" are bound to be different from "artificial light thoughts." And of course, our cognition is inevitably seasonal, especially at higher latitudes. The "short day thoughts" of winter are certain to be different from the "long day thoughts" of summer.

It's also safe to assume substantial differences between "indoor cognition" and "outdoor cognition." Indoor environments are likely to promote abstract thought, focused ideas, taxonomies, and categorization. This is where we excel at linear, executive, left-brain work. In contrast, outdoor environments promote relational, expansive ideas and fluidity of thought. When we're outdoors, we're less likely to be trapped in cognitive boxes, and more likely to be enchanted, inspired, and moved.

This indoor–outdoor distinction is bound to be a fertile area of research in coming years, but one thing seems certain: the transformation of human consciousness we so desperately need will not come with yet more time in cage-like indoor settings. Our indoor cognition has reached the limit of its usefulness and has actually made our problems worse. We've had our fill of taxonomies, abstractions, categorization, and spreadsheets. The next generation of powerful ideas will come to us in primal settings with open skies, natural landscapes, and running water. If you want to think creatively about a way forward, go outside.

HABITAT SHAPES OUR VIEW

The influence of the alien, manufactured world on human consciousness is far more pervasive, consequential, and destructive than most of us realize. The effect goes all the way to the core of how we relate to the universe as a whole. In every moment, we are constantly adjusting our awareness to be more or less receptive to the world. In essence, our sensitivity is an aperture that opens and closes in relation to survival demands and the perceived quality of our habitat.

When we're in a normal, ancestral habitat of plants, animals, soil, and water, our sensory–spiritual aperture opens to absorb and experience the world. The body wants to know and connect. This process not only enhances survival, but it also returns a lot of pleasant, meaningful information that's consistent with our deep evolutionary history. In this condition, it feels good to be aware of the larger, natural world. In turn, individuals and cultures are likely to see themselves as continuous with the world. It's all experienced as one vast, integrated process. This has been the dominant experience for the vast majority of human history. It's no wonder Old Way cultures are the way they are.

But when we live in an abnormal, alien world of noise, chaos, and sterile, manufactured habitats, our sensory–spiritual aperture begins to contract. Sensation and attention reach out to embrace the world, but the experience is often meaningless, chaotic, and distasteful. In the short term, we dismiss the encounter as mere unpleasantness, but when the experience becomes chronic, the mind–body–spirit begins to contract and isolate. We shrink, withdraw and protect. The aperture closes down, and we become hardened and self-centered.

This is bad enough for individuals and no doubt contributes to depression, loneliness, and narcissism, but it's an even bigger threat to the long-term welfare of society and culture. When millions of people contract their engagement with the world, our normal, ancestral experience of unity begins to break down. We begin to see ourselves as disconnected individuals, with no particular connection to the natural or social world. Our cultures move toward isolation, and individualism reigns supreme.

This is the tragedy of the manufactured, alien environment. Hostile, abnormal stimuli wear down our willingness to engage. Noise, traffic, concrete, and unnatural sensory inputs drive a contraction of attention and in the process, we become increasingly walled off from the world. We can mitigate some of this effect with better design, but it's hard to fool the ancestral body. No matter how brilliant our architects and urban planners, the body knows the difference between the normal and the manufactured. We can only endure so much sensory distress before we retreat into isolation and disconnection. As the human environment becomes increasingly manufactured and alien, there will be an even greater tendency for human awareness to contract and withdraw.

THE HEALTH–HABITAT CONNECTION

As domesticated Cartesians in the New Way tradition, many of us have come to believe that habitat is not particularly relevant to the state of our bodies. For example, it's almost unheard of for physicians to ask patients about their relationship to habitat. Health simply comes out of nowhere, as an inexplicable gift of genetics and lifestyle. If you've got it, you're lucky. If not, maybe the medical system can patch you up.

But in recent years, a host of research suggests a powerful relationship between our experience of habitat and health. In some cases, the relationship is causal and measurable. For example, we now know that rising carbon dioxide levels in the atmosphere lead to lower nutrient levels in agricultural crops, which can compromise our health.[65] We know that mountaintop mining in Appalachia spreads toxic dust over communities and leads to increases in cardiovascular disease, lung cancer, pulmonary disease, and birth defects in the surrounding region. We know that hydraulic fracking poses a significant local harm to human health[66] and that air pollution has been linked with cognitive decline.[67] We know that a warming environment increases populations of malaria-infected mosquitoes and that deforestation of tropical habitats probably releases new pathogens into human populations. We can even point to new evidence linking air pollution and type 2 diabetes,[68] and research that links increasing temperatures to rising suicide rates.[69]

But underneath these specific cases of cause-and-effect lies a deeper process, one that's more psycho-physical and even spiritual, but just as real in its ultimate destructive effect. Because we are of the Earth, our bodies and minds are inevitably affected by the health or degradation of the biosphere. Environmental destruction, experienced in the human psyche, lowers the threshold for every other injury, insult, or disease that might afflict the body. The Earth is stressed, and we're stressed with it.

In *My Name is Chellis and I'm in Recovery from Western Civilization*, Chellis Glendinning writes about "the screaming link between personal dysfunction and the ecological crisis." For many of us, that screaming link is obvious; it requires no proof, no academic research, no journal articles, and no further explanation. Since we are all children of the Earth, how could it be otherwise? When the whole is in trouble, so are the parts.

Studies of landscape preference are highly suggestive of this health–habitat connection.[70] Subjects are typically presented with a variety of photographs of various landscapes, and not surprisingly, most people tend to prefer ancestral environments that are human-friendly. That is, we tend to like savanna environments and semi-wooded mosaic grasslands, especially if there's visible water and places of refuge. These landscapes offer the prospect of good hunting and gathering, good range of sight, and easy walking. There can be no doubt that these kinds of scenes stimulate beneficial changes in the human nervous system. Likewise, it's no surprise that real estate prices are the way they are. Properties that mimic ancestral landscapes, even in some small way, are always more expensive; people are willing to pay top dollar to keep their bodies close to nature.

On the flip side, it's safe to assume that we also suffer negative health effects related to "landscape aversion." This has yet to be studied in detail, but there can be little doubt that the human nervous system rebels at the sight of urban sprawl, industrial domination of the land, factory farms, and clear-cut forests. Unlike the body-friendly scenes of the African grassland, these landscapes offer little in the way of refuge or the prospect for hunting, gathering, or vagility.

In *The Secret Life of Your Microbiome*, Susan Prescott and Alan Logan propose the existence of "gray zones," a play on the "blue zones," regions of increased human longevity made famous by Dan Buettner of National Geographic. Gray zones are areas of intense human activity and radical alterations of habitat. From the air, these urban areas, especially with miles of concrete and asphalt, actually appear gray—and it's easy to imagine they have a graying effect on human health as well. Our bodies and spirits recoil from the sight of degraded ecosystems, and we don't need an explanation to know that something is desperately wrong. We can be sure that constant exposure to these human-hostile landscapes drives chronic activation of our stress response, systemic inflammation, and in turn, negative health outcomes. Our habitat hurts, and we hurt with it.

On the positive side, a growing body of evidence points to a powerful relationship between intact habitat and health.[71] For example, we now know there's a relationship between residential "greenness" and birth weight.[72] Researchers compared birth registry data and vegetation data from satellites and found that "greenness is beneficial to fetal growth exhibited by higher birthweight." Other studies of the greenspace–health relationship show similar beneficial outcomes.

Likewise, a growing body of research demonstrates that time spent in natural environments is probably protective against stress. In particular, studies have shown that spending time in a forest environment can beneficially influence stress physiology, markers of inflammation, immune defenses, blood pressure, and heart rate variability. This is exemplified by shinrin-yoku, a Japanese practice that loosely translates as "forest-air bathing" or "absorbing the forest air" and places emphasis on the entire forest experience.

Similarly, a frequently cited study by Roger Ulrich is often presented as an example of the healing power of natural settings. Ulrich examined the hospital records of a suburban hospital and compared patients who had views looking out on a natural, garden-like setting with those who had no such view. Those with the nature view had "shorter postoperative stays, received fewer negative comments in nurses' notes, and took fewer analgesics than matched patients in similar rooms with windows facing a brick wall."[73] In the same vein, researchers have compared the effects of running on a treadmill while looking at views of either "rural pleasant" or "urban unpleasant" scenes. Not surprisingly, "rural pleasant" was the winner, with improved psychological outcomes and substantially reduced blood pressure.[74]

All of this makes perfect sense, but on the other hand, it's hard to know what to make of these kinds of studies. Does they tell us about the healing power of natural settings? Or do they tell us more about the health-negative effects of urban settings? And what should we make of the fact that we felt the need to do such studies in the first place? No native person or child would ever bother to ask the question. Of course your body is going to feel better when you've got a view of trees, plants, and water. Are we that far gone as a people that we need research to tell us going outside is good for us? Perhaps less research is needed.

The problem is that modern research and reporting on the health–nature link is all backward. That is, it starts from a civilized, modern New Way point of view—which is to say, it's civilization-centric. If you're distressed or depressed, all you need to do is add nature to the mix and you'll feel better. In this way, nature begins to sound like a nutritional supplement. "Just add vitamin N" to your life and everything will be okay.

This perspective is reinforced by a series of recent books about "nature deficit disorder" and "the nature fix." That is, we take civilized human experience as the reference point and work from there. We medicalize nature and promote it as a cure; in fact, some physicians are even beginning to write prescriptions for "green time." But is this really a step in the right direction? Even when such "treatments" or God-forbid, "interventions" provide actual benefit, they serve mostly to maintain and deepen our alienated relationship with the world. Nature may well be beneficial, but it's still *other*.

The obvious question: Should we focus on the healing power of nature or on the health-negative forces of the modern world? Medical commentators have increasingly described our modern environment as "obesogenic," "stressogenic," "depressogenic," and "inflammogenic." This is the fundamental issue. History tells us that our ancestral life ought to be our primary reference point. Wild, outdoor life has been the norm for 99 percent of our time on this planet; civilized living is the aberration. It's not so much that nature heals, but that modern civilized life causes us real, measurable harm. This is where we ought to put our attention and our action. It's all well and good to go for a walk in the park, but unless we deal directly with the psycho-physical challenges of the modern world, we simply aren't going to make much progress.

Once again, it's important to consider our language. "Nature deficit disorder" is somewhat vague, but "habitat deficit disorder" would get right to the heart of the matter. The reason our bodies and minds are suffering is that we're fast running out of healthy places to go and live in some kind of harmony with the world. In this sense, the real problem is not a "nature deficit," but rather a "civilization excess," especially our relentless, unquestioned devotion to growth and development. The equation is actually pretty simple: when you destroy habitat with industrial agriculture, shopping malls, roads, and new runways at major international airports, you're simultaneously destroying human health. It's perfectly sensible to recommend that people go outside, but at the rate we're going, there isn't going to *be* any livable outside to go to. And that is the real issue.

THE PRACTICE OF HABITAT

The fundamental problem of our day is that we've forgotten our primal relationship to habitat—which is to say, we've forgotten how to be normal. Clearly, we need some remedial education on this score, but we're up against some serious cultural obstacles. From our conventional, New Way perspective, habitat is just a two-dimensional plot of land, a parcel, a property to be exploited. It's real estate, a place to park our stuff or capitalize on an investment. It might have a few trees, maybe some water, but mostly it's just a building site. If it's level and has the proper utility hook-ups, you're good to go.

But habitat is rich, deep and constantly in flux. If we took the time to really learn, we'd see that even the simplest ecosystems have an extraordinary level of depth and nuance. Habitat, like the human body, is vast.

To get a sense of this depth, try a simple thought experiment: Start by taking an imaginary inventory of everything you know about the modern world:

- all the books and magazines, authors, and stories you've ever read

- all the cities, towns, and suburbs you've ever visited or read about

- all the highways, streets, expressways, bike paths, and subway routes you've ever traveled

- all the buildings you've ever lived and worked in

- all the movies, TV shows, plays, and songs you've ever heard or seen

- all the scientific knowledge you've accumulated

- all the technologies, tools, and products you've ever encountered

- all the cars, trucks, boats, and aircraft you've ever seen or traveled in

Obviously, this adds up to a staggering amount of information. It's impossible to measure, but it would surely add up to terabytes of data. But now for the twist: Take all of that neuro-cognitive capacity and apply it to your natural habitat. Imagine you could use all that "head space" to absorb every detail of the plants, animals, light, weather, water, and soils in your bioregion.

Your knowledge would be prodigious. You'd know the intimate details of all the creatures in your world, their characteristics and their relationships. You'd see thousands of things that are invisible to the untrained modern eye: the subtle influences of climate, weather, water, and wind. You'd be able to read the spoor of animals and navigate vast reaches of terrain with the faintest clues. You'd know the natural world in a way we can scarcely imagine today.

This is precisely the realization anthropologist Jared Diamond experienced in his early travels to Papua New Guinea. Diamond considered himself a competent naturalist, but was stunned by the knowledge of the locals, especially their encyclopedic understanding of the local bird population. But today our natural, physical knowledge of habitat is being replaced by intensive measurement, tracking, and analysis. We have reams of environmental data stored on computers, but we possess almost nothing in the way of personal, experiential, physical understanding.[75] This turns our normal way of knowing upside down. Instead of learning habitat through our bodies, we do it through our heads, especially the left side of our brains.

These days, everyone talks about the urgent need to "save the world," but in order to save it, we have to know it. And to know it, we have to spend time in contact with it. We have to feel the rhythms, the textures, the creatures, and the forces that are the very stuff of life. So imagine the immense sophistication of your nervous system brought to bear, not on the challenges we routinely experience in the modern world, but on the qualities of terrain, plants, animals, and weather that would have existed in a primal habitat.

Ideally, you'd be in a position to really learn a raw, wild habitat from birth, but for many of us this is simply out of the question. Most of us have moved several times in our life, and in all likelihood, our original birth habitat has been radically altered or even destroyed by development. So the next best thing is to find a habitat you like and immerse yourself in it. Choose some land that's accessible and walkable and go there often. Start observing the coarse-grained detail of the local plants and animals. Who lives there? How do they make a living, and how do they relate to one another?

Next, get your imagination fired up. Forget the fact that your backpack is full of yummy snacks and that rescue is only a few clicks away. Instead, remember your ancestry in authentic Paleo conditions. Imagine you're walking in a predator-rich environment where lions, leopards, and hyenas are common. In this world, you are not the alpha animal; you are part of the circle of life. You don't need to be terrified, but you do need to be wary. To complete the picture, imagine you haven't eaten in a couple of days and you're starting to feel it. Your attention is sharp, focused, intent on any sign of animal life or edible plants. You are fully engaged. This is a good place to begin.

Next, slow down. Speed is a sensation killer that obscures the world we're trying to learn. By slowing down, we see more and feel more. An indigenous farmer in Peru put it this way: "You can run and run at five kilometers an hour, but you will see nothing. If you walk, maybe one kilometer in five hours, you will see everything."

While we're at it, we'd do well to talk less and listen more. In a normal, ancestral environment, success in the hunt often hinged on the ability to keep a low profile and make as little noise as possible. Apprenticeship for young hunters would surely have included training in how to be quiet. To this day, native American elders in Alaska advise young people to WAIT, which stands for "Why Am I Talking?"

Naturally, this is a hard lesson for modern, New Way people to learn. To put it bluntly, we are loudmouths. We use our outdoor time as one more opportunity to express our opinions about everything under the sun. Not only does this compromise our ability to learn habitat, but in the Old Way it's also considered disrespectful to the land itself. Likewise, we might well ask ourselves, "Why Am I Thinking?" Let your monkey mind wind down, and start paying attention to the world of plants, animals, dirt, water, and weather.

Whenever possible, take your shoes off. The bare foot is an extremely capable sensory organ that tells important stories about the nature of habitat and the qualities of terrain, textures, heat, and cold. For modern urbanites, this practice will take some getting used to, but it's perfectly doable and enjoyable. After a few outings, the skin on your feet will start to toughen up *and* get more sensitive. Not only that, the proprioception in your ankles, knees, and hips will improve. In other words, your legs will get smarter and stronger.

As for electronics, the best practice is to leave your phone in the car. The mere presence of a smartphone is enough to hijack our attention and distract us from the goal of absorbing our surroundings.

By offering the prospect of instant navigation and rescue, the phone dilutes the experience, destroys our sense of adventure, and turns it into a superficial outing. If your phone is in your pack or even worse, in your hand, it's unlikely you'll ever enter a state of full immersion.

As for photography, you might want to give that a rest as well. We've all heard stories of outdoor photographers who report getting "closer to nature" through their art, and their claims may have some merit. But for the casual shooter, the camera is yet another distraction from full engagement. Remember, from a historical perspective, cameras are completely abnormal—not once did our Paleolithic ancestors look at a breathtaking sunset and wish they could get the shot. Even more to the point, the very act of searching for ideal images distorts our understanding and appreciation of habitat. In our quest to select the perfect shot, we bypass most of what we see, including many features that would have been essential for finding food and staying alive. In a wild, natural environment, the clues that are essential to survival won't necessarily make for good pictures.

Even worse, the spectacular imagery we do capture tricks viewers into thinking that nature is just one fantastic light show, there solely for our entertainment. When people go into the outdoors with this expectation, many are disappointed to find that nature fails to live up to its billing. In a paradoxical way, spectacular nature photography can actually turn us off to the genuine experience of enjoying the outdoor world. When tourists can buy spectacular postcards and calendars in the gift shop, there seems little point in actually going out into the park itself.

Ultimately, learning habitat is a question of attitude and relationship. To really learn the outdoor world, you'll have to abandon your cultural inclinations toward ownership, domination, and imperialism. You're not there to conquer the mountain, the land, or the river; you're a student, there to experience and learn. Forget what you know, and engage your beginner's mind. Open your attention to everything you see and feel.

Experienced birders tell beginners to "absorb the bird." Soak up the fine-grained details of weather, plants, and if you're lucky, animals. Use your skin, not just as a protective layer, but as a sense organ. Let your eyes relax by looking at distant features on the horizon. Let go of your mental chatter and feel your world.

Going further, get your imagination into the act. For our Paleolithic ancestors, tracking animals was a subtle and sophisticated art. Following hoof prints and tracks was an entry-level skill, easily mastered by any young apprentice, but experienced hunters practiced a higher art, what today we call "speculative tracking."[76] In this process, the hunter attempts to enter the body and spirit of the target animal and make predictions about how it will behave. The hunter doesn't think about the animal as an object; he actually identifies with it and attempts to feel what that animal feels. Imagination on fire, the hunter uses his entire body to sense the animal's experience. The more completely he can merge with the animal, the greater the chances of success. For modern-day hikers, this level of engagement is probably out of reach, but it's worth a try. Let your imagination run wild.

KEEP YOUR EYE ON THE AWE

Of all the pro-health effects of natural settings, one of the most intriguing comes directly from the magnificence of nature herself. Work by Dacher Keltner at UC Berkeley shows that even a mild sense of awe can change attitudes and behavior. People who watched a nature video that elicited awe were subsequently more ethical and generous and described themselves as being more connected to others—qualities that are commonplace in indigenous traditions.

Keltner's team also found that awe makes people happier and less stressed, even weeks later. Likewise, a landmark study by Jennifer E. Stellar and Neha John-Henderson found that "positive emotions, especially awe, are associated with lower levels of proinflammatory cytokines." Awe activates the parasympathetic nervous system, which works to calm the fight-or-flight response and dampen the production of toxic stress hormones. Awe also seems to help us break out of habitual thinking patterns and improves creativity. In other words, putting ourselves in contact with nature's magnificence is really good for us.

Research by psychologists at Stanford and the University of Minnesota also shows that experiencing awe can increase well-being by giving people the sense that they have more time available.[77] And there's even a pro-social benefit. Keltner and Jonathan Haidt have argued that awe is the ultimate "collective" emotion because it motivates people to do things that enhance the greater good. Research reported in the Journal of Personality and Social Psychology provides strong empirical support for this claim.[78] The authors found that awe helps bind us to others, motivating us to act in collaborative ways that enable strong groups and cohesive communities. Which, of course, is an ideal quality for both ancestral and modern life.

For those of us who've grown up in narcissistic, New Way cultures, the power of awe may seem counterintuitive. Most of us like feeling big and celebrating our status as the alpha species, but awe in natural settings does its work by making us feel smaller. It shrinks the ego and our sense of self and in turn, leaves more space in our attention for the rest of creation. Incredibly, Keltner found that when test subjects were awe-inspired, they actually signed their names smaller and drew themselves smaller. Other researchers have found that people who watched awe-inspiring videos estimated their bodies to be physically smaller than those who watched neutral videos.

All of which should give us pause. When we reflect on the radical differences between ancestral and modern environments, we're struck by what we might call an "awe gap." In a normal, outdoor, Paleo world, the experience of awe must have been commonplace. Our ancestors were in constant, daily contact with the magnificence and enormity of nature. Thunderstorms, lightning displays, and animal dramas played out in real time, right before our eyes each day, life and blood on the grassland, fighting and fleeing just outside our camps. With no light pollution, the night sky would have blazed with an intensity modern humans can scarcely imagine. And around a tribe's local habitat, vast reaches of unknown territory stretched to the horizon, home to whatever our imagination might conjure. Awe, in other words was a normal, health-promoting experience.

But today, few of us ever go outside in the first place, and when we do, most of our parks are highly domesticated, regulated, noisy, and light polluted. It's getting harder and harder to find nature's magnificence anywhere. Awe—and the health benefits that come with it—is becoming rare. We might even describe ourselves as "awe deprived."

All of which gives us yet another reason to get outside—way outside. Get out of yourself and expose yourself to the outrageous power of sky, earth, wind, and water. City parks and green spaces are all well and good, but to really find the awe, you've got to expose your body and spirit to the enormity of the living earth. Go to the big places, so you can feel really small.

A NEW–OLD BIOREGIONALISM

As our awareness of habitat deepens, we're likely to feel more at one with the world, but we're also prone to reach some highly disruptive and inconvenient conclusions about culture as usual. We've noticed the lay of the land and the ways vegetation, rocks, and watersheds combine in recognizable patterns, and we're struck by a profound sense of dissonance. That is, the political and legal boundaries of our day bear almost no resemblance to the actual features of life on the ground. The nations, states, counties, and jurisdictions that guide so much of our political and commercial lives have almost no relationship to actual living ecosystems.

The disconnect isn't just a curiosity; it also reveals something profoundly disturbing about our dysfunctional, imperialistic relationship with the planet and very often, one another. Our practice reveals not just an ignorance of habitat, but even a contempt for it.
When you're an alpha species, you lay down the lines wherever it
pleases you. This land is our land, that land is your land, but it's all
man's land. Earth is here to serve *us*.

Bioregionalism is the counterpoint to this flawed attitude. In the
modern era, the idea dates back to the 1970s, championed by writers such as David Haenke and Kirkpatrick Sale, and most famously
by poet Gary Snyder. But bioregional thinking has actually been the
dominant view for the vast majority of human history on Earth and
is implicit in the Old Way. Our current focus on arbitrary political
states, regions, and districts is a recent, abnormal, and arguably insane way to subdivide the biosphere.

Any child who looks at straight lines overlaid on a map is likely
to wonder what they have to do with the conditions she can see with
her own eyes. Her eyes see forests, watersheds, rivers, and oceans,
but the big people say that well, no, there are actually invisible lines
on the ground that must be honored. If you're standing on this side
of the line, one set of rules applies, but if you're standing on the other
side, it's another set entirely.

In fact, nature doesn't really care about our maps or our artificial borders. People who attempt to manage fisheries, water quality,
pollution, and regional issues are coming to realize that forests, animals, oceans, atmospheres, wildfire smoke, and infectious microorganisms simply have no interest in human boundaries. Life does
what it pleases.

Our New Way practice of indiscriminately drawing straight lines
over living landscapes is really a kind of violence and habitat abuse,
which is to say, self-abuse. The process is bad enough when it's used
to chop political districts into awkward pieces to benefit political

parties, but it's a thousand times worse when we use it to manipulate the biosphere for our own selfish ends. Naturally, artists have been quick to see the folly of our ways. In 1985, the Austrian artist Friedensreich Hundertwasser wrote a manifesto called "Paradise Destroyed By The Straight Line," declaring the straight line to be "godless and immoral."

Naturally, bioregionalism brings up a host of enormously inconvenient challenges. For example, nationalism begins to look like a defunct, outdated concept. National boundaries forced onto the land by conquest, war, or even negotiated agreement are almost always homocentric and out of sync with nature. Even worse, as nation states become firmly established, they give legitimacy to the idea that nature is nothing more than a two-dimensional stage for human drama. After a few generations of nationalism, the concept begins to feel increasingly "normal."

Likewise, bioregionalism puts an entirely new frame on modern discussions of gerrymandering, the manipulation of voting districts for political advantage. What if we drew up bioregional districts instead? Instead of arguing about party affiliations and which kind of voters live in which neighborhoods, we'd draw the maps based on the lay of the land, watersheds, vegetation and animal habitat. Forests would go with forests, and grasslands would go with grasslands. In the process, every encounter with a biologically based region would remind us of our life support system and the importance of the Earth.

The beauty of bioregionalism is that it gives us a positive path forward. We can't seem to agree on much in the modern world, but we should at least be able to agree on the unity of the plants, animals, weather, and watersheds we see in our region. In this way, bioregionalism would give us a sense of place and something real to rally around.

In the meantime, we can practice. Whenever possible, try to draw attention to the unique ecology of the region you inhabit. Look for local foods and materials, and the cultivation of native plants. Likewise, give some thought to your sports and athletics. Thinking bioregionally, it suddenly seems absurd to travel long distances to do our movement practices and sports. Each bioregion has its own terrain characteristics that challenge our bodies in particular ways. If you live in the mountains, skiing, climbing, mountain biking and hiking are the appropriate choices. If you live by the ocean, it's surfing. If you live in the plains, it's road biking and river sports.

The prime, original directive of the athletic enterprise is to move smoothly in context, in the habitat you actually inhabit, in conditions that actually exist. Ice hockey in Las Vegas is absurd; so too is snow making. If you have to get on an airplane to go play, you're missing opportunities right where you live. The time has come to stop with abstracted athletics and make our movement relevant to the places where we live. In short, "think globally, move locally."

The beauty of bioregionalism is that it inspires us to create new forms of culture that honor actual conditions on the ground: cuisine, flags, narratives, songs, and stories that celebrate the unique natural history of our home bioregions. Likewise, use bioregional maps whenever possible. These maps show layers of geology, flora, and fauna, and are powerful communication tools for advancing the bioregional narrative.

Bioregionalism is the way of our deep past, but it's also a path to a functional future. You may not be able to agree with your neighbor's political views, but you should at least be able to agree on the names of the plants that grow in your area, the animals that live there, and the way the weather comes and goes. It's common biological ground, and a good place to start. And, if modern infrastructure collapses, we may well have to think bioregionally, whether we want to or not. When food no longer comes to us by truck and airplane, we'll have to really pay attention to the land around us.

TRIBE

You can't be human on your own.

—Desmond Tutu

Imagine once again your birth day deep in prehistory, somewhere on the mosaic grassland of Africa. You're part of an ancient hominid band, not yet fully human, but highly intelligent and capable. The past few generations have been a time of prosperity and relative abundance, the climate has been friendly, the hunting and gathering have been good, and there's plenty of protein to go around. It's good news for everyone's health, but there's a surprising downside. As brains and heads have grown larger over the generations, it's become increasingly difficult for mothers to pass a child through the birth canal. Childbirth has become increasingly dangerous, and sadly, many women and children have perished.

But you are one of the lucky ones. Your brain and head are large, but by the luck of genes and a few mutations, your mother goes into labor early. Strictly speaking, your body isn't really ready for prime time, but there's no fighting the process, and suddenly you've arrived in the world, premature, but ready to make a go of it.

At this point, you've got some serious limitations. You can't walk, hunt, speak, or perform any of the functions necessary to make your way in the world. If left to your own devices, your life expectancy would be mere hours, so you've got to get some social life support right away. Specifically, you've got to attach to a caregiver as soon as possible. Ideally it's Mom, but any warm, caring human will do, someone who will keep you safe from danger, touch you, feed you, and keep you alive until you're fully developed. Attachment, in other words, is absolutely vital for your survival and development.

Back in today's modern world, you probably haven't given much thought to the premature nature of your birth, but your need for attachment remains strong and will have profound consequences that will reverberate for the rest of your life. Secure attachment to a caregiver isn't just important in infancy; it's a major predictor of how successful you'll be as an adult. If you're securely attached as a child, you have a good chance of going on to have a successful career, good health, and strong social relations. A powerful body of research, beginning with British psychoanalyst John Bowlby and validated by American psychologist Mary Ainsworth,[79] demonstrates that secure attachment is a better predictor of success than conventional measures such as IQ. And of course, insecure attachment goes the other way. Children who grow up insecurely attached are more likely to fall into dysfunctional behavior and disease in adulthood.[80]

It's hard to overstate the power of this process in the unfolding of human life. Attachment is a critical fork in the road for the developing human body, mind, and spirit. If the process is successful, the young animal body concludes that the world is mostly friendly and switches on a host of metabolic and growth functions that continue through life. But if attachment fails, the body concludes that the world is unfriendly and prepares itself for defense. Brain centers go on red alert and the mind crosses over into a state of vigilance or even hyper-vigilance. The body prepares for a life of danger and immediate action.

These findings confirm what indigenous people have known for thousands of years. Life on the grassland was dangerous and demanding, and personal survival was intimately linked to the welfare and functioning of the tribe. The tribe was a lifeboat on a perilous sea of wild land, open space, and hungry carnivores. Of course your body would be extremely sensitive to the status of the people around you. Of course native people would go to great lengths to sustain tribal function and integrity. It would be bizarre if it were any other way.

HYPER-SOCIAL BODIES

In the wild, tribal cohesion and membership was truly a matter of life and death, and it's no wonder we find loneliness and isolation intolerable. When we're alone for long periods, we're separate from our circle of life support, and in this sense, our lives are literally in danger. It's no surprise the body experiences rejection and isolation as a genuine physical emergency. This is also why solitary confinement is rightly classified as torture.

Given our survival predicament in the Paleo and our utter reliance on tribal life, it comes as no surprise to discover that our bodies are tightly linked with one another, all the way down to the deepest levels of physiology. A sense of tribal belonging is essential, not just for social amusement and friendship, but for the deep functioning of our bodies, brains, minds, and spirits. In fact, an enormous body of research in the fields of social neuroscience and interpersonal neurobiology has revealed astonishing levels of social sensitivity embedded in our bodies. We are so hyper-social that our bodies are, for all practical purposes, continuous with one another. It's no exaggeration to say that our social circles or tribes are literally life support systems for our bodies and our health. In a very real sense, our bodies and our lives are made of people.

NO SINGLE HUMAN BRAINS

Our social nature is far more than a simple desire to affiliate; it is deeply, fundamentally physical. Tribe is etched into the very tissue of our bodies and reflected in the deep structure and function of our brains. In *The Neuroscience of Human Relationships*, psychologist Louis Cozolino declares the brain to be "social organ" and even goes so far to suggest that "there are no single human brains." We are so inherently social, so dependent on one another for our very cognition, it makes little sense to view brains in isolation from one another. Even without digital technology, we are massively networked. As Robert Sapolsky put it in *Behave: The Biology of Humans at Our Best and Worst*, "No brain is an island." Or, as Steven Sloman and Philip Fernbach state in *The Knowledge Illusion*, "we never think alone."

CONTINUITIES

In essence, our bodies are highly sensitive emotion-detection instruments that absorb and express social information continuously. As modern, New Way Cartesians, many of us like to think our mental activity is autonomous and self-contained, but the body is always participating in our social interactions. The process is generally unconscious, but it's an extremely powerful force that's impossible to turn off. As job interview consultants sometimes put it, "Your body cannot *not* communicate."

Realize it or not, we are incredibly adept at reading one another's faces and bodies. A study in the *Journal of Nonverbal Behavior* found that study participants only had to watch about four seconds of basketball or table tennis games to recognize—from the looks on the athletes' faces—who was winning and who was losing. Participants were also able to quickly surmise whether the game was close or a blowout. [81]

Likewise, our bodies are quick to resonate with one another. According to a study published in the Proceedings of the National Academy of Sciences, holding hands with a loved one in pain not only synchronizes your breathing and heart rate, but causes your brain wave patterns to couple up too. The brains of close friends were also shown to respond in remarkably similar ways when they viewed a series of short videos. Researchers have found they can predict the strength of two people's social bond based on brain scans alone.[82]

And that's just the beginning. Children who dance together are more cooperative in subsequent games.[83] Adults who march, sing or dance as part of a church, army, or community group are more likely to work for the good of their group than those who don't. And when two people bop to a steady beat, they are more likely to rate the other person's personality as similar to their own than do couples who move out of time. Conversely, studies show that a bad marriage with frequent disagreement can seriously damage your health.[84]

Our hyper-social nature goes all the way to the deepest levels of our brains, where remarkably, social pain and physical pain are processed by the same circuits. This suggests that, from the body's point of view, social contact is vital for survival and that social rejection is just as much a threat to our lives as physical injury. Similarly, in both humans and nonhuman animals, social contact reduces physical pain.[85] Experiments summarized in the journal *Physiology & Behaviour* suggest that, given a choice of physical pain or isolation, social mammals will choose the former.[86]

Even the odors that waft off other people's bodies can affect us. Researchers took armpit swabs from two groups: one that had just completed an easy fun run, and another that had just parachuted out of an airplane. Subjects who sniffed the parachute sample showed increased activity in the amygdala, a bigger startle response, and increased sensitivity to angry faces. Likewise, a study of dental students suggests that dentists can smell when a patient is anxious, making them more likely to make mistakes and perform badly.[87] Our fear, in other words, gets around.

Even our stress is contagious. A 2018 study reported in *Nature Neuroscience* found that stress transmitted from others can change the brain in the same way real stress does. Working with mice, a research team removed one mouse from a pair and exposed it to a mild stress before returning it to its partner. They found that the networks in the brains of both the stressed mouse and naïve partner were altered in similar ways.[88]

Even our health habits and physical condition rub off on one another. Researchers have found that body weight within couples is highly interdependent. Spouses often enter marriage at a similar weight status and mirror each other's weight trajectories over time. When one spouse develops obesity, the likelihood of the other spouse developing obesity increases significantly. There is also evidence that weight loss can spread within couples. A study from the University of Connecticut showed that if one party in a couple is trying to improve a health outcome—in this case, body weight—it is likely that their partner will have a similar outcome, even if they had not intended to do so.[89]

Similarly, it comes as no surprise to learn that our long-term health outcomes are tightly linked to the quality of our social relations. This is the finding of the Harvard Study of Adult Development, a landmark seventy-five-year study of what makes us happy and healthy. Researchers followed 268 men who entered college in the late 1930s through war, career, marriage and divorce, parenthood and grandparenthood, and old age. The most recent leader of the study, psychiatrist Robert Waldinger, summed up the results this way: "Good relationships keep us happier and healthier. Period."[90]

In short, social influence is turning out to be a much bigger factor in human health than previously realized. Biomedical specialists have long been inclined to view the body in isolation, and until recently, most medical professionals believed that social standing had almost nothing to do with health and disease. But our understanding has matured in recent decades, and we now know that the "social determinants of health" are incredibly powerful. Work by epidemiologist Michael Marmot and others has shown conclusively that "health follows a social gradient."[91] For hyper-social primates—especially humans—being high in the hierarchy gives a sense of power and control, but low status carries the threat of exclusion and the stress of having to scramble to make a living. The effect is so powerful, in fact, that one's position in the hierarchy may be just as important for health as more familiar factors such as diet and exercise.

The implications are wide-ranging and highly inconvenient for culture as usual. In an egalitarian, Old Way culture, hierarchies were flat (or nearly so) and the feelings of inclusion would have outweighed the threat of exclusion. But in today's highly competitive environment, the pyramid is steep and exclusion is an ever-present possibility. In this radically unequal world, disease is essentially built into the system: status, money, and power flow uphill, while stress, cortisol, inflammation, and lifestyle disease flow downhill. This is how inequality kills. Unless and until we correct these inequalities, public health will continue to decline and people will continue to suffer.

TRIBE IN THE MODERN WORLD

Our bodies crave attachment, social acceptance, and inclusion. If we find our way into an authentic, functional human tribe, we'll probably thrive. Our bodies will feel safe, our autonomic nervous systems will conclude that the Universe is friendly, and our health will probably remain strong throughout our lives. But today our tribes are fragmented and often dysfunctional. Many of us find ourselves bouncing from one tenuous social circumstance to the next, never quite fitting in and never quite feeling confident the tribe will sustain us. It's no wonder so many of us feel anxious and insecure.

Recent centuries have radically altered our original social experience and our sense of inclusion. Agriculture, settled communities, food surpluses, growing populations, wealth, power, and hierarchy have all taken a toll. Dwellings changed us too, as people increasingly lived indoors, isolated from one another. In recent years, a tidal wave of population growth, migration, and technological innovation have dramatically transformed our social lives, and today, tribal affiliations come and go like the wind. We're always moving around, joining up, dropping out. We belong to many "tribes" simultaneously, but rarely are we "all in" with any of them.

We desperately need a sense of togetherness, but our social world is fast becoming incomprehensible. Internet "visionaries" like to say digital networks are the new communities that will unify people, but networks simply don't deliver. Our bodies want authentic contact with other bodies and voices, not blips on a screen. As networks grow, our attention becomes increasingly divided and scattered. Keeping up with our electronic "contacts" takes away from the meaningful relationships that are vital to long-term health and happiness.

In Western culture, our social distress is amplified by our laser-like focus on the individual. We live and die by our resumes. There's only so much success to go around, so you've got to do better than your peers if you want to have a shot at success. Social and academic competition have become so intense that millions of young people now feel the need for chemical enhancement in order to succeed in school and career. It's no surprise so many of us now feel alienated and lonely. In a high-competition environment, the possibility of exclusion always lurks in the background. If you miss a beat, you're out on the street.

Adding to our alienation is the highly transactional nature of our modern world. Commerce is everywhere, and most of us spend a substantial amount of our lives in some kind financial exchange: buying, selling, managing, and accounting. But when it's all about the money, we just don't feel felt. When everything's transactional, our first and sometimes only question is "What can I get out of this?" Companies tell us they value us as customers, but rarely do we feel valued as people. To put it another way, in a capitalist system, our interest in one another is highly conditional. The system is designed for economics, not for humanity. And the body knows the difference.

Money itself is a profoundly disruptive, anti-social force. Kathleen Vohs at the University of Minnesota primed subjects with reminders of economics, finance, prices, and costs, and discovered that "money-primed people behave more selfishly and show a greater reluctance to be involved with others ... Even in intimate relationships and collectivistic cultures, reminders of money weaken sociomoral responses." Likewise, a 2015 review of money-priming experiments found two major effects:

> Compared to neutral primes, people reminded of money are less interpersonally attuned. They are not prosocial, caring, or warm. They eschew interdependence. Second, people reminded of money shift into professional, business, and work mentality.[92]

These are hugely disturbing findings. Obviously, people who live in the modern world are massively and continuously "money-primed." Immersed in a world of twenty-four-hour commerce, advertising, special offers, and discount pricing, we're reminded of money hundreds of times each day. If those priming events incline us even slightly away from a pro-tribal, pro-social orientation, the overall effect is destructive on a planetary scale. Is it any wonder so many of our modern social relations are strained? To say money is the root of all evil may be a stretch, but there can be no question it's the source of some serious tribal dysfunction.

This leads us to another inconvenient realization. That is, capitalism—with its focus on self-interest and individual welfare—goes sharply against the grain of human history and the natural social inclinations of our bodies. Our bodies crave contact and connection, but capitalism turns our priorities upside down, declaring that anti-social behavior is actually pro-social. This flies in the face of our ancestry and our natural, pro-social wiring. And since affiliation is essential to the functioning of our bodies, it's not a stretch to say capitalism—especially its modern, extremist form—poses a threat to public health. By relentlessly driving people toward self-interest, it destroys communities and robs us of opportunities to connect. A transactional society is no society at all, merely a set of self-interested calculations. In other words, Ayn Rand was dead wrong—selfishness is not a virtue. The invisible hand doesn't provide. It hands out some free samples and outrageous promises, then drives us apart into isolation, dysfunction, and ill health.

To make matters even worse, our social connection is also being degraded by the almost universal use of electronic communication devices. In normal, Paleo circumstances, human communication begins in the body and our physically embedded "resonance circuit." That is, we don't just exchange words or units of information; our nervous systems actually absorb tone of voice, physical postures, movement, and intent, processing it through mirror neurons in the brain, down into the gut and back to the prefrontal cortex.

In all probability, this circuit is a trainable, "use it or lose it" system that we might well describe as "muscular." When we practice resonating with people in authentic, face-to-face encounters, we get better at absorbing nonverbal elements and understanding emotion. This is precisely what actors and drama students learn in theatre. But when this experience is displaced by flashing lights, icons, and beeps, our skills begin to atrophy. We become increasingly oblivious to what people are trying to tell us with their bodies, which of course makes communication increasingly awkward, ineffective, and even counterproductive.[93]

Obviously, this does not bode well for the future. Every time we choose electronic communication over genuine face-to-face encounters, we compromise our ability to feel with our bodies and to interpret the feelings we experience. In effect, we're amputating the body from our social relations and in turn, eliminating huge swaths of meaning and capability. This amounts to a planet-wide dumbing down of our social intelligence. It's a terrible price to pay for speed and convenience.

In short, the modern world is socially abnormal, and the body knows it. We do our best to reach out across the fragmented social landscape for authentic connection, but when this effort fails, many of us fall into the quagmire of loneliness and depression.[94] Our hyper-social minds and bodies wander the modern landscape, desperately looking for connection and too often finding none.

All of which sounds bad enough, but it's actually worse than it looks. Not only does a dysfunctional social system affect the health of isolated and excluded individuals, but it also compromises the experience of *everyone*. Social angst and alienation are contagious conditions that extend beyond the boundaries of our skin. Even well-connected individuals feel the effects. And when the deeply social nature of our bodies is compromised, we lose the ability to find solutions and create meaning in common. Faced with the prospect of biospheric disaster and the urgent need for unprecedented levels of cooperation, we need to do more than just get along. We have to remember how to relate.

HOW TO BE NORMAL

In normal, Paleo human life, the foundation for communication and social relation was nonverbal gesture and then sometime later, conversation. There was food to be hunted and gathered, shelter to be built, and fires to be stoked, but people had lots of time to simply be with one another and gossip about their adventures. Conversation would have been central to their existence, their cohesion, and their happiness.

But today, conversation is in danger of disappearing altogether.

A large proportion of our social interactions are now transactional, scripted, and premeditated. Some companies brag that "you can talk to a real person," but when you actually reach a live person, it's obvious they're reading from scripts, scarcely an improvement over an automated chat bot.

An immense amount of information gets transmitted around the world each day, but the amount of actual conversation is declining. People are talking almost nonstop, but most of us are talking *at* one another or *to* one another, not *with* one another. And even worse, many of us are trying to sell one another with almost every waking breath. Many of us go for days or weeks without having an engaging, authentic conversation with anyone.

And even when we do talk, our conversations are often rushed, skewed, or colored by ulterior motives. Some people hardly talk at all, while others can't stop. We've forgotten the rhythmic give and take that makes conversation so engaging and rewarding. Once again, we need some remedial education. What does genuine human conversation sound like? And even more important, what does it feel like?

Far more than an exchange of information, a healthy conversation feels alive, shared, and reciprocal. A good conversational partner is attentive and responsive, and shows signs of life. He's receptive to your gestures and meanings, and most importantly, he's capable of being transformed in some way. If all goes well, he'll remember your story and integrate it into his own experience.

To put it simply, we recognize a good conversation when we feel heard and most especially, when we *feel felt*. We're satisfied when we come away with the impression that our partner experienced not just the informational content of our words but the emotional reality behind them.

This makes perfect sense in terms of our history. As a helpless, premature infant in a wild environment, your survival would have depended entirely on successful attachment to an attentive human being. Naturally, you'd have been extremely alert to the quality of that person's attention, and one question would have been right at the heart of your experience: "Do I feel felt?" This is the gold standard for effective, functional conversation. If the answer is yes, you've got a shot at secure attachment and a solid relationship. But if the answer is no, you've got to keep looking.

Naturally, this is about far more than spoken words or information transmission. The body is constantly alert for human engagement and attention, something that's communicated with posture, tone, and general demeanor. We feel felt when people are authentically present, listening, curious, and available. They're not checking their phone, tapping their feet or looking away; they're focused entirely on the matter at hand. This is why modern conversations so often go astray. We may well say precisely the right words in the right order with the right informational content, but unless we are fully engaged, the outcome may well surprise us.

Attention is vital to a successful outcome, but equally important is our willingness to take time. If you want to engage and feel felt, you've got to slow down. If you're stressed or in a rush, you might mange to transmit some bit or byte of information, but it won't be a conversation. Obviously, this will take some getting used to. In a world that's constantly pushing us to move on, we're likely to find ourselves hounding one another to get to the point, to condense our messages into smaller and smaller fragments so that we can turn to other things. But the cost is immense. When conversations are rushed, no one feels felt, and in turn, stress, misunderstanding, and alienation are not far behind.

Likewise, we build a sense of conversational rapport by creating an atmosphere of safety. This is taken as bedrock in the world of counseling and therapy, where therapists sometimes say, "Safety is treatment." When the body feels safe, everything goes better. When the autonomic nervous system concludes that the world is friendly, the body relaxes and the mind becomes receptive. So how do we help one another feel safer? A few possibilities spring to mind:

Show functionality and competence. "This person seems to know what she's doing and isn't going to lead me into a crisis."

Show receptivity and a nonjudgmental attitude. "This person isn't going reject me based on how I look or what I say."

Show predictability and consistency: "This person isn't going to jerk me around or drive me crazy with wild, erratic behavior."

Show playfulness and curiosity: "This person feels safe enough to have fun, explore, and laugh."

Show a sense of temporal affluence: "This person is going to take enough time to listen and won't abandon me as soon as something comes in on his phone."

Taken together, these qualities will set the stage for meaningful encounters and strengthen your life as a conversational activist. So get out of the transactional rut and look for opportunities to engage. Absorb your partner. Soak up his or her meanings, emotion, and life experience. See your partner with fresh eyes and treat her story as if it were the most important thing in the world. With each act of receptive attention, you're actually contributing to your health, your partner's health, and in turn, our health.

THE DARK SIDE OF US

As hyper-social animals, it's easy to romanticize the warm, fuzzy benefits of tribal affiliation. We talk a good, seductive game about belonging and inclusion, and we love the benefits that come with secure attachment, social acceptance, ubuntu, and the "tend and be-friend" response. But there's a dark side to tribe, and we'd be fools to ignore it.

Consider the now-famous hormone oxytocin, often celebrated in the popular press as the "love hormone" or the "trust hormone." Advocates call it an empathogen and point to its many virtues. It promotes trust, relaxation, social bonding, and affiliation. It decreases fear and anxiety and even decreases inflammation and promotes wound healing. Even the idea of oxytocin makes us feel good.

But there's more to the story. While oxytocin does produce the trusting, pro-social effects we love, it also stimulates some nasty out-group behaviors. Robert Sapolsky describes the effects in *Behave: The Biology of Humans at Our Best and Worst*, citing research showing that when interacting with strangers, oxytocin actually *decreases* cooperation. "Oxytocin makes us more prosocial to Us and worse to everyone else." In other words, it sharpens our in-group, out-group distinctions. When we're under the influence of oxytocin, we're all about Us, but have little interest in the welfare of Them.

Another notorious dark side is obedience, famously described by Stanley Milgram in his legendary *Obedience to Authority*. Shocked by the atrocities committed by ordinary citizens in World War II, Milgram recruited volunteers to participate in a fake experiment of "social learning." Subjects were instructed to administer tests to "learners" located in another room. If the "learners" answered incorrectly, the "teacher" was to administer increasingly painful shocks. Individuals who questioned the process were pressed by an authority figure in a white coat who ordered that "the experiment must continue."

The findings were profoundly disturbing: A substantial percentage of volunteers submitted to authority and continued shocking the "learner," even going so far as to administer (fake) lethal doses of electricity. Milgram called this mental condition "the agentic state." In this state, the subject gives up his own judgment and sense of responsibility and becomes an instrument of an authority figure. If enough people lapse into this agentic condition, atrocity becomes increasingly possible.

Equally troubling is the problem of conformity, famously explored by Solomon Asch in the 1950s. His experiments demonstrated that a sizeable minority of people were willing to adjust their personal perceptions to fit the dominant estimates of the group. In other words, a lot of us are willing to reject our own judgment for the sake of getting along.

Closely related is groupthink, a process by which individual ideas tend to coalesce within a group. When we're under the influence of groupthink, we avoid raising controversial issues or alternative solutions and as a consequence, individual creativity and independent thinking begin to disappear. Like obedience, groupthink can also lead to dehumanizing and violent behavior against others. Irving Janis, an early pioneer on groupthink theory, warned:

> The more amiability and esprit de corps there is among the members of a policy-making ingroup, the greater the danger that independent critical thinking will be replaced by groupthink, which is likely to result in irrational and dehumanizing actions directed against outgroups.

These findings force us to confront a monstrous dilemma for effective living: Tribal affiliation is essential for keeping us happy and healthy, but mindless obedience, conformity, and loyalty are a recipe for atrocity. The dark side of tribe isn't just unpleasant; it holds the seeds of disaster, for both people and the Earth. Tribalism nurtures us, but it can also destroy our future.

The problem goes well beyond human–human relations. In most circles, the problems of obedience, conformity, and groupthink are considered matters of social relationship, but they also impact our relationship with the biosphere at large. Just like Milgram's subjects, we are willing to do violence against the natural world, so long as someone else is taking responsibility. Just as a significant percentage of subjects were willing to shock innocent "learners," so too are millions of people willing to chop holes in the planetary lifeboat under direction of authority. It's impossible to measure how much environmental destruction is committed under the influence of authority, but we can assume it's substantial. Concerned employees may well attempt to do the right thing, but authority issues the command that must be obeyed. "The experiment must continue."

In this sense, historian Howard Zinn might well have been speaking on behalf of the biosphere when he wrote, "Civil disobedience is not our problem. Our problem is civil obedience." When rich corporate interests hold the biggest megaphones, the dangers of conformity and groupthink are multiplied. When advertising becomes omnipresent and neurologically sophisticated, we're under the influence almost constantly. We go along to get along, and before you know it, we're doing as we're told, mindlessly destroying the future on command.

DISSENT AS SOCIAL HYGIENE

The lesson here is that dissent is an essential force for social hygiene and the creation of a functional future. Many of us tend to dismiss activists as cranks, contrarians, and rebels, but their voices are vital antidotes to the perils of obedience, conformity, and groupthink. Activists are essential to our health and survival and should be respected as such. In other words, dissent is a pro-social act that should be celebrated and honored. As James Baldwin put it, "I love America more than any other country in this world, and, exactly for this reason, I insist on the right to criticize her perpetually." So too for Howard Zinn and others who have written, "Dissent is the highest form of patriotism."

The practice begins with curiosity and inquiry. Why are things the way they are? What is the history? How does power and culture work? What are the assumptions and values that drive the status quo? What are the conventional explanations, and how can we do better? In this practice, we bring our beginner's mind to the world of culture, society, and politics. In turn, we put ourselves in a position for more intelligent, even sapient action.

In this practice, it's essential to remember that complaining is not the same thing as dissent. Complaining is sometimes satisfying and can even be mildly cathartic, but it doesn't move the world in any significant way. In fact, complaining mostly serves to drag the rest of us down into the muck of discontent. It makes no contribution to social hygiene, health, or the creation of a functional future. In contrast, dissent is focused, intentional, and honorable. It challenges assumptions, power, and culture through acts of exposure and risk. It engages the world and stands up for health and sapience. In essence, dissent is a wake-up call to a society that is always in danger of falling asleep.

Unfortunately, our courage sometimes fails us. As a modern, domesticated species, we've grown accustomed to obedience and conformity and lost some of our willingness to push back. We go along to get along and stop asking why; we fall asleep to the world and the conditions around us. But this is where our physicality and wildness can help us stay awake. Don't forget: it wasn't so long ago we were wild animals, ready and willing to step up and speak out for what we believed in. This ancient, primal courage can still serve us. Love your tribe, but don't assume it knows the true path. Love your people, but be prepared to disobey. Respect your leaders, but be ready to question their judgment. Standing up feels dangerous, but it ultimately makes us smarter, stronger, and more functional. Your rebellion is vital to our survival and our health.

ONE WORLD TRIBE?

All this talk about tribe makes us wonder. We know our bodies are primed for living in small groups, but what are we to do with a vast human population that now inhabits the entire planet? Can we make the jump from small tribal bands that number in the dozens to a massive planetary tribe that numbers in the billions? Can we look at foreigners and outliers with the same sense of inclusion we reserve for those in our immediate circle?

Spiritual leaders advise us to do just that, but we might well wonder if the human brain is up to the task. Anthropologist Robin Dunbar has proposed that there's a cognitive limit to the number of people with whom we can maintain stable social relationships: the legendary "Dunbar's number." By calculating the average human brain size and extrapolating from the results of other primates, he proposed that humans can comfortably maintain up to 150 stable relationships. In other words, we're wired for the small tribes that were typical in prehistory. In this kind of social environment, we're fully capable of inclusivity and pro-social behavior.

But what happens when the human "tribe" numbers in the billions? In evolutionary and neurological terms, the challenge is completely unprecedented. On our good days, we'd like to be inclusive and welcoming, but perhaps our brains can only stretch so far. When faced with the prospect of bringing millions of people into our circle, we balk and revert to primitive in-group/out-group distinctions, xenophobia, and exclusion. We threaten to build walls and deport people by the millions.

PRACTICE

No one knows the ultimate solution, but a good first step in transcending our small-tribe view would be to focus on human universals, the features and qualities of life experience we all share. Donald Brown and other anthropologists have done great work on this score, some of which appears in his 1991 book *Human Universals*. According to common estimates, there are sixty-seven human universals, but you don't have to be an anthropologist to guess what they might be. Every human culture ever studied includes language, abstract symbolism, art, music, play, food preparation, and other activities we would all recognize no matter where we come from. Everyone sleeps, dreams, wakes, eats, talks, mates, fights, and makes up. This is common human ground.

But even more important is our common experience of simply being alive in this impermanent and mysterious world. No matter where we're from or what culture we inhabit, we're all faced with the same ambiguous predicament. Everyone is surprised by life, and everyone fears death. Everyone fears abandonment and longs for attention and attachment. Everyone wants to learn and achieve a sense of mastery and control. Everyone loves a story and longs for an explanation of why we're here. And most of all perhaps, everyone needs to feel felt.

We're also united in our shared neurobiology. Every human brain is a kludge, an assembly of neurological and psychological components, assembled over the course of millions of years. Each of us contains multitudes and those multitudes are constantly in flux. We're wired for love and fear, for approach and vigilance. We're vulnerable to traumas that shape our bodies, our nervous systems, and our behavior and we all get stressed, anxious, and afraid. We all come up with awkward, unskillful responses to our predicaments, and we're all extremely fallible.

In a fundamental sense, we are all doing the same thing in life, regardless of culture, history, or upbringing. We're trying to be happy, safe, and secure. We're trying to satisfy our needs for friendship, abundance, and love. Our strategies for meeting these needs vary widely, and many of them are awkward, misguided, and ignorant, but this too is a human universal.

When we focus on human universals, our fear diminishes and our compassion deepens. Everyone is living the same predicament. We build defenses and keep up appearances of confidence, but at the core, we all share the same uncertainties, frustrations, and desires. In this, we are never alone. As we open ourselves up to our own hardships, fears, and follies, we begin to understand that these are also shared. Everyone in the world, no matter their appearance or their history, feels these things too.

To connect with the human universals, treat everyone you meet as a fellow traveler. Imagine you're on a walkabout in a distant land and you've encountered a stranger. You feel a certain apprehension, but you're also curious. Both of you are on a journey into the mysteries of life, and both of you are in possession of incomplete knowledge. This person has seen things you've never seen and has stories you've never heard. Open the conversation with the most human questions: "Where are you from? Who are your people? Where have you traveled? What makes you laugh? Do you have any stories? What are your aspirations?"

Ask these questions and listen carefully. With luck, your new friend will feel felt and in turn, will share their humanity with you.

ACTION

Resistance is not only about battling the forces of darkness.
It is about becoming a whole and complete human being. It
is about overcoming estrangement. It is about the capacity
to love. It is about honoring the sacred. It is about dignity. It
is about sacrifice. It is about courage. It is about being free.
Resistance is the pinnacle of human existence.

—Chris Hedges

All is not well on the pale blue dot. We know—consciously or otherwise—that something is desperately wrong with our world. Climate change, habitat destruction, fresh water depletion, corporate tyranny, social inequality—every day the drumbeat continues, and every day we're confronted with a thousand calls to action. At the same time, many of us are grappling with issues of illness, pain, and trauma. Our hospitals and clinics are overwhelmed with an exploding caseload of obesity, diabetes, heart disease, neurological disorders, and stress-related conditions.

But what, if anything, do these two domains have to do with one another? The conventional view holds that health is one thing, activism another. Health takes place in a gym, studio, or clinic or on a sporting field, but activism takes place in the streets, in courtrooms, and in the halls of power. Health is managed by physicians and medical experts, while activism is led by passionate volunteers and organizers. Physicians have little or nothing to say about politics, and activists are mostly concerned with the mechanics of power, government, and legislation. Rarely do these domains overlap.

But it doesn't have to be this way. In fact, this division of attention is fundamentally flawed and compromises both our health and our ability to create change. So consider this possibility: What if activism and health were actually elements of a single practice? What if engagement in the issues of the day actually made our lives and bodies stronger?

In fact, these domains have far more in common than most of us realize. Activism is powerful, not just for the ends it sometimes produces, but also for the sense of meaning and purpose it brings to our lives. By taking responsibility for the state of the world, our experience becomes more meaningful and in turn, healthier. In the process, our health practices become a thousand times more interesting and relevant. What we eat, how we sleep, how we move: we're not just doing these things for ourselves. We're doing these things for the world.

One of the most robust findings in modern health research is that a sense of meaning is essential for maintaining vitality and resilience. Meaning is a psycho-physical force that carries us through adversity and buffers us against the inevitable frustrations of life. Activism harnesses that sense of meaning, puts us into a virtuous cycle of vitality and in turn, makes us stronger. As journalist Chris Hedges put it: "This is not only a fight for life—it's also a fight that gives life."

From this perspective, political inactivism begins to look like a health-negative behavior and maybe even a risk factor for disease. To be sure, there's plenty to be depressed about in the world of politics and a million reasons not to be engaged, but the bigger risk is passivity. By removing ourselves from the field of action and retreating into the comforts of our personal lives, we risk more than we think. Without something to fight for or against, we lose our vitality. The comfort feels good for a time, but ultimately, life becomes gray, shallow, and pointless.

Even worse, passivity is an act of complicity, a vote for the status quo and culture as usual. It's a vote for corporate rule, social injustice, and the continuing assault on the biosphere. The consequences of non-engagement are doubly vexing: Not only do the bad forces win, but our lives become pale, irrelevant, and unhealthy. As Hedges put it, "If we don't rebel, if we're not physically in an active rebellion, then it's spiritual death."

Inaction may look like a safe strategy, but the consequences go all the way to the deepest levels of our identity and life experience, an effect that's been widely recognized by spiritual leaders and activists across the spectrum. Martin Luther King Jr.: "The way of acquiescence leads to moral and spiritual suicide." Eleanor Roosevelt: "When you cease to make a contribution, you begin to die." Likewise Edward Abbey: "Sentiment without action is the ruin of the soul."

In short, the time has come to get out of our pigeonholes and start thinking of health and activism as two sides of the same practice. Activism, for all its frustrations and challenges, is simply a better, healthier way to live.

THE SPIRIT OF ACTIVISM

Activism may look like many things, but at its core, it's really one thing: the radical acceptance of responsibility. Everything flows from this stance. Once we take ownership of our lives and the state of the world, things begin to unfold.

To get a sense of how this process works, consider the drama triangle, a model of human relationship first described by psychologist Stephen Karpman in 1968. Often used as a tool in counseling and psychotherapy, it has powerful applications across the entire range of human experience.

There are three basic roles on the triangle: victim, persecutor, and rescuer. The trouble begins when a person identifies himself as a powerless victim in the face of circumstance. According to the victim's narrative, the primary source of his unhappiness lies with other people, agents, forces, and events. He pins the blame for his predicament on a persecutor, or if that doesn't work, he goes in search of a rescuer, someone or something that will extract him from his predicament and save the day.

Of course, it's essential to remember there are genuine victims in this world and, just as obviously, authentic persecutors who deserve justice. But here we're talking about attitudes, identities, and orientations. What roles are we claiming in the world? Who is creating our lives? These are questions of agency and responsibility. By reflecting on our roles in the triangle, we gain a sense of clarity about our stance and our relationship to the world.

The drama begins when we stumble, get hurt, or fail to get what we desire. Looking for a way out of our unhappiness, we claim victimhood. We blame our parents, our genes, our childhood, our jobs, our bosses, and our partners. We blame modern culture, government policy, the opposition party, stress, and overwork. These accusations may well contain some elements of truth, but this is beside the point. The real issue is our orientation. By claiming the role of victim, we give away our power. No longer are we acting in the world—the world is acting on us.

Going to the other point of the triangle—toward rescue—is no better. In our unhappiness, we look for people, substances, ideas, or organizations to bail us out of our predicament. To be sure, sometimes we're in genuine need of assistance and support, but when we compulsively seek out rescue, we give away our power once again. The more we seek to be propped up by the world, the weaker we become.

Many of us have heard this story before, and it's easy to assume that victimhood is something reserved for the underbelly of society; alcoholics, drug addicts, and criminals come to mind. But victimhood is alive and well at every level, and no one is immune. After all, it's an easy, seductive trap. There's plenty of blame to go around, and excuses are always handy: The economy is in recession, our parents were flawed, our neighborhood was in turmoil. Bullies abused us, the schools failed us, the system didn't provide the kind of employment we deserved. That's why complaining has become a national sport, with entire media empires dedicated to round-the-clock finger pointing. When things aren't going well, there's always a handy perpetrator we can blame, right across the aisle.

Not only does victimhood weaken our sense of power and agency, it's also bad for our health. When we see ourselves as powerless agents in a sea of influence, we simply go along with whatever lifestyle choices are presented to us. We lose contact with the strength and vitality of our primal bodies and hand our fate over to the forces of marketing, advertising, and corporate culture. It also set us up for stress. When we cast ourselves as victims, we give up our sense of power and control, the very qualities that would protect us from adversity. Ultimately, adopting a victim orientation may be even worse for our health than widely recognized behaviors such as smoking and physical inactivity.

ESCAPE FROM THE DRAMA TRIANGLE

The way out of the drama triangle, as many teachers, therapists, and coaches have suggested, is the creative orientation. This is where we exercise responsibility and start building a vision of what we want to become. As we move beyond habits of blaming, complaining, excuses, and wishful thinking, life begins to open up into a world of opportunity, power, and freedom. In this practice, we actually change our identity. Instead of blaming circumstance or hoping for a rescue, we ask a new set of questions: What can I do today, right this moment, to advance my creation? Where can I exercise control? Where does my power lie?

why's it gotta be a she?

At its core, activism is about taking full responsibility for our lives. But the activist doesn't just take responsibility for his own life and behaviors; she takes responsibility for the state of the entire world. She takes responsibility for climate change, habitat destruction, and every other insult we inflict on the natural world. She takes responsibility for social injustice, racism, sexism, and every other abuse that people inflict on one another. She takes responsibility for lifestyle disease, diabetes, and depression. In short, she owns it all.

To be clear, the activist didn't cause these things, and just as obviously, she will never be able to fix most of these problems by her own hand. But this is very much beside the point. The activist isn't concerned about the specific causal chain of events that led to some particular problem, and she's not inclined to spend her time working out the fine-grained details of who's to blame for every human calamity. Instead, she concentrates on what's possible, and in the process finds a wellspring of meaning and energy.

Not surprisingly, this willingness to accept responsibility is the defining quality of our most popular heroes, heroines, and superheroes, both real and imagined. These people are not complainers, nor are they seduced by rescue agents, substances, or ideas. They may well be fighting epic battles against powerful forces of destruction and injustice, but they keep their energy focused. It's hard to imagine Jackie Robinson, Martin Luther King Jr., Nelson Mandela, Mahatma Gandhi, or the men and women of Standing Rock blaming, complaining, or looking for a rescue. They're too busy creating the future.

Ultimately, it's all about our orientation. Yes, some predicaments are inherently challenging and even maddening, but no matter the nature of the adversity, we are free to choose our interpretations of events. We are free to choose our stories. We are free to move beyond blame and rescue. And however we choose, our willingness to abdicate or accept responsibility is contagious. When people start giving away their power through blaming and complaining, others are quick to follow and before long, everyone is pointing fingers, ducking responsibility, and blaming the world for their misfortunes. But when people step up, others are inclined to do the same.

EXTRAORDINARY FORCES

…the resources of those skilled in the use of extraordinary forces are as infinite as the heavens and earth, as inexhaustible as the flow of the great rivers, for they end and recommence—cyclical, as are the movements of the sun and moon. They die away and are reborn—recurrent, as are the passing seasons.

—Sun Tzu
The Art of War

Being an activist on this blue-green lifeboat is no simple matter. The entire enterprise is fraught with dilemmas, ambiguities, and world-class frustrations. In the first place, it's a highly unconventional battle. There are some genuinely bad actors on the lifeboat who must be opposed, but in many cases it's not at all clear who or what the adversary is. In fact, a substantial percentage of environmental and social destruction is caused simply by humans being humans. Only half aware of what we're doing, we blunder our way through the world, sometimes being sapient, but mostly just being awkward in our relationships to our bodies, our planet, and one another.

At the same time, activists are up against a titanic imbalance of power. Future-hostile forces are immensely powerful, well connected, and aggressive in protecting their interests. Corporate Goliaths are protected from liability and sealed off from dissent. In this environment, our ability to create change often feels insignificant.

Fighting back seems hopeless—but giving up is no better. It's no wonder so many people give up on activism and go back to their normal abnormal lives.

But perhaps we can draw some inspiration from the Chinese military strategist Sun Tzu and his enduring classic, *The Art of War.* One of Sun Tzu's most intriguing themes was his distinction between the "normal" and "extraordinary" forces in battle. As he put it: "That the army is certain to sustain the enemy's attack without suffering defeat is due to operations of the extraordinary and the normal forces." Sun Tzu's focus was on battlefield tactics, but his observations are equally relevant in the world of political power, influence, and culture.

In the world of activism, normal forces operate within conventional, mainstream channels. We identify an issue, set up a nonprofit, raise money, build a mailing list, recruit volunteers, hire lawyers, and craft legislation. It's all pretty ordinary work. If you're effective in organizing these normal forces, you might be able to move the needle on policy and legislation or recruit better candidates to elected office. But even if your pro-future nonprofit is well-funded and well-organized, the battle is still supremely difficult. Corporate agents of destruction are massively funded, highly aggressive, and mostly free of ethical constraints. If we try to confront these actors with conventional forces, we'll usually come up short.

This is where the activist turns to the extraordinary forces—the domain of art, storytelling, and culture. Instead of challenging the status quo directly with legislative power, these arts target the human imagination and spirit. They work with ideas, sensations, and relationships that lie outside the halls of power. In this sense, art is the ultimate workaround.

The extraordinary forces of art work in subtle but powerful ways. Paint a poster with provocative message and maybe no one notices, today. Or maybe someone notices, but does nothing overt. Maybe consciousness shifts just slightly, just enough to move a behavior down the line. It's never a sure thing, but inspiration flows and ideas cascade. Hyper-social animals are always sharing. Art, especially something new and exciting, gets around.

The power of art lies in the way it speaks to the deepest, most influential layers of brain and body. Art is wild, ancient, primal. It bypasses left-brain rationality and the New Way's obsession with logic and speaks directly to our oldest selves. It leapfrogs convention and gets to the heart of the matter. We might well say a well-crafted picture is worth a thousand wonkish facts.

Art is an expression of freedom and a longing for the vagility we've lost with the development of roads, cities, and suburbs. It refuses to be constrained by convention. It leaps over fences, and fights back against templates, pigeonholes, automation and conformity. It's our Paleo spirit, speaking to us from deep within our animal core.

The power of art lies in its ability to transcend the ordinary as it moves our minds and spirits out of habit. When it works, art becomes a monkeywrench in human imagination and culture. Great art is an antidote to boilerplate, cliché, and corporate consciousness. It derails entrenched assumptions and expectations, clearing the way for new insights. And that's precisely what makes it so valuable.

ARTIVISM AND CULTURE

It's no surprise that artists and activists are natural allies, exemplified in the emerging movement called *artivism*.[95] In *It's Bigger Than Hip Hop*, M. K. Asante gives us a typical definition:

> The artivist uses her artistic talents to fight and struggle against injustice and oppression—by any medium necessary. The artivist merges commitment to freedom and justice with the pen, the lens, the brush, the voice, the body, and the imagination. The artivist knows that to make an observation is to have an obligation.

In normal society, we're conditioned to believe that art is something we do with paints and brushes, wood, metal, and glass, something that lives in museums, galleries, and gift shops. But for the artivist, art is all about the human encounter with life and culture. As Joe Brewer, the cofounder and research director of Culture2,[96] a culture design lab for social good, sees it, "ALL of our problems arise through pathologies of culture." He advocates "culture hacking" with new rituals, new art, new writing, and new relationships. Says Brewer, "If we want to design our way through this maelstrom of crises we will have to become culture designers who learn how to guide and shape the evolution of entire societies." Culture is our canvas.

THE CREATIVE IMPERATIVE

To be an artivist is to stand at the leading edge of culture and point the way to something better. It requires that we remain alert and awake to the meaning and consequences of our actions in context. Unfortunately, it's easy to fall into a state of reactivism. We wait for someone in power to do something abhorrent, then we strike back with venom, satire, or ridicule. It's hard to resist, but this kind of effort usually goes nowhere and accomplishes nothing. Even if our snark is right on target, we haven't really created anything of value. Impulsive reaction to the issues of the day is not artivism.

To put it another way, our resistance to destruction and injustice is necessary, but is not sufficient. As Naomi Klein has put it, *No Is Not Enough*. Outrage, indignation, and protests are good first steps, but by themselves, they don't go very far. We must stand in the way of bad policies and bad behavior, but we've also got to be building something of value. And if you can't say what it is you're building, maybe you're just being a reactivist.

Calls to action are all well and good, but what we really need are calls to cultural creativity. As we've seen, New Way culture has yet to develop a curriculum for dealing with mismatch, lifestyle disease, social inequality, or a functional future, and it simply isn't delivering the kind of teachings we need to craft a long-term relationship with the planet. Activists must fight the good fight against planet- and future-hostile actors, but even more important is the need to create curriculum. What can we teach each other about building a functional future? Can we show the way through the chaos to something that actually works?

As artists, we need to illuminate what's wrong, but even more importantly, we need to show what's better. Use your art to draw attention to bad actors, highlight foolishness, and speak truth to power, but more than all this, use your art to revive and extend our health and sapience.

TRUST YOUR BODY

Art is more important now than ever before, but we're in serious danger of losing touch with our creative capacity. The rise of the STEM curriculum (science, technology, engineering, and math), threatens to eclipse the humanities as more and more schools devote their resources to practical, economic concerns. Art, along with dance, history, language, physical education, and music, is being left in the dust.

This puts us in serious danger. Our planetary crisis presents us with a long list of inconvenient truths, not the least of which is that, whatever happens in the coming years, we are almost certainly going to have to live in new ways. The hockey stick graph tells us that radical change is imminent, but lacking faith in our creative capacity, many of us are terrified of the prospect. We assume that our familiar, modern system of employment, commerce, legal relationships, private property, and technologies is the only possible way to live.

Lacking confidence in our ability to create, we double down on convention and our continued reliance on traditional tools, machines, roles, and relationships. But our imagination is failing us. We behave as if there's no other way to add value to a community or sustain life. As if there's no other way to enhance human welfare or succeed. As if there's no other way to make a living or be happy. Our unwillingness to act on the crises of our day is due in large measure to our inability to trust our creativity, our adaptability, and our bodies.

This is precisely why art is so vital. It's not so much that it produces great museum pieces or even something to post on the refrigerator door. Rather, the value lies in the way art teaches us to draw on our inner capabilities. The process of drawing, painting, or crafting gives us experiential proof that when we make the effort and take a chance, we can almost always come up with something. It may or may not look like much, but the experience shows us that creation is possible. In short, art teaches us to trust our bodies. In this sense, art is arguably the most important subject in today's educational curriculum. It gives us vital confidence in our adaptive powers and our ability to imagine new possibilities.

IT'S ALL MATERIAL

So the time has come to get serious about art. It's time to get over the idea that art is for a certain kind of people with a special kind of attitude. It's time to get over the idea that our creative efforts have got to pay off in some financial way. And most of all, it's time to get over the belief that you don't have what it takes. In fact, anyone can take a chance on a new form, pattern, or idea. Anyone can make a mess, then another mess, then a refinement, then another iteration, and then eventually, something that works.

Perhaps you don't think of yourself as an artist. Perhaps you believe artistic skill is a special aptitude that's reserved for gifted people. Perhaps you've had the creativity squeezed out of you by a school system dedicated to perfection, right answers, and preparation for corporate serfdom. If that's the case, get over it. In the context of human history—for at least the last hundred thousand years—artistic ability has been commonplace. For the vast majority of our time on earth, there was no special class of individuals called "artists." Everyone had the muse and the potential. Anyone could craft and create.

Every human being has the capacity to make something. From the cave paintings of our ancestors to the explosion of modern forms, we are fundamentally, outrageously capable. It's simply a matter of exercising what's already there. Just start with what you've got on hand. The entire messy, broken world is your medium. Every facet of your chaotic life is a candidate for expression and transformation. The paints and brushes are just a metaphor. The material that's really interesting is our relationships, our values, our decisions, and our culture.

Think of the whole world and the totality of your life as an art project. Open your mind to the unusual, and free yourself from the bonds of familiarity, routine, and neuroplastic habit. You're living on a planet of raw material, and possibilities are everywhere. If you want to access the core of human experience and do the work of personal and cultural transformation, this is the place to go. When in doubt, keep your eye on the art.

ENDS AND MEANS

> Cause and effect, means and ends, seed and fruit cannot be severed; for the effect already blooms in the cause, the end preexists in the means, the fruit in the seed.
>
> —Ralph Waldo Emerson

On the face of it, activism seems like a simple proposition. We start with a set of beliefs and try to advance the truth as we see it. We choose an issue, lay out a plan, and choose our methods. But every time we attempt to exercise power or influence in a system, we soon discover there are no surefire methods, strategies, or tactics. Complexity and judgment calls are everywhere, and every time we turn around, we're confronted with that age-old conundrum: How adversarial should we be in the pursuit of our objectives? Should we fight back directly with force and outrage? Should we monkeywrench the machines of destruction under the cover of darkness? File lawsuits? Or should we work inside the system for incremental change? How should we play this game? Flowers or pitchforks? Naughty or nice?

On one hand, the case for naughty, militant action is strong. If you're on a lifeboat and someone is actively chopping holes in the hull, it's right, necessary, and intelligent to take the fight directly to the perpetrators. If you were on an actual boat, it would be foolish to do otherwise. Inaction means death, not just for yourself, but for everyone on board. By this metaphor, it makes perfect moral sense to take swift, decisive action against agents of destruction. Incrementalism just isn't going to do it.

But of course, it's never so simple. Direct militant action might be emotionally satisfying and even effective in the short term, but it's also likely to be counterproductive in its side effects. Acts of vandalism and destruction ratchet up the stress, fear, and inflammation in the social system. And it doesn't take much imagination to see what would happen if even small pieces of modern infrastructure were compromised by direct action. When people get desperate, saving habitat and building community is the last thing anyone's inclined to do. People are already under major stress as it is.

So what about nice? As we learned in kindergarten, polite and respectful behavior is the preferred path for building productive, long-term relationships. Nice creates a sense of safety and inspires others to be more open-minded and receptive. All of which sounds wonderful, but depending on your orientation, it's either highly sophisticated or hopelessly naïve. At its best, playing nice builds good will and social capital while laying the groundwork for solving wicked problems. But at its worst, it wastes precious time and leaves us feeling duped. The perpetrators shake our hands, say the right words, and go back to their ghastly work of destroying the planet.

So what are we left with? Naughty causes too much destruction, but nice doesn't work fast enough and maybe not at all. How do we modulate our intensity? How do we adjust our activism to be effective while still maintaining the goodwill we need to live on the boat?

ACTIVISM V. ANTAGONISM

There is no ultimate answer to the activist's dilemma, but a good first step would be to understand the difference between activism and antagonism. Activism is an essential, noble, and meaningful pursuit that's vital for cultural hygiene and a functional future. Antagonism is simply trash talk, a reactive attempt to heap dirt on those we disagree with. Unfortunately, many would-be activists fail to understand this distinction and labor under the belief that the only way to change the world is to destroy the opposition.

Today we see this attitude all across our polarized, modern world. Humans have always had an antagonistic streak, but Donald Trump set the standard for incivility in his 2016 campaign and threatens to drag our entire culture into the gutter. Antagonism has now become a mean-spirited national sport, whipped into a frenzy by talk radio and the internet. Civility seems like ancient history.

But antagonism is not activism. Activism is creative work, focused on creating some new, more functional way of being in the world. It's about building culture, policy, and relationships. In contrast, antagonism only seeks to humiliate and provoke the opposition. Points are scored through ridicule and, if that fails, repetition and volume. If you can make your opponent look bad, you've succeeded.

But antagonism only makes bad situations worse. Inflammatory rhetoric makes our social systems less intelligent; when people feel attacked, they become less receptive and less likely to reflect on their own behavior. Curiosity and growth come to a standstill.

This is where metaphor meets reality. Knowing what we know about mind–body interdependence, we begin to see that political language can have genuine consequences for physical and cognitive health. The tone of political speech actually shapes the flow of information within our bodies. Inflammatory speech, in other words, may well cause actual inflammation in the bodies of listeners. The old childhood rant that "sticks and stones can break my bones, but words can never hurt me" is just plain wrong. In fact, hurtful words can fire up the same neural pathways that operate in physical injury.[97,98]

So instead of looking at antagonism simply as a matter of political speech, we might well look at it as a public health issue. As antagonism ripples through a social system, bodies and minds become more inflamed and in turn, cognition narrows. We become more fearful, anxious, xenophobic, and even paranoid, all of which make our efforts at creative activism that much more difficult. In the end, antagonism makes the activist's work harder.

There are no perfect answers for our naughty-or-nice dilemmas. Being overly strong and hawkish can set off inflammation, pushback, and unforeseen side effects, but being passive and dovish sets us up for ineffectiveness and abuse by superior forces. The middle way—the way of the owl—is no guarantee either, but it does focus our vision on skills and perspectives such as balance, judgment, and poise in the face of conflict. The owl is wary of extremes and well aware of the pathologies of power and passivity. Aggression fails; acquiescence also fails; but assertiveness sometimes works. The middle ground is ambiguous, difficult, and often stressful, but this is where the art lives. Don't try to escape this place. Inhabit it.

KEEP YOUR EYE ON THE WAY

Ultimately, the art lies in our perspective and spirit. As activists, we focus on objectives and look for particular outcomes; we feel good when we achieve a success and depressed when we don't. But attachment to outcomes can actually distract us from the vital work we do along the way. In a highly dynamic, interconnected world, we actually have very little control over ends. Even the simplest issue has lots of moving parts, and our best efforts can easily be overwhelmed by power players and unknowable forces. The battles are tough, defeats are common, and victories are rare. Try as we might, we have little control over the final result.

In contrast, we have almost total control over the means by which we conduct the battle. We can choose to act with dignity, balance, proportion, and sapience. We can choose to act with honor, skill, and sincerity. Our effort may be inadequate to secure a victory, but in the long run, the quality of our effort often proves to be the most important part of the game. People pay attention to the way we engage. If they witness us fighting with sincerity, decency, and sapience, they're likely to follow our lead.

According to legend, football coach Vince Lombardi once told his players that "Winning isn't everything; it's the only thing." Likewise, modern culture has become infected by a similar "ends are everything" attitude, and we've managed to turn almost every aspect of society into a competition. From grade school through grad school and the corporate ranks, we're expected to win at whatever we do while the means are increasingly left by the wayside. The most important thing is the victory and the achievement.

But we could just as easily turn this view upside down, replacing our focus on ends with a focus on means. This is a common theme in Eastern traditions, especially in disciplines like Zen archery, where actually hitting the target is very close to being irrelevant. Instead, it's the quality of our attention and experience that matters. We can well imagine a Zen coach advising an archery student to worry less about the outcome and more about the totality of the experience. "The process isn't everything," he might say. "It's the only thing."

Out in the messy real world, outright wins are rare, and if we focus exclusively on outcomes as the standard for success, we'll be frequently disappointed. But when we focus on means, we can win every day. A battle fought and a life lived with dignity is a victory of its own, regardless of the particular outcomes. From this perspective, there is no shame or disgrace in defeat. We are fallible human animals. But no matter the outcome, we can always engage in sincerity. Defeat is undesirable, but if we fight with courage and resolve, the effort stands on its own. People are watching. Even in defeat, we can move the world.

Today we're faced with the prospect of losing the battle for a functional future and a long-term relationship with the Earth. In our passion and fear, we may well be moved to drastic, impulsive action, but we cannot and must not take our eyes off the means. How we fight this fight is vitally important, not just for victories we might achieve today, but for the long future. Will we go down in a spasm of partisan name-calling, petty grievance, and bitter tribalism? Will we close our eyes and take refuge in denial and amusement? Or will we fight with dignity, honor, courage, and sapience? The difference will tell a story of our spirit and will serve as a powerful gift to our descendants. We may not be able to give them a functioning atmosphere or a world rich in biodiversity, but we can give them a story of our courage and our effort. And that will be worth a great deal.

So worry a little less about the ends and a little more about means. If we keep the means beautiful, we win. The way, you might say, is the way.

TAKE A KNEE FOR THE PLANET

In the popular imagination, we tend to think political activism is all about protesting in the streets, filing lawsuits, or getting elected. It's about knowing the mechanics of power and deploying the best strategies and tactics. These elements have their place, but at its core, activism is all about our willingness to expose ourselves to risk and ambiguity. It's about courage, especially our willingness to pay attention, exercise judgment, and act with sincerity. Will we retreat into the safety and comfort of a narrow view or will we have the strength to keep our eyes and minds open to larger, more difficult realities?

As usual, it's a matter of attention. As we grow into adulthood, the scope of our awareness widens and reveals more about the world, including the problems and suffering of those around us. In turn, we feel a responsibility to act. As the artivists say, "To make an observation is to have an obligation." The obvious solution is to actually step up and take action, but this means risk, commitment, and uncertainty, so most of us opt for an easier "solution"—we simply contract our awareness. Instead of taking in the state of the planet as a whole, we reduce our field of vision. We become specialists in some narrow domain: a single country, a single profession, a single issue, or more often, the details of a personal life. And the narrower, the better. If we can contract our awareness far enough, we'll never have to take on the really nasty human and environmental dilemmas of our time. It's a great labor-saving tactic, you might say.

But of course, it's also a recipe for long-term failure at every level. Narrow vision is simply antithetical to the holistic systems-based thinking we so desperately need. When millions of people contract their attention and shrink into specialization or self-interest, it becomes almost impossible to even have a conversation about large-scale problems and integrated solutions. When people retreat to their psychological and personal silos, nothing moves.

This suggests a new focus for activism. Knowing the nuts and bolts of political change is necessary, but the real challenge is to build and sustain our personal and cultural courage so we can keep our eyes open to the big pictures of our day. In this sense, our challenge isn't technical, legal, or political; it's profoundly spiritual. To see big, we've got to stay strong—physically, psychologically, and spiritually.

PROFILES IN STRENGTH

Of course, we're always impressed by highly visible acts of courage in the service of some grand objective. We honor those who've stood up and exposed themselves in dramatic defiance of adverse conditions, those who've made highly conspicuous sacrifices for the common good.

We think of Martin Luther King, Jr., Gandhi, Rosa Parks, and Jackie Robinson. We think of the 1968 Olympic Games, when sprinters Tommie Smith and John Carlos raised a human rights protest salute during their medal ceremony.[99] We think of Colin Kaepernick taking a knee against racism at NFL games. We think of Emma Gonzalez, David Hogg, and student activists who spoke out after the mass shooting at Marjory Stoneman Douglas High School in Parkland, Florida.

Likewise, we're reminded of the founders of Greenpeace, who confronted Soviet whaling vessels on the open ocean, and resolved to "place our bodies between the whales and the harpoon." We think of Ken Ward and the climate activists who in October, 2016, closed valves on pipelines carrying tar sands crude oil into the United States.[100] We think of the men and women of Standing Rock.

In 1973, Paul Watson was a medic for the American Indian Movement (AIM) during the occupation of Wounded Knee, South Dakota. As he tells the story,

> We were hopelessly outnumbered and surrounded, and the Federal agents were firing thousands of rounds into the village every night. There was zero possibility of us winning. I went to AIM leader Russell Means and I asked him why we were continuing to resist because we could not possibly win. His answer stayed with me the rest of my life. He said, 'We

are not concerned about winning or losing. We are not concerned about the overwhelming odds against us. We are here taking a stand because it is the right thing to do and the right place to do it.'

These acts of visible courage are important and inspirational, but they tend to overshadow the equally important but invisible acts of courage that move the needle on the world every day. This is the courage no one ever sees: the simple, daily choices we make about what to buy, what to read, what to eat, what to drive, what to talk about, and how to relate to the world.

It takes guts to live against the grain of commercial culture, especially when no one is watching. It takes guts to buy less and consume less. It takes guts to live simply and dedicate attention to the welfare of the seventh generation. In all likelihood, your unseen acts of courage will not be recorded for posterity. No one will glorify you or celebrate the fact you made a sacrifice for the future, but your acts still count. A million acts of invisible courage ultimately amount to some real, highly visible change. And so the koan for our day: Would you be courageous even if no one was looking?

PUT YOUR BODY WHERE YOUR MOUTH IS

On the face of it, activism looks and feels dangerous. Blowing the whistle on bad actors exposes us to public scrutiny, and speaking out makes us vulnerable. If you advocate for the future, people will even attack you for your "radical" pro-lifeboat position. Your career and your personal life may well suffer.

It's a risky business, to be sure, but inactivism and passivity are equally hazardous. Stand up and you're exposed, but sit down and you might just be obliterated by the blind, powerful forces of the status quo. Inaction gives environmental atrocity and social injustice a place to grow, and when it does, there's no hiding from the

its own kind of healing [handwritten marginal note]

consequences; passivity only delays the reckoning and leaves us with nothing. As Greenpeace founder Bob Hunter put it, "If we wait for the meek to act, there isn't going to be any earth to inherit."

No matter what path we take, safety is an illusion and an impossibility. Danger lurks on the grassland and in the streets and boardroom of the modern world. But when action and inaction are equally dangerous, the choice becomes obvious. We can sit back, do nothing, and suffer the physical and spiritual consequences or we can stand up in honor and courage. Courage may seem exceptional and rare, but in another sense, it's really the only sensible way to live.

The good news is that courage is muscular. We get good at standing up by standing up. We get good at speaking out by speaking out. Acts of courage are expressions of health, and in all likelihood, they also build health. Given what we know about the interconnected nature of mind, body, and spirit, it could hardly be otherwise. Every time we act courageously, we prove to our bodies that we're capable of living and thriving in this world. In turn, power and confidence flow through our veins and our tissue. So take a knee for the planet and your health. Take a knee for social justice and a functional future. No matter the outcome, your courage will be its own success.

LIFE

But unless we are creators we are not fully alive. Creativity is a way of living life, no matter our vocation or how we earn our living. Creativity is not limited to the arts, or having some kind of important career.

—Madeleine L'Engle
Walking on Water: Reflections on Faith and Art

From all outward appearances in today's world, it looks like activism is all about the money. Every day we're confronted by a steady stream of appeals for contributions to environmental and pro-social causes, and every "call to action" is really a call to click the "donate now" button. To make a difference, it seems we've either got to give money or raise money, but does this mean that only rich people can be activists? What if I'm broke? I can't possibly give enough to move the needle on the world. It's no wonder so many people drop out.

Money, like it or not, is necessary. It costs a lot to rent office space, do research, and hire lawyers and staff to move legislators and policy makers. Without some kind of well-funded opposition, corporate Goliaths would simply have their way with the world. But this focus on fund-raising obscures the possibilities for more interesting work. By telling a story based exclusively on the ability to fund campaigns, conventional activist groups distract us from the fact that even without money, our lives can still be powerful.

To really succeed, we've got to shift the emphasis onto the way people live. Not everyone has money, but everyone has a life. Everyone makes choices, and everyone has at least some influence on the people around them. We may not have enough to make significant financial contributions to pro-habitat, pro-social, and pro-future organizations, but we can always move our lives toward pro-habitat, pro-social, and pro-future behaviors. If we do it right, our lives become the activism.

So how are we supposed to construct an effective, healthful, and meaningful life? Everyone wants to know the recipe, and experts are happy to step up with simple answers and formulas, but if you've ever tried to construct a life according to conventional recommendations, you've probably discovered things just don't add up. Literally.

Try a back-of-the-envelope calculation: Start with eight hours of sleep every night, then add in another hour or so for basic hygiene and self-care. Then another hour for your dwelling, cleaning and repairs. Maybe an hour or so for food shopping and preparation, another hour for exercise, another few hours for child care and hanging out with family and friends. Add another hour for homework, reading, and hobbies and yes, don't forget the commute and your day job. No matter the specifics, it all adds up to a lot more than twenty-four hours.

This is why formulas don't work. Our lives are messy and constantly in flux. Every morning brings new challenges to our adaptation, and monkey wrenches are everywhere. We try to get our lives organized into well-ordered sequences and hierarchies of activity, but something always seems to come up. We plan out our lives carefully with day planners, calendars, and digital programs, but in the end, no plan survives contact with the chaos of modern life. Unless you're a professional athlete or wealthy executive with a lifestyle support system in place, you're going to have to find your own way. And a good place to begin is to treat your life like an ongoing art project.

The art of choice is called bricolage, from the French verb *bricoler* ("to tinker"). The idea is to craft your art from whatever happens to be available. The work is not premeditated, structured, or choreographed—it's improv. Use whatever you've got on hand: your family and friends, your work, your possessions, your history, and your values. There's no right way to do it. Just try for an arrangement that pleases your eye, your ear, and your heart, then stay with the process. As conditions change, rearrange the elements as necessary. You're an artist, not a technician.

Start with movement opportunism. Look for gaps in daily life when you can get up out of your chair, out of your vehicle, and out of the office. This isn't going to be a warrior workout, but a burst of physicality in context. You might find yourself in the backyard, a parking lot, a lobby, or a playground. Conditions won't be ideal, but they don't have to be. There's always stairs and steps, curbs, poles, walls, rocks, and trees. Make something up.

Then, practice food opportunism. Be on the lookout for the real stuff that makes up your food-based diet. Become a hunter and gatherer of quality. If you see something real and tasty, grab it before it gets away. Next, practice rest opportunism. If there's a break in the action, look for a place to let go of your striving. Keep your eyes open for a lull in the schedule when you can breathe, meditate, and let your body ease into a quiet, parasympathetic state. Next, practice some social opportunism. Stay alert for a chance to have a genuine conversation with a fellow human traveler. Find out where they're from and what they've learned about the world. Listen and learn. And finally, look for opportunism in activism. Keep your eyes open for a chance to make a case for planetary health, interdependence, social justice and the seventh generation. Find a crack in the system, and start working.

RHYTHM

The same stream of life that runs through my veins night and day runs through the world and dances in rhythmic measures. It is the same life that shoots in joy through the dust of the earth in numberless blades of grass and breaks into tumultuous waves of leaves and flowers.

—Rabindranath Tagore

The goal of life is to make your heartbeat match the beat of the universe to match your nature with Nature.

—Joseph Campbell

As always, life is about movement, and once again it's time to remember our lives in prehistory. Imagine you've been sleeping out with your tribe, clustered around the campfire, dreaming of animals and roaming the spirit world. As the first light appears in the sky, you awaken, and someone tells you it's time to move. The elders have decided that today you'll join a hunting party to explore a distant valley to the East. It's going to be a big day.

Your party leaves camp at a brisk pace, traversing a familiar wash you've explored many times before, and by midday you're on new ground, alert for predators, scanning for tracks, scat, and any other signs that will tell the story of animal life. As the afternoon unfolds, you've crossed miles of open ground, navigated some hilly terrain, and forded a crocodile-infested river. By the time the sun reaches the horizon, you realize you're going to be out that night and all day tomorrow as well. You're feeling strong, but the exertions are beginning to draw down your reserves.

It's three long days before you finally circle back to camp. The hunt was successful, and you return with a small antelope, some scavenged meat, and a new understanding of your bioregion and the ways of the animals who live there. You're excited to be back, but after the welcome, some stories, and a feast, you're feeling the effects. Your feet are tender, your legs are sore, and you've got a nasty bruise from when you slipped on the river crossing. Now you're ready to relax.

Which is exactly what you do. For the next three or four days, the whole tribe takes it easy, lounging in the shade, sleeping as much as possible, gossiping, eating, and observing the world. There's no urgency to do anything, and plenty of time to just rest. Your body takes full advantage of the lull and begins the work of repairing damaged tissues and replenishing energy stores. After a few days, you're ready to head out once again.

In their 1988 book *The Paleolithic Prescription*, anthropologists Eaton, Shostak, and Konner described this oscillating pattern of activity and rest in native people, and dubbed it the "Paleolithic rhythm." Without question, this pattern the norm for human beings. Our bodies thrive on this kind of pattern. If we're going to restore our vitality, this would be very good place to begin.

PLANET OF RHYTHM

The history of our rhythmic experience goes all the way back to the origins of life on earth. From those earliest moments in that "warm shallow pond," every organism would have been exposed to alternating patterns of light and darkness, the waxing and waning of tides, and daily and seasonal oscillations of temperatures and moisture. Everything was constantly changing, driven by the tilt of the Earth and the beat of natural light. LUCA and her descendants would have generated some extremely sophisticated adaptations based on those rhythmic patterns. LUCA didn't have a heart exactly, but we can be sure she had a pulse.

Today, our rhythmic ancestry lives on in the bodies of every animal, deep in the physiology of cells, organs, and tissues. Even plants feel the beat.[101] Researchers at Aarhus University in the Netherlands used a form of laser scanning to observe twenty-two species of trees on windless nights. The findings suggest the trees are actively pumping water upward in stages, and that trees have a slow version of a "pulse." Presumably, all plants have similar oscillations in activity. After all, their history, like our own, is rhythmic.

Today, every aspect of our physiology is linked to ancient circadian patterns. There's the flux and flow of hormones that rise and fall throughout the day and over the course of seasons. Our blood pressure, digestion, and mental acuity wax and wane from dawn to dusk. Even our cognitive performance fluctuates by season. Andrew Lim, a neurologist at the Sunnybrook Health Sciences Centre at the University of Toronto, has found a seasonal pattern in cognitive ability and gene expression.[102] "We found a peak in cognitive performance near the Fall equinox, at the end of summer," says Lim. The precise mechanism is unclear, but the study's authors speculate that factors such as light and temperature, vitamin D, and hormone levels are involved.

Likewise, a growing body of research suggests that our bodies function optimally when we align our eating patterns with our circadian rhythms. *The Circadian Code* by Satchin Panda, a professor at the Salk Institute and an expert on circadian rhythms research, argues that people improve their metabolic health when they eat their meals in a daily eight- to ten-hour window, taking their first bite of food in the morning and their last bite early in the evening.[103]

Incredibly, the rhythmic nature of our bodies even extends to processes such as wound healing. Researchers have recently discovered that wounds sustained during the daylight hours heal significantly faster than those sustained at night.[104] Similarly, the body's inflammatory status shows a marked seasonal variation, with higher levels of inflammation in European people during the winter months.[105]

Rhythm is in us and around us, but sadly, modern culture has forgotten the ancient beat. In our arrogance and rush to succeed, we've chosen to work and live against the rhythm of the biosphere.

If there's one word that defines our modern work environment, that word is *chronic*. We work during the day where a common lament has it that "I'm chained to my desk," and when we get home there's even more work to be done. Sometimes it's chores and child care; sometimes it's more work-related work. It just keeps coming, a relentless onslaught of things to do. Take a workaholic culture, add in digital technology, artificial light, and a globalized, always-on commerce system and the result is a long, grinding plateau of effort that degrades our health, our activism, and our happiness. In more ways than one, we become flat-liners.

This is what some might call an "epic fail" of modern culture. Our bodies crave rhythm, but modern work and commerce forces us into opposition to the most primal forces of life. When you live on a rotating planet with a pulsing, throbbing biosphere, a static lifestyle is fundamentally out of step with the nature of the world. As flat-liners and workaholics, we are without question the worst musicians on the planet. The master drummer—the Sun—lays down a regular beat of natural light, but we march to the beat of a mechanical, commercial metronome that never sleeps. While every other species on earth adjusts its behavior to the beat of the light and darkness, we forge ahead, oblivious.

We see it in our schedules and our calendars. Regimented work weeks and holidays have almost nothing to do with human physiology, seasonal variation, or the rhythms of the biosphere. Much has been made of the fact that middle and high school start times don't line up with normal, healthy teenage sleep patterns, but this is just the tip of a very large iceberg. When we look deeper, it soon becomes obvious our conventional work patterns are nothing more than cultural artifacts, products of the Gregorian calendar and the religious dictate to rest one day out of seven.

It's no wonder we're stressed. We've chosen to ignore the natural beat of the biosphere and replaced it with arbitrary cultural markers, alarm clocks, and official holidays, all of which are experienced by the body as random, disconnected events. There's a rhythm of sorts, but it has nothing to do with our bodies or our deep history.

It takes a lot of energy to go against the pulse of the biosphere, so it's no surprise to find the stress reflected in our bodies. We know, for example, that shift workers are at risk for a host of health problems. Likewise, flight attendants, with their constant working against the natural beat of day and night, show increased rates of a variety of cancers. Disrupt an animal's circadian rhythms enough times and things will start to break down.[106]

In the world of spy thrillers and real-life espionage, writers sometimes describe interrogations that feature radical alterations in normal human rhythms. Diabolical torturers intentionally distort circadian patterns of light and dark to break down their prisoner's sense of coherence, resilience and sanity. Just imagine the experience: your first night in lock-up is sixteen hours, the next is four, then ten, then twenty-four. Just when your body thinks it's time to sleep, the lights come on. To add to the chaos, breakfast comes at noon, dinner at 2 a.m. As the body becomes progressively weaker, the prisoner becomes increasingly disoriented and supposedly, more inclined to talk. The metaphor is distressing: as inhabitants of a chaotic modern world in which light and experience often come at random intervals, we might well wonder about our own disorientation. In effect, it's as if we're torturing ourselves.

TRAIN HARD, REST DEEP

As we've seen, the lives and bodies of our Paleolithic ancestors were tuned to daily and seasonal cycles of activity and rest. Likewise, children and dogs are masters of the play–rest cycle and light–dark rhythms. Left to their own devices, they explore, play, and run, then rest deeply until the urge to move returns. Similarly, we see the power of rhythmic engagement in modern athletic training. If you're a professional athlete or serious amateur, you know the formula for success: When you're training, hit it really hard, but when resting, rest really deep. Go to the gym, the track, or the pool and put in your best possible effort for a couple of hours, then spend the rest of your day listening to music, napping, and lounging.

Athletic coaches recognize this pattern as an ideal way to build and repair tissue and reorganize the body's nervous system for maximum performance. The body thrives with this kind of oscillation, and the higher the contrast, the better. To put it in technical terms, challenge plus rest equals "supercompensation," the process by which the body remodels tissue in anticipation of similar future challenges. Typically, we think of muscle, but supercompensation takes place throughout the body: bone, connective tissue, and nervous system circuits all become more robust with oscillations of effort. When we keep this beat, our bodies respond by giving us more of what we need.

HIGH-CONTRAST LIVING

The rhythmic beat of athletic exertion and rest is powerful and no doubt therapeutic, but the body seems to thrive on all sorts of rhythmic contrast. For example, temperature oscillation pumps our tissue, increases circulation, and makes us feel good. Hot, then cold and repeat. We see this in various home remedies and hydrotherapy practices, but it's also a normal feature of an ancestral environment. Life on the grassland was always a high-contrast experience: hot during the day, cold at night, always changing, always promoting circulation and adaptation. This is also why going to the mountains is so incredibly health-promoting. Contrast is everywhere: terrain goes up and down, temperatures go from hot to cold and back again, and the sky goes from intensely light to intensely dark. It's no wonder outdoor athletes thrive in these conditions.

Even in the worlds of high-intensity cognitive and professional labor, performance experts routinely recommend a high-contrast pattern for success. Engage completely with focused effort, then disconnect.[107] Just like muscle tissue, the nervous system needs time to rest and re-energize. Instead of grinding out long, chronic sessions of partial engagement, focus on your work with the maximum possible intensity, then step away. It may feel less productive in the short term, but your body and your brain will function at a much higher level. Think of it as a kind of cognitive athletic training. Work hard, then rest deep.

KEEPING THE BEAT

As every musician knows, the beauty of rhythm is that it makes everything easier. When you've got a sense of the beat, your body knows what's coming and can mobilize for the appropriate action. You're either gathering your energies for action, or you're relaxing and relinquishing effort. When you're synchronized with the dominant rhythms of your world, life is a thousand times easier. So the obvious question: How do we get back in rhythm? How do we get our activity back in harmony with the natural music of the biosphere?

It's a serious conundrum. Perhaps you're working an anti-rhythmic, chronic, life-hostile day job where you're expected to maintain a twenty-four/seven level of engagement. Perhaps your managers and overlords have no interest in your deep, primal need for rhythm, oscillation, contrast, and rest. You can try to tweak things around the edges and modulate your activity within the system, but it may not be enough. You might have to look elsewhere for something that's consistent with your biology and your desire for a healthy future. You might even have to quit your day job and find something truly rhythmic.

In the meantime, the place to begin is by listening to the beat of the biosphere, especially natural light. The sun, not the clock, is your metronome. Artificial light has its uses, but try to minimize it. Above all, try to get natural light early in the day and let it do its work, synchronizing all the systems of your body.

Likewise, it's essential that we destigmatize rest and prioritize biology. In the industrial era, rest got a bad rap because it seemed to undercut productivity. But today we're suffering a hangover in values. We continue to worship people who work insane hours, denying their bodies and the beat of the biosphere. Elon Musk claims that he works 120-hour weeks, and some of us celebrate his dedication, but we really ought to know better. The research is piling up, and it's becoming clear that rest is vital, not just to individual brain health and work performance, but to the healthy functioning of lives, relationships, and communities. Without adequate rest, we lose our sense of perspective, our patience, our willpower, our adaptability, and our sapience. Rest is not just pro-health; it's pro-social and a gift to future generations.

In the meantime, do what you can to build a culture of rhythm. Remind your family, your coworkers, and your community that the body needs contrast and oscillation. Take a good, hard look at your rituals, policies, schedules, and values and recast them in musical terms. Are they keeping a beat? Are they adding to the flux and flow of normal animal physiology? Or are they contributing to the chronic, flat-line culture that inevitably leads to illness and unhappiness?

In the process, we'd do well to strive for rhythm in everything we do. Look for cognitive rhythms between linear and holistic orientations. Look for artistic rhythms between freedom of expression and discipline in craft. Look for a whole–part–whole rhythm when studying any kind of interconnected system. Imagine yourself as a master bicycle mechanic, working to true a wobbly wheel. Look at the totality of the wheel or system in motion, focus your attention on the offending spoke or element, then return your attention to the big picture. Don't get stuck in a single perspective. Keep the beat.

Finally, try living a normal, Paleolithic rhythm. For this, the backpacking model is ideal. Hike in, set up camp, explore a mountain valley or forest preserve, then head back to camp. Sweat the uphills with a heavy pack for a good long day, then spend a day or two relaxing with the tribe. Get up early with the light and do it again. Research from the University of Colorado Boulder published in the journal *Current Biology* shows that as little as one weekend of camping helped reset circadian rhythms and promote sleep.[108] "These studies suggest that our internal clock responds strongly and quite rapidly to the natural light-dark cycle," says author and integrative physiology professor Kenneth Wright. At the risk of medicalizing it, we might even say that camping is medicine.

PACE

Omni festinatio ex parte diaboli est.

(All haste is of the devil.)

If we're going to make peace with our bodies and the modern world, it's essential we learn to adjust our tempo. Unfortunately, New Way culture has little appreciation for this simple life skill. We're in love with speed, and we rarely stop to consider context, habitat, environment, or setting. Whatever we're doing, we simply assume that faster is better. We love fast cars, fast food, fast aircraft, fast computers, and people who can get things done as fast as possible. When given the choice between two identical products, devices, or services, we reflexively choose the one that's faster. We don't really know where we're going, but we're determined to get there as fast as we possibly can.

Our obsession with speed extends all the way to activities traditional cultures would normally consider sacred. Beginning in the 1970s with Nathan's Hot Dog Eating Contest, an annual holiday tradition on Coney Island, competitive eating has grown into a recognized sport, with official tournaments, governing bodies, and yes, a code of ethics. The International Federation of Competitive Eating hosts nearly fifty "Major League Eating" events across North America every year, many of which are aired on ESPN.[109] Competitors are glorified as "food warriors," and engage in rigorous training to prepare for competition. All of which leaves us wondering that maybe Michael and Ellen Kaplan had it right with the title of their book *Bozo Sapiens*.[110]

To put it another way, the modern world has begun to feel like one vast Jason Bourne movie: We wake up with a case of amnesia and start running. We've got no sense of history or understanding of how we got into this predicament, but we do know one thing: people are chasing us, and we'd better start moving as fast as possible.

In the process, we've become clockaholics. No matter the activity, we're constantly checking our status and our progress against some kind of timepiece. Even runners, who in an earlier age would have paid close attention to terrain, weather, and animal life, now reflexively check their watches at every intersection.

To medicalize it, we might say we're suffering from a kind of "time sickness" or "temporal pathology." Symptoms include a chronic, impulsive need to hurry from task to task, even when no actual need exists. We lunge toward the future, never sitting still, never lingering. Stressed to the gills, we define our lives as emergencies and work from an assumption of scarcity. Abundance, if we think of it at all, becomes a dream of some distant, utopian future.

As with so many things, our modern relationship with time is historically abnormal. For the vast majority of our time on Earth, humans have experienced time as organic, rhythmic, and flexible. The passage of time was marked not by the regular ticks of mechanical devices, but by the movements of planets, weather, plants, and animals. Time moved, but it was not tyrannical.

In fact, many native cultures had no words for time, past, or future. In *A Sideways Look at Time,* Jay Griffiths writes about the Karen, a hill tribe in the forests of Northern Thailand: "To the Karen, the whole forest was a clock." Time was alive, local, bioregional, and grounded. So too for the Pirahã people of the Amazon. As described by Daniel Everett, author of *Don't Sleep, There Are Snakes*, the Pirahã spoke only in the present tense and had virtually no conception of "the future" or "the past," not even words for "tomorrow" and "yesterday," just a word for "other day," which could mean either one.[111]

In these settings, time sickness would have been nonexistent. Relationship and context were always more important than punctuality or precision. Success in hunting and gathering depended on observation and integration with natural cycles. It would be folly to go faster than the speed of habitat; to hurry would be to do violence to one's relationship with the natural world.

In contrast, modern time is synthetic and completely divorced from the natural world. Our lives are experienced as standardized moments that slip through our fingers with each passing second. If we "waste" time in some unproductive manner, we're losing our allotment of life experience. Mechanical time removes us from the waxing and waning of nature just as surely as if we were locked indoors or rocketed into outer space. Nothing has been so destructive to the human–nature relationship as the clock.

If we slowed down for a minute, we might well realize that speed has some serious downsides. Pushing the pace alienates us from the world and in the process, destroys our skill and our sapience. As our speed increases, awareness contracts. The faster we go, the more disconnected we become. We get to our destinations in record time, but we get there in pieces.

Needless to say, it's an unhealthy way to live. In our state of artificial urgency, we close ourselves off from the wonders of the world and withdraw into an ever-tighter circle of tasks, calculation, strategy, and management. At this level, success consists of nothing more than meeting the demands of the current crisis; the focus is on survival, not experience.

In this way, we begin to see that linear time is a very real threat to human health and the quality of our experience. The constant urgency, the relentless activity, and most of all, our radical de-synchronization with the natural rhythms of the living world—these things extract a destructive toll on the human body and spirit. By giving us a sense of scarcity and shrinking opportunity, linear time increases our stress and our anxiety. Inevitably, these mental states are reflected in our bodies.

In this sense, linear time and speed addiction constitute a genuine public health problem. The consequences are just as destructive as the poisoning of the modern food supply by Big Sugar, the epidemic of gun violence in the United States, and the growing threat of antibiotic resistance. In other words, it's time we took time seriously.

A familiar parable would be a good place to begin. According to Aesop, the hare ridiculed the short feet and the slow pace of the tortoise, but the tortoise would have none of it: "Though you be swift as the wind, I will beat you in a race." We laugh, but then wonder. We know that the tortoise wins in the end, but what gives him the edge? And what will it take to move from our frantic hare-culture to one that's more in keeping with the ways of the tortoise?

A good first step would be to stop with the glorification of busyness. In today's hyper-kinetic culture, many of us have bought into the belief that "busy equals important." We idolize the entrepreneur who works around the clock, or the supermom who raises a family, holds down a career, and runs triathlons in her spare time. If we get really busy, so our story goes, maybe we'll be important too.

But this obscures the fact that by itself, busyness is not a strategy for anything. More likely, it's an expression of the anxiety and insecurity we're feeling. As one meditation teacher has put it, "We are not restless because we are busy; we are busy because we are restless."

Once we learn how to relax, our busyness will begin to fade away. As a result, we'll be far more powerful in the things we choose to do.

There's another solution that often escapes our hare-brained notice. That is, we can actually make time by scaling back our ambitions and doing less. Once we cut our to-do lists down to size, things start to loosen up. Our bodies and our minds begin to relax, and in the process, we become far more effective at the things we choose to do. The beauty of doing less is that it actually creates a sense of temporal affluence and all the benefits that go with it. No longer are we so desperate. We can breathe, look around, and study the world. Our actions can be targeted and precise. Doing less means doing better, and doing better means being happier.

The art lies in honoring context and setting. Look at the clock as a necessary tool, but keep your eye on the real action: the flux and flow of habitat, people, and your work. As Sir Roger L'Estrange put it in 1699: "There is a proper time and season for every thing; and nothing can be more ridiculous than the doing of things without a due regard to the circumstances of persons, proportion, time and place."

Knowing this, the tortoise takes the time to savor experience. This may sound like a luxury, but it's actually a necessity for sensitivity, understanding, sound judgment, and yes, performance. The tortoise understands his world in a way the hare cannot. The hare covers a lot of ground, but in his haste, he fails to feel. And in his failure, he makes foolish mistakes.

The tortoise knows that slowing down is a universal solution for most of what ails us, and a recipe for success in almost every human endeavor. Of course, success in the modern world demands some level of attention to the ticking and tocking of linear time. But still, we can't let it tyrannize us. Remember your ancestry and imagine you grew up in a normal, indigenous culture that just didn't do linear time, clocks, and calendars. In this kind of life, your attention would be focused on immediate experience and events in habitat. You'd be in direct contact with life on the ground.

In the end, tortoise wisdom is subtle and often invisible. His success comes with the not-doing, things left undone, challenges left unmet, projects relinquished. Non-action creates time, abundance, and in the end, room for his mind and body to function at their best. It's okay to relax.

MEDITATION

Here's another Paleo thought experiment: Imagine you're sitting on a hill in East Africa, tens of thousands of years ago. You're out with your hunting party and you've been observing the animals for most of the day. It's an incredible scene: thousands of wildebeest migrating, birds by the millions, carnivores resting up, elephants and hippos bathing. And it's just another day in your life.

If you'd time-traveled to this point, you'd be awestruck, not just by the vista of plants and animals before you, but by the silence. No vehicles, no aircraft, no construction crews, no car alarms, no leaf blowers. The only sounds are the voices of your friends, the calls of the animals, and the wind on the grass. Inevitably, you'd find this silence calming in a profound way. The so-called "normal" stresses of your modern life would dissolve, and you'd sink into a state of relaxation.

Just imagine the peace. No assaults on your attention. No interruptions. No advertisements, no special offers, no pop-up windows. No homework, accounting, or record keeping, no symbols to be absorbed and processed, no technologies to be mastered, no calculations to be performed. Only direct sensory engagement and participation in the natural world.

In obvious contrast, today we live on a planet of noise, only some of it acoustic. Today's world has become a twenty-four-hour distraction machine, a conspiracy against focused attention, every day a blizzard of beeps, buzzers, hyper-normal colors, and flashing lights, all intruding in our lives at almost every moment. All of this presents an unprecedented challenge to our cognitive resources and our ability to pay attention. If you add up all the books, manuals, podcasts, radio shows, posts, and advertisements we're exposed to each day, they amount to vastly more cognitive load than we've had to deal with before in human history.

YOUR LIFE ON COMPLEXITY

This acoustic and cognitive onslaught is no mere nuisance. It's a serious threat to our health, our happiness, and our ability to create a long-term relationship with this planet. As noise escalates, it becomes harder and harder to hear and appreciate the essential signals in our lives–signals from habitat, relationships, and the people around us. Over time, our overconsumption of cognitive content depletes precious neurological resources and drives us into a state of nervous exhaustion.

This mental–spiritual overload has profoundly negative consequences for both individuals and society as a whole. According to the legendary psychologist Daniel Kahneman, author of *Thinking, Fast and Slow,* "people who are cognitively busy are more likely to make selfish choices, use sexist language, and make superficial judgments in social situations." Willpower is also depleted, which of course leads to all manner of poor behavior and impulsive decisions.

We try to keep up with it all by multitasking, but most of us have gotten the memo from the neuroscience world by now. That is, the brain only attends to one thing at a time. When we attempt to manage multiple tasks, the brain simply increases speed in switching from one point of attention to another. In moderation, we can manage it, but this rapid alternation of attention eventually takes a toll on the whole mind–body. Over the course of months and years, we become increasingly vulnerable to stress and in turn, depression.

When complexity and cognitive overload become extreme, we triage out everything except immediate demands and lose sight of our life support systems: the Earth and the people around us. Worst of all, noise and chaos drown out the awe we'd normally experience in our engagement with life's mystery. When we're constantly managing tasks, we become oblivious to the immensity and magnificence of life itself.

THE POWER OF NOTHING

Overwhelmed by modern life and frustrated with conventional approaches, many of us turn to meditation for relief. Research suggests that regular practice reduces inflammation, lowers levels of the stress hormone cortisol, and reduces anxiety, depression, anger, and fatigue. It also stimulates the vagus nerve, a powerful player in the autonomic nervous system that helps us activate metabolic processes that are vital for healing, tissue repair, inflammation control, and psycho-physical rejuvenation.

Meditation even has a powerful epigenetic effect. Work by Herbert Benson, documented in *Relaxation Revolution*, showed that a modest six-week training program turns on clusters of beneficial genes, while turning off pro-inflammatory pathways. Meditation may even improve the function of the brain's prefrontal cortex by giving it some time off from chronic executive activity. By giving the prefrontal brain a rest, we also improve our emotional regulation and our ability to modulate fear.

This list of benefits is impressive, but it's important to frame our discussion in the right way. In our highly individualistic culture, meditation is often presented as a means to high performance and self-improvement, but this perspective may actually be a step in the wrong direction. The very act of trying to improve ourselves strengthens our sense of self, which in turn sets us up for more duality and conflict. A better approach would be to think of meditation as a practice of self-release. That is, we aren't trying to make ourselves better; we're trying to let go of our ego and merge ourselves with the world. When we succeed, we experience less self, less duality, and in turn, less suffering.

In any case, meditation gives us a chance to step outside the complexity of our normal, daily lives and observe exactly what we're up to. In the process, it gives us an increased understanding of our bodies and our experience. When we allow the chattering, judgmental mind to come to rest, we begin to actually feel what we're feeling. As we let go of the noise of the modern world, we begin to feel the life coursing through our bodies, via the breath.

Meditation improves our awareness and our performance by providing an essential sense of contrast with the "normal" chaos of our abnormal daily lives. The visual artist might say meditation is the negative space on the canvas of our lives, a content-free space that allows the rest of our actions to stand out in sharper relief. This gives us a chance to see what we do more clearly. With regular meditation, the quality of our tasks and behaviors becomes increasingly obvious to us, giving us the opportunity to revise and adjust our behavior.

In essence, meditation gives us a chance to meet the first beginnings of our mental activity. It's a precious opportunity to get in at the earliest instant, before the mind gets wrapped up in its own momentum. When we're in at the beginning, we can make adjustments easily. A little nudge here, a little pull there, and the mind comes back into balance.

From a mind–body point of view, the power of meditation lies in the experiential proof it gives us that we can coexist with ourselves. We sit quietly for a while, and behold—nothing bad happens. Our minds might get distracted, and we might waste some time ruminating on the dramas in our lives, but these things tend to fade away. In turn, it begins to dawn on us that it's not really necessary to spend every waking moment running away from ourselves or our predicaments. It's not really necessary to surround ourselves with distraction and compulsive activity. It's okay to just be. This is a liberating insight.

The beauty of regular meditation practice is that it takes us deeper into the human experience. Some teachers say meditation is all about being in the present moment, but we might also say it's like going back in time, all the way back to the preliterate, preverbal days of deep history. Once we let go of our verbal soundtrack and mental ruminations, we return to our primal, ancestral experience. We return to the Great Integrity, the Tao, the time before words. We return to our normal, aboriginal state of mind.

The experience is calming, but it's far more than even that. When we abandon our internal chatter and focus on our bodies and our breath, we reunite with the totality of life on Earth and all the power that goes with it. When we relinquish our compulsive narration about life and our troubles, we're left with a direct experience of a body that's literally millions of years old and continuous with all life. This takes us out of our isolation and back into integration. In this sense, the medical benefits of meditation pale in comparison. Reducing your blood pressure is undoubtedly a good thing, but even better is the chance to unite with the totality of life itself, all the way back to LUCA.

LET IT BE

Unfortunately, meditation is often presented as a complex, daunting practice that takes decades to master. There are dozens of styles, hundreds of books, thousands of teachers, and according to some, layer upon layer of sophistication. This diversity makes for some interesting conversation, but it also distracts us from the essential simplicity we're trying to nurture. Why take something inherently simple and make it complicated?

In fact, there's no wrong way to do it. Just sit still in one place for a while. Turn off the phone and abandon your concerns about work, your to-do list, and all the things nagging at your mind. Forget about proper posture, breathing technique, attention, mindfulness, compassion, and loving kindness, at least for the moment. Keep it as simple as you can. As one meditation teacher puts it, "Just sit down, shut up and pay attention." If you can do this, you're halfway there.

Now, let things settle. Take a few good breaths, and imagine a glass of muddy water. As you relax, the particles of dirt will sink to the bottom of the glass and you will become calm. This is a well-known Buddhist image, but not exclusively so. In *The Art of Worldly Wisdom*, Baltasar Gracián also recommended the power of non-action: "To give way now is to conquer by and by. A fountain gets muddy with but little stirring up, and does not get clear by our meddling with it but by our leaving it alone."

As you settle down, focus your attention on your breath, the vital spirit, life force, or prana that animates our bodies and our lives. Breath is your most intimate ally, a safe and reliable friend that will show you the way to equanimity and calm. By merging your attention with your breath, you'll move toward a state of integration.

Of course, if you're anything like a normal human being, your attention will begin to wander almost immediately, and this is the moment of truth. If you try to strong-arm your attention back to your breath, you'll simply produce more noise and wind up even further away from your target. But passivity also fails. If you simply allow yourself to be swept up in whatever thoughts and imagery your mind cooks up, you'll never learn how to stabilize your attention. You'll simply have a nice daydreaming session.

The tricky part is that distraction feeds on itself. We drift off our focal point, and each thought generates another association, memory, or image. Before we know it, we're light years from our original intent. The solution, as the Buddhists so often point out, is compassion. There's nothing to be gained by abusing yourself for getting distracted. Every time you drift off target, you get another chance to practice. Just let it go.

Next, stick with it. When pain or distraction intrudes on your experience, relax. Don't try to change anything. As Pema Chodron, author of *When Things Fall Apart* advises, "soften and stay." Relinquish effort, but maintain focus. Note the pain, note the distraction and the emotion, then return to your breath. Maintain the role of a compassionate, nonjudgmental observer. Observe the way your mind goes on journeys into the past and future. Observe the chatter, the commentary, and the random images that appear as if from nowhere. Observe all this, and return your attention to your breath.

Whatever you do, keep it simple. In the popular imagination, many people suppose meditation is a path to some kind of higher, altered state of consciousness—and some of us seek it out precisely for this reason. We want the special thing, the extraordinary state of awareness we believe will take us to a new level of experience and contentment. Just as with almost everything else in the modern world, we want the exceptional, the incredible and the elite.

But we've got it entirely backward. Meditation is not an altered, exceptional state; it's our normal state. Our frenzied, fragmented modern condition is the altered state. When we meditate, we simply return to our historically normal, Paleo condition of mind and body. In other words, the meditative state—being still and feeling the breath—is the baseline, the reference point. It's a safe home base. It's not exotic; it's normal. It's who we are.

So instead of reaching for something rare and astonishing, maybe we'd do better to reach for something modest. Don't worry about sophistication, advanced techniques, or mystical experiences. Stick with simplicity. It's reliable, accessible, and effective.

Of course, most of us claim to be too busy to bother with meditation. The practice takes time and produces no immediate, spectacular payoff, so most of us simply avoid it in favor of more impulsive activity. But seen from another perspective, this makes no sense whatsoever. After all, we seem to have plenty of time for activities that bring noise, confusion, and complexity into our lives. Why not something that's proven to give us a sense of clarity, depth, and equanimity? Why not something that offers the possibility of stepping out of the chaos, if only for a few minutes each day. It's worth a try.

MINIMALISM

Simplicity is the ultimate sophistication.

—Leonardo da Vinci

In conventional conversations about health, the lion's share of our attention goes to diet and exercise. We talk about cardio and protein, gyms and gluten, kettle bells and CrossFit, but we rarely get around to talking about our relationship to our material possessions. This is a major oversight, because our relationship with our stuff actually has a great deal to do with how our bodies function, as well as the quality of our life experience.

Unfortunately, New Way culture pulls us in precisely the wrong direction. Every time we turn around, some new thing is coming into our lives, cluttering up our homes and our consciousness. Commercial culture never sleeps, constantly seducing us with the promise that consumption and ownership will bring us everything we desire. It's no wonder we're afflicted by what the Greeks called *pleonexia*: the endless hunger for more and more. Or, in Walt Whitman's words, "demented with the mania of owning things." Many of us take the phrase "He who dies with the most stuff wins" not as a joke, but as a guiding principle for success in life. But today, some of us are beginning to realize that material affluence isn't what it's cracked up to be. And beyond a certain point, it's positively destructive to our health and our future. We are literally consuming our planet to death.

PALEO

This state of affairs is a far cry from our Paleo experience. Not so long ago, our ancestors lived their entire lives with almost nothing we would call property or possessions. People lived by their physicality, their attention, and their wits, plus maybe a few stone tools, a fire-starting stick, and an animal skin for warmth and protection—only what they could carry.

Even today, the Bushmen (and women) of the Kalahari are the undisputed masters of simplicity. Theirs is the oldest, most sustainable culture on earth, an "economy" premised on having very few needs. As described by James Suzman in *Affluence Without Abundance: The Disappearing World of the Bushmen*, these people have "modest needs, easily met." When you trust your habitat and have confidence in your skills, there's no need for a lot of stuff. And until recently, these people never felt deprived or poor. On the contrary, they got to live in the middle of a glorious, natural habitat every day, which is a powerful kind of affluence in its own right.

Even in the modern world, many of us are coming to realize that material affluence follows the famous inverse-U curve. In small amounts, material possessions clearly make our lives better. We become more powerful and more secure, and for a while, more affluence gives a bigger payoff. But once we pass the tipping point, the returns diminish and material wealth becomes a literal and psycho-spiritual drag. There's more stuff to be managed, more stuff to maintain, and less freedom to move. Instead of empowering us, our stuff becomes a burden, pinning us to the ground and inhibiting our vagility. Even worse, our mania for possession contributes to the continued degradation of the biosphere. In this sense, unrestrained material affluence in the present adds up to poverty and chaos for our descendants.

WRONG ABOUT STUFF

This is one of the most fundamental delusions of the New Way: we're wrong about stuff. Living under siege by commercial advertising and marketing, we've come to believe having more is the key to everything we desire: happiness, health, and admiration. This shifts our attention away from core human values and drives us into "extrinsic living." Whipped into a frenzy by brightly colored images and hyper-normal stimuli, we spend our days chasing material ghosts.

This is bad news for our health and happiness. In *The High Price of Materialism*,[112] psychologist Tim Kasser describes research showing that when people organize their lives around extrinsic goals such as product acquisition, they report greater unhappiness in relationships, poorer moods, and more psychological problems.

So what if we turned it around? What if having less stuff actually made us *more* powerful and happy? Given the prevailing narrative of our day, this may sound like crazy talk, but the case is strong. As we cut back our possessions to the minimum, those possessions become increasingly valuable and we're free to spend our time doing meaningful things. In this sense, less stuff means *more* affluence.

The beauty of minimalism is that it calms us down and frees us up. At the risk of medicalizing it, we might say simplicity is a kind of balm for the distressed mind and body. Simplicity gives us a sense of order and predictability, which lowers stress. It's safe to assume that people who imbibe in simplicity enjoy neurological and cardiovascular benefits. Less stress means better health and better decisions.

And contrary to popular belief, simplicity also makes us more powerful. With less complexity in our lives, we can pour more of our energy into fewer tasks. And if you buy less stuff, you can buy better stuff–possessions that provide authentic pleasure of use and ownership. Consume less, and you'll be less stressed about money. Own less, and you'll have fewer management tasks on your list. As your cognitive load goes down, you'll have a bigger mental surplus for appreciating the awe of being alive in a mysterious universe. When we crawl out from under our possessions, we can find out who we really are.

ALPINE STYLE

This is where we can take some powerful inspiration from the world of modern alpine climbing, a sport in which it's essential to have a good relationship with your gear. In the early years, climbing was done strictly in "expedition style." It typically took months to plan an expedition, secure the material, and transport it all to base camp. From there, teams of climbers and sherpas would establish a series of camps and fixed ropes, climbing higher and positioning themselves for the final push to the summit. Climbing was a major work project.

But then the game changed. Equipment got lighter and more functional, and suddenly it was possible to climb big mountains in a single, lightweight effort. No camps, no fixed ropes, no hauling loads—just climbing. This came to be called "alpine style." Famously advocated by Yvon Chouinard, the founder of Patagonia, the goal was to design beautiful, well-crafted tools and clothing to deepen the alpine experience and reduce the impact. As he famously put it, "He who dies with the least toys wins. Because the more you know, the less you need."

The beauty of this orientation soon became obvious to climbers around the world. Alpine style puts climbers in direct contact with the essential ambiguity of the mountain experience. No longer supported by fixed ropes and numerous camps, climbers were fully exposed to the dangers and beauty of the route, forced to rely on their skills, endurance, and wits. Less work, more sport.

This was a powerful win–win. There's joy in crafting, owning, and using simple, high-quality tools. It's a process of creative subtraction.

While expedition style asks, "How much stuff can we take with us?" alpine style asks, "How light can we go? Do we really need this extra stuff? Can we put ourselves into direct contact with the experience we seek? If in doubt, throw it out, give it away, fix it, or recycle it. Less is the new more.

Alpine style is an incredibly valuable metaphor for our time and a practical answer to the problem of consumerism. It teaches us a fundamental, commonly overlooked life lesson: how to own things. It teaches us to savor experience over possessions, to value what we do own, and to reject the voices constantly shouting at us to buy more.

Moreover, alpine style teaches us to appreciate quality. As it stands, a common rap is that modern culture is "too materialistic," but perhaps it's precisely the opposite. The reason we buy so much stuff is because we don't really value what we've got. In this sense, we're not materialistic enough. If we really paid attention to the quality of the things we owned, we wouldn't have to go looking for more. If we took the time to savor good craftsmanship and prime materials, we'd be more content. A few simple, beautiful possessions would satisfy us.

ESCHEW SURPLUSAGE

The practice of simplicity is well, simple. We start by buying less, consuming less, and owning less. Does this thing add meaning to my life? Is it well crafted? Is it an appropriate use of technology? What meanings come along with it? If the item in question fails to bring meaning into your life, get rid of it. If it fails to inspire you by virtue of its quality, materials, and form, sell it or give it away. If you haven't used it in twenty years, it's safe to assume you're just not going to use it. It may have cost a lot to buy it in the first place, and you'll be reluctant to take a loss, but remember, continued ownership also extracts a cost in the form of a cluttered mind and a cluttered life.

In the same vein, the time has come to rethink our cultural habit of giving material gifts on holidays, especially that annual state of retail madness known as Christmas. Most people already have enough stuff as it is, and there's a good chance your recipient is already trying to dig out from under his own pile of excess. In this sense, giving material gifts can actually be a burden. ("If you really want to give me a gift, come to my house and help me get rid of some of my stuff!") Better to give the gift of your presence and your time. Cook a meal or make a contribution to a worthy cause in your recipient's name. Enough with the stuff.

MINIMALISM AS METAPHOR

The beauty of minimalism is that it suggests a way, a Tao, for conducting our entire lives. Trimming down our stuff inspires us to reduce complexity everywhere. Clear out the garage and the closets, clear out the mind and spirit. Author Greg McKeown calls this practice "essentialism," the disciplined pursuit of less. We're reminded of the teachings of Thoreau and the Zen masters. Keep it simple. Chop wood, carry water. Stay close to experience, and don't get distracted by complexity or possessions.

In this practice, we lean toward monotasking and single-focus activities. We set up our days to minimize interruptions and distractions. Scale back your ambition. Put one very important thing on your to-do list and do that thing. Don't try to master every skill, sport, or discipline. Survey the options, choose one, and make it your own. Likewise, focus your activism. Don't try to address every crisis or injustice in the world. Instead, concentrate your energies on one issue at a time. Precision activism, like precision living, is a powerful way to make a difference.

DIGITAL MINIMALISM

Minimalism isn't just about shedding the big stuff like TVs and RVs. It's also about the computer world and our ability to keep our digital lives under control. Unfortunately, the "visionaries" of the late twentieth century sold us a promise that computers would take all the complexity and cognitive overload in our lives and condense it into a form that would be easy to manage. Computers were going to be a solution.

But the promise was false. Computers don't tame complexity and cognitive overload; they make it a thousand times worse. Every day, we're confronted with a million websites and social media platforms that suck our attention and derail our focus. Email tsunamis, phishing attacks, spam, fake news, and endless appeals for money—we spend hours each day simply trying to sort the meaningful from the sinister, the valuable from the ridiculous. For every labor-saving feature of the modern computer, there's a thousand details we have to chase down. The displacement costs are enormous; every hour spent on the computer is one less hour you could spend actually living.

But like it or not, some digital engagement is necessary for survival. We can't simply opt out, but vigilance, discipline, and containment can keep us from getting sucked into the quagmire. Like all power tools, computers and smartphones have legitimate uses, but we must protect our time and our physicality. Every now and then, take a good hard look at your machine and its capabilities. Focus hard on the things you want to do, then do only those things. Don't even try to use all the features and capabilities of your system. Don't be lured into the latest and flashiest. Turn off every application, notification, and complication you can. Computers should be like the power tools in your garage: use them for important projects, appreciate their power, and then put them away.

SMALL STEPS, BIG CHANGE

The lifestyle arts of meditation, rhythm, minimalism, and movement are vital and powerful, but they do their work in a surprising and subtle way. In the beginning, you may not notice the benefits at all, and you might even be tempted to abandon the practices altogether. But a few years from now, you'll wake up and notice your body and your life are substantially different from those of your peers who failed to make the effort.

Small benefits, multiplied by large numbers, add up to substantial improvements in our vitality, our physicality, and our relationship with the world. This reminds us of *kaizen*, the Japanese concept of small improvement over time. Beautifully described in *One Small Step Can Change Your Life: The Kaizen Way* by Robert Maurer, kaizen is a modest but persistent approach to transformation. The power of this approach lies in its humility. As Maurer puts it, "the small steps of kaizen disarm the brain's fear response" and give the mind–body room to adapt. Kaizen doesn't intimidate us or ask us to make abrupt changes to our lives; it nudges us toward a better way of living.

To be sure, some research and anecdotal evidence suggests that change is stickiest with big disruptions to life, events that really shake up the personal and organizational status quo. People who join the military or move to foreign countries sometimes report their habit patterns are completely and permanently altered. And we might well argue that, in the context of climate change and imminent planet-scale catastrophe, radical lifestyle change is precisely the thing we need at the moment. We simply don't have time for "small changes over time."

But people can only tolerate so much change, and if the challenge is too severe, many will simply reject the entire prospect and double down on old patterns. To propose that people instantly drop their familiar, fossil-fueled lifestyles and adopt a primitive life of austerity and sustained physical labor is just too big an ask for most. This is why kaizen remains a valuable practice. The transformations we seek may not come as fast as we'd like, but small, persistent efforts, sustained over the course of months and years, add up to meaningful change.

Legendary basketball coach John Wooden was a passionate advocate of this incremental approach and used it as a foundation for developing one of the greatest athletic programs of all time:

> When you improve a little each day, eventually big things occur. Don't look for the big, quick improvement. Seek the small improvement one day at a time. That's the only way it happens—and when it happens, it lasts.

In turn, this suggests an answer to the question commonly posed by aspiring exercisers who ask their trainers and coaches, "How long will it take to get healthy and back in shape?"

The honest answer: "The rest of your life."

STRESS

The tipping point on Planet Earth may well come, not when the heat waves become unbearable and our ecosystems collapse, but when the noise in our own heads becomes unbearable and our psychosystems collapse—when mood disorders, distraction, and psychosis reach a point where we cannot think clearly anymore.

—Adbusters

It's not easy being mismatched in the modern world. Our deepest biological inclinations drive us toward nature, tribe and robust physicality, but our culture often forces us in the opposite direction. At every turn, we're required to suppress our natural instincts, inhibit our physicality, and abandon our ancestral heritage. The stress plays out in the millions of microtraumas that bedevil us over the course of our lives. Your body wants to move, but you're stuck on the airplane. Your body wants to rest, but you're besieged with nonnegotiable work. Your body wants to engage with authentic social time, but you're locked into an electronic system that's jagged, unpredictable, and disembodied. Over time, these minor insults to our ancient bodies add up to major threats to health.

To be sure, there's plenty of comforting qualities to the modern world, but the body knows the difference between ancestral reality and today's pressure cooker. Even if your life is working pretty well, you're already prestressed simply by being an aboriginal primate in an alien world. Add the stresses of an exclusionary, highly competitive social order, time pressures, economic uncertainty, and epidemics of anxiety and fear, and you've got a body in trouble.

Humans have always experienced stress, but today's challenge is a far cry from what we experienced on the grassland. In a primal setting, stressors were sometimes acute, but they were always congruent with habitat and the nature of our bodies. Natural challenges such as heat, cold, and predator attacks triggered appropriate physiological reactions that contributed directly to our survival. Conditions may have been harsh, even brutal at times, but they always made physical sense. In contrast, modern stressors attack us more or less at random: the phone rings or the email arrives, not in any relationship to the natural functioning of our bodies or habitat, but whenever. This random, arbitrary stimulation of our stress response system is highly disruptive. Our bodies look for patterns, but in many cases, no patterns exist.

Even worse, we're now forced to confront stressors that are remote in space and time. Until quite recently, all stresses were local and immediate, but today we're in constant contact with conflicts, dramas, and disasters around the world. Even more challenging, we now have the ability to predict massively disruptive events—like climate change and sea level rise—that lie in our immediate future. This ramps up the stress load a thousandfold.

In fact, if a diabolical engineer set out to design a high-stress environment from scratch, he couldn't do much better than the modern world. Economic uncertainty dominates many lives, jobs are vulnerable, and few people have enough savings to weather a storm. Many people lack a sense of power and control, while rigid hierarchies and social injustice leave many feeling excluded. Medical bankruptcies are not unusual, and many people live in fear of becoming ill. Many of us feel isolated by an individualistic culture and the "every man for himself" ethos that has come to dominate modern life.

All of these stressors are plenty daunting enough, but when we add activism to the mix, the challenge escalates even further. Going against the grain of society and culture means making yourself vulnerable to attack, ridicule, financial hardship, and even incarceration. By definition, activists work in domains where their power and control is minimal. This is a classic recipe for psychological stress.

STRESS ME OUT

No matter the source, stress is hard on our individual bodies, minds, and spirits. The good news is we now understand the fundamentals of stress physiology and the ways it shapes our tissue, our cognition, our behavior, and our health.

By now, many of us have heard the story of the autonomic nervous system, the deep, ancient wiring that controls the basic regulatory functions of our bodies, and in turn, our minds and spirits. Two branches extend from the brain, deep into the body, one devoted to action, the other to restoration and repair. These nerves regulate everything from breathing to digestion, cardiac function, arousal, and even the long-range trajectory of our health.

When we perceive a threat, the action branch of the autonomic system stimulates our bodies for vigorous physical movement such as fighting, climbing, or running. Every organ and tissue in the body goes on alert; heart rate goes up, digestion is suppressed, blood pressure increases, and glucose is released into the bloodstream. Pain is dampened, and immunity is stimulated. In short, the body prepares itself for a physical encounter with the world. This is the famous fight-or-flight response.

The repair system essentially does the reverse. When the world feels friendly, heart rate and blood pressure go down, digestion picks up, and nutrients are delivered to the cells that need to be patched up. In short, the body begins to put itself back together in what Robert

Sapolsky describes as "long-term rebuilding and development projects." In popular culture, this is sometimes described as the rest-and-digest or feed-and-breed response. (When we're relaxed, we like to eat and have sex.)

Of course, there's more to the stress response than a binary, on–off reaction to the world. In real life, the process unfolds along a classic inverted-U-shaped curve. On the left side of the curve, stress hormones are low and we're in a state of relaxation. As stress hormones rise, good things happen to body and cognition. Metabolic fuels are released into the bloodstream to feed our attentive brains. At the same time, our brains secrete "neurotrophic factors," chemicals that actually stimulate the growth of new nerve cells, dendrites, and synapses. In this sweet spot, learning is engaging, memory is sharp, and attention is focused.

As stress increases further, benefits increase, but beyond the tipping point, the effect reverses itself and stress becomes destructive. Our cognitive, psychological, and spiritual resources begin to drain away, and our bodies are slower to recuperate from workouts, injury, and illness. In turn, this makes us increasingly vulnerable to other stressors, even those we would normally weather without a second thought. Aches and pains seem worse than normal, and we begin to worry about the trajectory of our health.

Over time, chronic activation of the stress response inhibits the growth and connectivity of precious neurons, and can even damage brain centers involved in learning, memory, and impulse control. Key neurotransmitters such as dopamine become depleted, which leads to a loss of pleasure. If stress continues, our mood becomes increasingly serious, then grim. Our sense of humor declines, then disappears entirely. We stop laughing. We stop loving life.

At this point, we enter the dark world of disease, dysfunction, and depression. Stress hormones may become neurotoxic, endangering neurons and even killing them outright. Chronic exposure erodes the structure and function of the hippocampus, a crucial brain center involved in explicit, short-term memory and learning. In turn, this can lead to a host of neurological disorders, ranging from minor attention problems all the way to full-blown dementia. At this level, stress hormones also become psychotoxic, leading to impulse control problems and substance abuse. We fall into a state called "learned helplessness" and begin to generalize our lack of control to other circumstances, even to those cases when control is in fact possible.

LIFE LESSONS

The inverted-U curve provides some powerful life lessons. In the first place, it teaches us that stress has real value. In moderation, it's essential for learning, performance, and a good life. So instead of trying to make our lives stress free, the superior strategy is to seek an optimal level of stress: the right kind of stress, in the right intensity, for the right duration. In other words, look for precision, not eradication. Whenever possible, fine-tune your adversities. Expose yourself to stress strategically in service of your goals and purpose.

The second lesson is to recognize the point of diminishing returns. As stress increases and you approach the top of the curve, be alert for these warning signs:

- Anhedonia (loss of pleasure)
- Neophobia (avoidance of new things)
- Perseveration (mindless repetition of established habit patterns)
- Reduced ambiguity tolerance, increased extremism and black–white thinking.
- Social withdrawal and isolation; excessive focus on the self
- Cognitive distortions, especially overgeneralizing and small-picture, short-term thinking

- Physical lethargy, poor sleep quality, decreased resilience
- Irritability, "making mountains out of molehills"
- Catastrophizing; going straight to the worst-case scenario
- Decreased sense of humor and play
- Poor concentration and attention span
- Impulsive behaviors, reduced self-control
- Decision resistance, procrastination and impatience.

If this sounds like an accurate description of your life, take heed. You're well on your way to going past the tipping point, and it's time to try a different approach.

TRANSLATING THE VOICE OF STRESS

By now, most of us understand the basics of stress physiology and the way that chronic exposure to stress hormones can have a negative impact on our health. But stress isn't going away, nor do we really want it to. A better approach is to understand what stress is trying to tell us.

Back in prehistory, the voice was almost always clear. If you were feeling stressed, it was probably because there was a direct and immediate threat to your survival: you were under stress because a rhino just gored your best friend and is rampaging through your camp. In cases like this, it's easy to understand what the body is saying, but for most of us in the modern world, stress is often a garbled and sometimes incomprehensible voice. The problem is that stress just isn't that articulate, and doesn't have much of a vocabulary. Sometimes it assaults us with dramatic bursts of sharp, metallic anxiety, but other times it grinds away in the background, chewing on our bodies, our cognition, and our spirits. We know something is wrong, but we can't say exactly what it is.

What we really need is an interpreter or stress translator that can tell us what our stress is trying to say. For example, stress might be trying to tell you about a direct threat to your body or more generally, a threat to your life support systems. If your home, habitat, tribe, or culture is under attack, stress is going to let you know something is wrong.

If your body senses an erosion of personal power and control, stress is going to start talking, first in nagging whispers and then in full-blown demands for action. Maybe you're running into financial problems or suffering a loss of options. Maybe you're suffering from cognitive overload or temporal poverty. If the mind–body senses that it's at the limit of what it can absorb, stress will start yelling its head off.

Or, stress might be telling you that your status in the tribe is under threat. As we've seen, this comes straight from our ancestry, where exile from our social circle is something very close to a death sentence. As a hyper-social species, we live and die by our relationships, and when those relationships dissolve into conflict, our bodies start acting up.

Stress will also start speaking out if your identity and sense of meaning are under attack. Meaning is vital to human life and even abstract threats are taken seriously. If your sense of value and purpose is being undermined by someone else's narrative, stress is going to start raising its voice.

Or, more generally, stress might be telling you you're in an adversarial relationship with the world at large. You've otherized the world and set yourself in opposition to people and events. Naturally, this position puts you in a feedback loop and keeps the voice of stress going almost continuously. The more you otherize the world, the more isolated and stressed you'll feel.

Finally, the voice of stress might be telling you you're doing genuinely creative work in the world and meeting the inevitable resistance that comes with art and activism. In this case, you're simply experiencing what any creative activist would experience. The stress comes with the territory. In other words, you're on the right track.

Naturally, it can be hard to sort it all out. It could be all of the above; sometimes multiple stressors are in motion simultaneously. It would be great if we all had a decoder ring to make sense of it all, but until that time, we've got to listen carefully and rely on our experience. Pay attention. It's not enough to simply say, "I'm stressed." Dig in and find out why.

STRESS US OUT

Everyone knows chronic stress is bad news for our individual bodies and health, but we're now beginning to realize it's also bad for us collectively. As highly social animals, feelings of stress can spread like wildfire. Humans are always on alert for signs of danger or safety, communicated through words, gestures, postures, and even odors. We're always wondering: Is the world friendly or not? If there's fear or anxiety in the air, we feel it. And obviously, the process is amplified by our always-on media environment. Stress gets around, fast.

As stress circulates through a community, it generates a wicked, destructive cycle that feeds on itself and makes solutions increasingly difficult. The effects are corrosive on a planetary scale:

First, stress and fear make us more likely to "otherize" the world. Fearing for our welfare, we lean toward xenophobia. Our sense of continuity with the world dissolves, ego becomes dominant, and we become increasingly selfish and antisocial. In *Behave: The Biology of Humans at Our Best and Worst*, Robert Sapolsky summed up the research about moral decision-making after a social stressor: "Stress made people give more egoistic answers about emotionally intense moral decisions; the more glucocorticoid levels rose, the more egoistic the answers." [113]

Not surprisingly, stress also shifts our perspective away from abundance and toward scarcity. In our stressed-out minds, there's less of everything: less wealth, less time, and fewer resources to work with. We're more likely to see life and society as a competitive, ze-ro-sum game. Hoarding behavior—by individuals and organiza-tions—becomes increasingly common. There's only so much to go around, so we'd better get what we can, when we can.

Stress even affects our sense of time. When stress escalates, we begin to undervalue tomorrow and overvalue today. Stressed peo-ple aren't thinking about their health twenty years from now; they're thinking about the pleasure they can get today. They aren't thinking about the welfare of the seventh generation; they're thinking about the welfare of the first generation, right here, right now.

Stress also contributes to a siege mentality. It drives us into our bunkers and narrows our sense of tribe. The world is against us, so we must defend ourselves at all costs. Social trust declines, and we become increasingly risk averse. We cling to the conventions of Mother Culture and the status quo. Deviations from business as usu-al and culture as usual strike us as dangerous, inconvenient, and out of the question.

Likewise, stress also pushes our political inclinations to the right. In 2012, a research team found they could move people in a conser-vative direction by distracting them and putting them under time pressure.[114] At the same time, stress also drives many of us to adopt a victim orientation. Instead of taking responsibility for our lives, we seek out rescue and/or blame perpetrators. In the process, we be-come less creative and less effective in moving the world.

Finally, stress erodes our willingness to participate in civic life. When pressure becomes too extreme, many of us simply withdraw. In 1950, US novelist John Dos Passos described apathy as "one of the characteristic responses of any living organism when it is sub-jected to stimuli too intense or too complicated to cope with." This description, of course, is a dead ringer for life in the modern world.

In short, stress robs us of our humanity, drowns out our sense of awe, wrecks our communities, and diminishes our sapience. Social resources such as trust, reciprocity, and cooperation diminish at the very time we need them most. Even worse, the effect is intergenerational; waves of stress are passed from fathers to son, from mothers to daughters. From this point of view, it becomes increasingly obvious that stress is a public health problem on a planetary scale.

ANTIDOTES

So what are we to do with our personal and collective stress? It might seem that these are completely different levels of angst, but in fact, they're radically interdependent. The good news is whatever works at one level should give us relief at the other. Just as stress is contagious, so too are feelings of equanimity and calm.

Starting with our individual lives, most of us have heard about the recommended remedies and antidotes. We think of deep breathing, visualization of relaxing settings, progressive relaxation of the body, mindfulness, and a more receptive attitude toward life in general. But in fact, there are actually two completely different strategies for success, a yin and a yang. Practiced together and in oscillation, these practices make for a more effective, integrated approach.

THE YANG ARTS

The yang arts begin with the recognition that all animals need some sense of power, control, and predictability. When nonhuman animals are placed in situations that decrease their sense of control, they show biological evidence of stress,[115] but when control is granted, they do better. Not surprisingly, a rat that can turn off an electric shock does better than a rat that can't. Even fake buttons and levers that offer the appearance of control reduce the stress effect.

Predictability helps too: a rat that gets a warning light before the shock does better than one that gets no such warning, even when the levels of stress are precisely the same. There is no question on this score: a sense of control and predictability is vital to long-term health.[116]

In this sense, the solution to stress may lie not in relaxing and letting go but in focusing our attention and executing the work at hand. When our lives are in chaos, we need to accomplish some vital tasks that will help us get a grip on the situation. In these circumstances, it makes little sense to imagine you're lying on a beach in the South Pacific, breathing in the fresh air and contemplating the gentle waves as they caress the shore. No, we've got to redouble our efforts and get the work done.

There's no real mystery here. The practice begins with familiar task management and mastery of the fundamentals of modern living: planning your days and your weeks, using a calendar, budgeting your time, making to-do lists, and keeping your schedule in order. Do the planning, get the work done, gain a sense of control, and in turn, your stress will diminish.

Naturally, money helps. A fat wallet dampens uncertainty and gives us a sense of power and control. In this sense, money might be the ultimate stress-relieving agent and even a form of medicine—it's no wonder we fight so hard to get it. Likewise, having the right tools gives us a sense of leverage. Good tools—whether physical or digital—help us get our work done and in turn, give us a feeling of mastery. Education also increases our sense of power and control, especially when it's relevant to actual circumstances on the ground. Knowledge gives us options, and in turn, makes the world seem less arbitrary and more predictable. Even strength training can give us a feeling of mastery. When we work our bodies against gravity and build our physical competence, the rest of world begins to feel more manageable by comparison.

As vulnerable animals in a dynamic and sometimes unpredictable world, we need some sense of mastery to feel safe and comfortable, but there's an inverted-U curve here as well. Some mastery is good, and more is usually better, but we can also go too far. A sense of proportion is vital, and nothing is so sad as an individual or a culture that, having gained some basic sense of mastery, continues the pursuit relentlessly and impulsively, without purpose. In fact, a little mastery goes a long way toward health and serenity. We don't need to control the world, only a corner of it. Develop enough power and control to secure a sense of equanimity and then move on.

THE YIN ARTS

Power, control, and predictability are great antidotes to stress, but we also need to know the art of letting go. And as usual, we'll work with the body, mind, and attitudes. Anything that creates an atmosphere of safety is a good place to begin. Massage is excellent. Meditation is perfect. Just sit and observe your breathing. Just be with whatever state your mind–body happens to be in. Accept the world, accept your body, accept the turbulence in your mind and spirit. It's all okay as it is.

Progressive relaxation is also powerful. Lie down on the floor, and let yourself go limp. Allow the floor to do all the work of supporting you, then start with your breath. With each exhalation, let go of any holding or areas of tension. Now go system by system: Feel all the bones in your body, and let them go limp. Feel all the muscles in your body, and let them relax. Feel your heart and all the blood vessels in your body; let these relax. Let every cell in your body relax. Or, go part by part: Feel your feet, and let them relax. Feel your lower legs, knees, upper legs, pelvis, and so on, all the way up to your neck, skull, face, and scalp. With every exhalation, relax a little more. Think of your hands as heavy and warm. Imagine all the space inside your body as large and expansive. Your chest and abdomen are as a vast chamber. And then relax some more…

Above all, get your mind and spirit in on the process. As your body relaxes, let go of whatever it is you're holding on to. Turn the quest for power and control around, and simply let the world be as it is. No matter the pain and confusion in your spirit, let your life be. Relinquish your expectations, your grudges, your outrage, and your ambition. Forgive and let go. Breathe and let go. For this moment, at least, all is well.

PLANETARY PRACTICES

Personal stress relief practices are vital, but what of our stress on a larger scale? What can we do to turn down the fear and anxiety that's circulating through modern society? A good place to start is by moderating our consumption of modern media. The problem, of course, is that electronic devices now give us the "luxury" of knowing about conflicts, danger, and disasters that are far removed from our immediate location, and even help us make accurate predictions about looming disasters. The hyperactive pace, instant reactivity, and inclination toward conflict and strife, tend to whip us all into a frenzy of angst, most of it unnecessary. From an ancestral perspective, this is positively abnormal.

In a way, it's no surprise. Our primitive grassland minds have always been alert for novelty, danger, gossip, violence, and sex. Producers and creators of media are well aware of this inclination, and know how to capture our eyeballs and ears. Turn up the conflict, chaos, corruption, and scandal, and you'll keep your audience engaged. And once we're hooked, we come to the conclusion that the entire world is nothing more than an ever-tightening knot of stress, ready to explode into catastrophe.

This leads to an obvious prescription for calming down: judicious, disciplined consumption of media, especially forms that exploit our sensitivity to fear, anger, and outrage. If the content and tone are filling you with fury and indignation, you might do better to simply turn it off. In fact, we might well say reducing our consumption of media is a pro-social act that's also good for our health. And given the power of the mind to influence the body, we might even rank "media hygiene" alongside more familiar health factors such as diet and exercise.

But to be more precise, the thing that's really tightening the ratchet of stress in our collective consciousness is not something called "the media," but rather the narratives that circulate through our culture. Stories act directly on the autonomic nervous system, telling us if the world is friendly, or not. This suggests that the real antidote for planetary stress should be stories of belonging, of sharing, trust, togetherness, and unity. These stories can be top-down, spoken by leaders of governments and organizations, or they can be bottom-up, shared by ordinary people in regular conversation. Words matter. Leaders who spread messages of xenophobia and division aren't just playing politics; they're inflicting real damage on human bodies, minds, and our collective future. To shape a better future, we can start by telling better stories.

THE POWER OF MEANING

The most important days of your life: The day you are born and the day you find out why.

—Mark Twain

Our conventional stress-relief practices are all well and good, but far and away, our most powerful antidote to stress is a sense of meaning and purpose. Again we're reminded of Viktor Frankl's *Man's Search for Meaning*. Frankl often quoted Nietzsche: "He who has a *why* to live can endure almost any *how*." Or, as we might put it today, "He who has a why to live can tolerate almost any stressor."

A small, vague sense of "why" leaves us vulnerable to every passing annoyance, but a strong, powerful why can carry us through the most serious challenges and adversities. We might well say having a strong why is an essential element in health, perhaps even more vital than our conventional prescriptions for diet and exercise. We might even say, "She who has a powerful why can remain effective and even happy, even in the face of injury, illness, and the tragedies of trauma, divorce, and social turmoil."

We're reminded of Sisyphus, sentenced to push a boulder up the hill, over and over until the end of time. If Sisyphus has a strong sense of meaning and purpose, pushing the ball is endurable and maybe even satisfying. But without a powerful sense of why, it's just chronic, punishing adversity that grinds down our bodies, minds, and spirits. This is what makes our fragmented modern world so challenging. Today, we're pushing the ball up the hill in the form of conventional work and roles, but many of us are skeptical that the process has any long-term value. We're starting to suspect that a lot of our ball pushing is inflicting damage on the world and putting our future in jeopardy. This kind of anti-meaning is a recipe for disaster. If you don't have confidence in the value of your work, you're a sitting duck for a stress-related catastrophe.

The power of meaning has long been recognized in traditional cultures and is very much part of the Old Way. In Japan, people often speak of *ikigai*, often translated as "that which makes life worth living" or having a purpose in life. It's similar to the French *raison d'être*, meaning, "reason for being." In the culture of Okinawa, ikigai is thought of as "a reason to get up in the morning." Dan Buettner, author of *The Blue Zones*, has suggested that ikigai is one of the reasons people in this region have such long lives.

A growing body of evidence confirms the power of purpose and meaning in health. In 2017, *New Scientist* summarized the findings:

People with a greater sense of purpose live longer, sleep better and have better sex. Purpose cuts the risk of stroke and depression. It helps people recover from addiction or manage their glucose levels if they are diabetic. If a pharmaceutical company could bottle such a treatment, it would make billions.[117]

Victor Strecher, a public health researcher at the University of Michigan and author of *Life on Purpose* writes that

> Over the past 10 years, the findings about the health benefits of purpose have been remarkably consistent—revealing that, among other advantages, alcoholics whose sense of purpose increased during treatment were less likely to resume heavy drinking six months later, that people with higher purpose were less likely to develop sleep disturbances with age, and that women with more purpose rated their sex lives as more enjoyable. These findings persist "even after statistically controlling for age, race, gender, education, income, health status and health behaviours.

So how do meaning and purpose actually improve our health? The answer may lie in a distinction between two types of well-being: *hedonic*, which comes from the pursuit of pleasure and rewards, and *eudaemonic*, which comes from having a sense of purpose. Steven Cole, a researcher at the University of California, Los Angeles, asked participants to rate their well-being over the previous week, in terms of how often they felt happy (hedonic) or that their life had a sense of direction (eudaemonic). He found that people with higher measures of hedonic well-being had higher expression of inflammatory genes and lower expression of genes for disease-fighting antibodies, a pattern also seen in loneliness and stress. For people scoring highest on eudaemonia, it was the opposite. "There were surprises all around," Cole says. "The biggest surprise being that you can feel similarly happy but the biology looks so notably different."

Cole suspects eudaemonia—with its focus on purpose—decreases the nervous system's reaction to sudden danger that increases heart rate and breathing and surges of adrenaline. Overactivation of this stress-response system causes harmful inflammation. A similar study indicates that people with higher eudaemonic well-being have lower levels of the stress hormone cortisol. "There may be something saying 'be less frightened, or less worried, anxious or uncertain,'" says Cole. "Things that you value can override things that you fear."[118]

The power of meaning is so vital to health that it ought to be included as a routine part of every medical exam; in the long run of a person's life, it's probably at least as important as body weight, blood pressure, and lab results. In fact, most of us can easily weather minor biomedical abnormalities, but when meaning is weak or absent, our resilience, stress resistance, and vitality are all compromised. If modern medicine is to catch up with the times, it needs to make meaning a regular feature of practice. We might even look forward to the day when "sense of meaning" is given its rightful place as a diagnostic sign, recorded on medical records, and updated regularly. Hippocrates would surely consider this as a step in the right direction.

But where does our sense of meaning come from? Most of us already know the answer. Across the planet, our most powerful "whys" come from serving other people, especially our families and friends. Or from serving our communities or our country. Or from serving the future. Across all these perspectives, the common theme is serving and sacrifice. The act of giving integrates the mind–body–spirit and in turn, sustains us. This is why self-centered pursuits so often fail. If narcissism is your why, you might succeed for a time, but it won't be long before the ball crushes you.

This is yet one more reason why capitalism poses such a threat to human health and happiness. By justifying and promoting self-interested behavior, it displaces and dilutes the traditional "whys" of community, sacrifice, and altruism. It's no wonder we're so often depressed. If my reason to get out of bed in the morning is simply to gain a slender advantage over a competitor or increase the market share of my company, I'm going against the grain of some of humanity's deepest whys. If I'm lucky, I've got a good sense of why via my family and my friends, but if not, I may be in real trouble.

WHAT'S MY WHY?

Knowing your why is possibly the single most important thing you can know about yourself. It's the story of your life, the reason to persevere when times get hard—and in this sense, bigger is better. Small whys take us a little ways up the hill, but big whys take us on powerful journeys into experience and meaning. Big whys go right to the heart of the human experience. They're bold and ambitious in their reach for moral and spiritual possibilities. In turn, big whys can power us through immense adversities.

The same principles hold true for culture as a whole. That is, "a culture that has a why to live can endure almost any how." Having a strong sense of cultural meaning—a big why—would surely go a long way in helping us navigate the wicked challenges of our day. Which brings up the obvious question: what is our cultural why in the modern world?

Judging from our current behavior, it's obvious our why is almost exclusively economic. As a people, we've decided that "growth," "internalizing profit," and "increasing shareholder value" are some of our most important values. As a society, we gauge our progress and success against measures like GDP and the Dow Jones Industrial average. For many, profit has become our dominant why.

But money is over-rated. In modest proportion, it can buy us essential goods as well as valuable power and control, but beyond that, there's not much to be said for it. When the profit motive is your only motive, you're bound to miss out on the magnificence of life, community, and health. As the song goes, money "can't buy me love," but even more to the point, it can't buy sapience or healthy relationships with the world. Money might help Sisyphus get the ball up the hill for a while, but this kind of why ultimately fails to sustain us.

Obviously, we need a better why. That is, we need to shift our focus from "making money" to "making meaning." If we put as much energy into making meaning as we do into making money, our world would be transformed in short order. Meaning without money is challenging but endurable, and may even prove to be rewarding, but money without meaning is simply ridiculous.

While we're at it, we can look for new whys that will carry us into the future. Possibilities abound: "Working for the seventh generation." "Creating a functional future and a long-term relationship with the Earth." "Promoting health and sapience."

Perhaps we need a cultural vision quest or a planetary retreat to refocus our priorities. Lacking that, we need leaders, writers, speakers, and teachers who are willing to step up and help us build a better why. This is some of the most vital work we can do on the planet right now. Without a better why, the boulder is simply going to roll back downhill and destroy us.

IS THE UNIVERSE FRIENDLY?

In essence, the human stress response is built upon Einstein's legendary question: "Is the Universe friendly?" If the answer is yes, the body sends its systems into action, preparing for exploration, affiliation, curiosity, growth, and learning. If the answer is no, it becomes vigilant and prepares for action and defense.

This is where things get interesting. Not only do we have the ability to sense genuine physical threats directly, but we also have the ability to imagine them in ways that are completely independent of reality. Mind, story, and culture are always getting into the act, interpreting the meaning of events at every turn.

Acts of imagination have very real physiological consequences; every thought, every mental image, every muse has a downstream physical effect. This is why stress researchers are careful to say the trigger for the stress response is not a threat to the organism, but rather a *perceived* threat to the organism. In other words, belief matters. If you believe some circumstance constitutes a threat to your life or your status, your body will buy your story. If you believe in the safety and friendliness of your world, your body will believe that as well.

Perception and interpretation are everything in this art. If we perceive our capability to be adequate for the challenge at hand, it's going to be an easy day. But if we judge our capability to be insufficient, it's going to be a struggle, no matter the actual nature of our circumstances. Work by June Gruber at Yale University has shown marked physiological differences between stress events, depending on how they are perceived. When a stressor was perceived as a *challenge*, subjects showed increased cardiac output, increased diameter of circulatory blood vessels, increased blood flow to the brain, and increased cognitive and physical performance. In contrast, when a stressor was perceived as a *threat*, subjects showed decreased cardiac output, decreased diameter of circulatory vessels, decreased blood flow to the brain, and decreased cognitive and physical performance. Even a subtle shift in interpretation can add up to big physiological and performance consequences.[119]

This suggests a narrative strategy for dealing with potential stressors and big events on the horizon. Perhaps you're called upon to step up to speak in public, manage some chaos at work, or navigate the turmoil of a difficult personal drama. Instead of simply reacting to the pressure, try this story:

This situation isn't a threat; it's simply a test of my

adaptability. And the good news is I come from a long line of highly adaptable animals that have been adjusting to difficult and even life-threatening circumstances for millions of years. My body has a rich history of adaptation. My ancestors have found ways to live in outrageously challenging circumstances. If they can do it, so can I.

Interpretation is such a powerful driver of human experience and physiology that it even affects our long-term health outcomes. Stanford professor Kelly McGonigal describes a study conducted at the University of Wisconsin School of Medicine and Public Health[120] in which researchers asked two very simple questions: "How much stress are you under?" and "Do you believe stress is harmful to your health?" Years later, they compared death records, and found a marked difference in mortality. Those who believed "stress is bad for you" were significantly more likely to die than those who held a friendlier view. The authors concluded:

> High amounts of stress and the perception that stress impacts health are each associated with poor health and mental health. Individuals who perceived that stress affects their health and reported a large amount of stress had an increased risk of premature death.

In other words, the belief that stress is bad for your health is bad for your health.

When faced with a universe that's both friendly and unfriendly, many of us are inclined to lean toward the darker interpretation. As we see it, the world is a dangerous place and the outlook is bleak. Evil forces are ruthless and out to destroy everything we hold dear. This is the NRA vision of life, a world filled with adversaries, criminals, and bad guys with guns. In this world, the only solution is to "harden up" our schools, our world, and our lives.

The problem is that we don't see reality clearly. Our history as vulnerable bipeds in predator-rich habitats of prehistory has skewed our attention toward vigilance, even hyper-vigilance. That rustling in the bushes could be anything, but if you interpret it as a dangerous predator on the prowl, you're more likely to live to see another day and pass your psychological disposition down to your descendants. Treat that rustle as something friendly and you're more likely to wind up in the gut of a hungry carnivore. And so, even in a modern predator-free environment that's generally safe, we tend to see events and conditions as more dangerous and unfriendly than they actually are. In a sense, we're wired for paranoia.

The consequences of this disposition are far-reaching. What was an asset in the Paleo becomes a liability in a modern world that's swarming with stimuli. When you're living in the bush, there's not much of a price to be paid for "false positives." If that rustle in the bushes turns out not to be a leopard, you can simply take a deep breath, laugh it off, and return to your walkabout. But in the modern world, the false positives add up. Our fears that are triggered by a news headline, social media post, or ambiguous social encounter may turn out to be unfounded, but when it happens often enough, the repeated activation of the stress response begins to feed on itself, corroding both our bodies and our cognition. Our vigilance intensifies, and the world begins to look deadlier than it really is. Our lives become filled with false leopards.

The good news is, once we understand this ancient inclination toward vigilance, we're in a position to think more clearly about the world. Yes, there are genuine threats, but we almost always exaggerate. Our negativity bias tries to keep our bodies safe and alive, but in today's world, it actually makes our problems more intractable. We blow things out of proportion and turn molehills into mountains. Knowing this, we can remind ourselves that things are probably not as bad as they seem. We can calm down, take a deep breath, and rest assured that things are probably going to work out.

This frees us up to see more of the friendliness around us. In recent years, researchers and therapists have pointed to the beneficial effects of gratitude, kindness, and the intentional practice of focusing on the nurturing qualities of the world. This advice bears repeating, because for many of us, it does not come naturally. Our ancient, slightly paranoid brains need to be reminded that yes, there are plenty of things to celebrate, to savor and be grateful for. Predators are real, but so too are the spectacular qualities of the natural world, the friendship and love of the people around us, and the richness of human culture. In this sense, we're actually swimming in a sea of friendship. Friendliness is the norm; unfriendliness is the exception.

Likewise, we're reminded of our creative responsibility. Everyone we meet is continually wondering about the friendliness of the world, scanning the environment for clues about danger and potential. We are part of that creation. We can sculpt one another's attention toward danger, duality, and hostility, or we can show people the friendliness that exists in almost every moment. This is not just a good thing to do; it's a very smart thing to do. When the people around us see friendliness, they relax. They become more receptive and maybe even a little more sapient. Being friendly is far more than just being nice; it's vital work of health activism.

To be sure, the universe has its share of dangers, but don't let that fact obscure your vision or your capability. Keep one eye on the beauty. The friendliness will sustain you.

REALITY IS NEVER WRONG

Ultimately, stress is about perspective. Sometimes we experience direct threats to our physical survival, but more often our stress is a consequence of the way we explain reality to ourselves. When there's a mismatch between story and reality, our bodies and minds begin to feel uneasy. This suggests a strategy: if we could just give up some of our expectation and our judgment, we might feel and perform a whole lot better.

This is precisely what we see in the world of martial art, where teachers sometimes advise their students to shift their perspective and remember that "the enemy is never wrong." This may well sound preposterous, but the lesson is sound. The idea is to remain fluid and adaptable—don't get wrapped up in some expectation about what your opponent should or shouldn't be. The enemy—the adversary, the situation—just is. Abandon your psychic resistance and your anger. Observe that reality, and adapt accordingly. Fight for what you believe in, but don't get caught up in unnecessary judgment and evaluation. Don't be trapped by your own mind.

This is not to say we should simply accept everything about the world as it is. Rather, it's an argument for freedom and adaptation. It's an argument for letting go of expectation and working with the world as it presents itself. The fight remains essential, but the indignation and stress are optional. In the long run, "reality is never wrong" might well be the ultimate koan for stress relief and resilience, the ultimate expression of adaptive psychology. Think of your favorite opponents, grievances, and pet peeves. Now imagine abandoning your judgment; these things and people simply are what they are. It's a powerful thought experiment that might just free you up, dissolve your stress, and put you in a position for more skillful action.

Please don't take this the wrong way. Of course climate change, habitat destruction, fracking, social injustice, and racism are wrong. Of course your unemployment, childhood trauma, divorce, and cancer diagnosis are wrong. Of course the presidency of Donald Trump is wrong. But in our quest for sapient behavior and effectiveness, the rightness and wrongness of these things is beside the point. The challenge is to bring our skill and intelligence to circumstances as we find them.

Outrage has its place, but there comes a time when the best course is to play the situation as it stands. Life is capable of anything. We'd all like to have things a certain way, but our preferences are not the real issue. Our job is to create and recreate adaptations on the fly. When we get too wrapped up in the wrongness of people or events, we become rigid and lose our sapience. We lose our ability to move and in turn, become even more vulnerable. If we can let go of our indignation, we can start fresh and return to the encounter with a clear vision.

We all have expectations about reality and relationships, but it's essential to remember that the word *ought* is a product of the human imagination. For every other animal on earth, and for the vast majority of human history, *is* has been the reference point for action. For every other primate and every other mammal on earth, there is no ought and thus, less stress. Life is what it is.

As a stress-relieving practice, this reframe is almost magical. As soon as we say, "Reality is never wrong," our minds turn around and a lot of our angst simply disappears, at least for a while. The conflict and the danger may persist, but the anger and indignation lose their ability to tyrannize us. In turn, this frees us up to bring more of our resources to bear on doing what needs to be done. So whatever you do, keep your eye on the *is*.

MEDICINE

One of the weaknesses of the Western medical approach is that we have made the physician the only authority, with the patient too often a mere recipient of the treatment or cure.

—Gabor Maté
When the Body Says No: The Cost of Hidden Stress

For the vast majority of human history, the body was naked to the world. Like all wild animals, we were exposed to the elements and vulnerable to heat, cold, trauma, and predation. Serious injury or illness was an ever-present danger, and medical care as we know it today was unimaginable. If your body was hurting, you might get some relief from medicinal plants or a shaman, but mostly you'd have let your body do the work of getting back on its feet. It's no surprise our hunting and gathering ancestors were strong and resilient. They had to be.

Things began to change when Hippocrates arrived on the scene in the fourth century BCE. Sometimes referred to as "the father of medicine," Hippocrates rejected mysticism and advanced the idea that diseases had natural, explainable causes. His detailed observations and emphasis on professional conduct were powerfully influential for hundreds of years and remain so today.

But for all of Hippocrates' vision, the average patient continued to suffer. Throughout the age of agriculture and deep into the age of industry, effective medicine was little more than a fantasy. Folk remedies sometimes eased people's suffering, but much of this was little more than a placebo effect. Early surgery and dentistry were horrific events, conducted without the aid of antiseptics, analgesics, or anesthesia. Hunters, farmers, settlers, and native people were on their own, face-to-face with the physical world. If something went wrong, they had no recourse but to fight their way through it. And whatever didn't kill them often made them stronger.

Starting in the late eighteenth century, a wave of discoveries opened the door to germ theory, antibiotics, antiseptics, and anesthesia. In 1860, Louis Pasteur debunked the concept of spontaneous generation, and a decade later, Joseph Lister developed the practical use of antiseptics in surgery. Penicillin was discovered in 1928 by Alexander Fleming, but the big bang of modern medicine didn't actually take place until 1942, when physicians began using penicillin on a wide scale. Almost overnight, medicine went from being a matter of wishful thinking to a reliable scientific practice that worked in spectacular ways. Suddenly, medicine took on a new meaning, and the possibilities seemed endless.

THE AGE OF MEDICALIZATION

With success came a new mindset. Over the second half of the twentieth century, physicians became increasingly confident in their powers and began to apply the medical model more broadly. Before long, every human condition and experience became a candidate for medical interpretation and intervention: childbirth, athletics, minor afflictions, mood disorders, aging, wrinkled skin, and of course, death. For the vast majority of human history, we fought our way through these experiences on our own, but today we turn to medical care by reflex. If you've got an affliction—no matter how minor—there's a cure for that.

This process of creeping medical intervention in human life is known as medicalization, famously described by social critic Ivan Illich in his landmark 1976 book *Medical Nemesis*. His idea was simple. As modern medicine extends its reach into more and more areas of human life and hands more responsibility for the body over to an expert class, it takes away our sense of personal power and control. We receive some obvious benefits, but the existential and experiential costs are immense.

Today, medical and health professions lay claim to every cell in the body and almost every aspect of the human experience. Most obviously, we medicalize exercise: "Before beginning an exercise program, see your doctor" goes the absurd, ominous warning. But that's just the beginning. Today we attempt to medicalize nutrition, sleep, meditation, stress, family and social time, work–life balance, music, travel, and even education. It's all fair game for modern medicine. If it touches the body or human life in any way, we attempt to track it, diagnose it, treat it, and profit from it.

The rise of medicalization is reflected in the wave of overtesting, overdiagnosis, and overtreatment in clinics and hospitals across America. Physician and author Atul Gawande describes this as an "epidemic of unnecessary medical care." As he puts it, "Virtually every family in the country, the research indicates, has been subject to overtesting and overtreatment in one form or another."[121]

The industry has taken on a life of its own. A 2007 essay in the *New York Times* put it bluntly: "What's Making Us Sick is an Epidemic of Diagnoses."[122] At about the same time, a *New Scientist* essay observed how a rising tide of "cures" for diseases people didn't think they had is "turning society into one big hospital."[123] Similarly, *New York Times* columnist Gina Kolta has written about the rise in "disease mongering" and concluded, "If you've got a pulse, you're sick."[124][125]

The consequences of medicalization go far deeper than most of us realize. As a patient population, we've grown accustomed to visiting experts and professionals for every ache and pain. We've become dependent upon their expertise, methods, machines, and prescriptions. The end result is that, while some of us get better, many of us are doing worse. As Illich put it,

> ...dependence on professional intervention tends to impoverish the non-medical health-supporting and healing aspects of the social and physical environments, and tends to decrease the organic and psychological coping ability of ordinary people.

By turning entire populations into patients, our robust animal nature is compromised; we become shadows of our ancestral selves.

When used in excess, modern medicine becomes a kind of prosthetic, an artificial prop for people who may not truly need the help. When every ailment is treated, people no longer need to fight their way through difficult or painful experiences. And when there's no fight, there's no adaptation. When the challenge disappears, the body has no incentive to reorganize itself to a higher level of function. In this way, modern medicine can deprive us of the very stimulus our bodies need to find their own solutions.   • • •

As medicalization has become pervasive, it's actually altered our popular understanding of health itself. Today we think healing comes from substances, procedures, products, and providers. Health is something that comes in a bottle, ordered via the internet. In the process, we've forgotten the ancient and immensely sophisticated healing power that lives in every cell in our bodies. In fact, animal bodies have been actively healing themselves for hundreds of millions of years. This legacy still lives in our history, our tissue, our relationships, and our experiences.

Medicalization turns our powers upside down and confronts us with an inconvenient truth. That is, medicalization may well constitute a significant public health problem in its own right. Maybe what we really need is less medicine, not more. Maybe what we really need is more challenging, physical experience, especially in natural outdoor environments, real food, more sleep, and meaningful work.

FIRST, DO NO MEDICINE

> The endgame is to return the control of our health back to ourselves.
>
> —Ellen Langer
> *Counterclockwise: Mindful Health and the Power of Possibility*

To be sure, modern medicine provides a valuable service, and we can be grateful it works as well as it does. The discoveries of germ theory, antiseptics, anesthesia, and antibiotics surely rank as some of the greatest advances in human history. But at the same time, medicalization stands as a real threat to our health and personal power. So, to borrow an idea from medicine itself, perhaps the solution lies in getting the dose right. Physicians often speak of a dose–response curve for various drugs and medical treatment. This simply means effectiveness varies, sometimes dramatically, depending on the amount administered. As toxicologists often tell us, "the dose makes the poison." Likewise, "the dose makes the medicine."

We can say the same thing about modern medical care itself. A small amount can be extremely helpful, and a moderate amount even more so, but after a time the returns begin to diminish and even reverse themselves. The trick for maintaining our health and personal power is to focus on our innate powers first, then turn to the medical system as needed.

Obviously, we'd be fools to avoid modern medicine entirely. There are plenty of perfectly valid reasons to make use of wonder drugs, technologies, and knowledge that can make our bodies whole again. But in the main, our goal should be to use modern medicine as little as possible and to shift the challenge of adaptation back onto our bodies.

Of course, it's always a judgment call. When you're suffering a minor injury or illness, it's tempting to go straight to the health care professional and get the fast-acting substances that will make the unpleasantness go away. But there's value in fighting the fight and delaying the medicine as long as possible.

This is where the conventional wisdom changes polarity. Instead of adding the mandatory tag line "see your doctor" to every report and advertisement, we might well advise one another to stay away. Stay away from physicians, specialists, hospitals, health care providers, and most especially, pharmacies. Keep your body in the adaptation game as long as you can and give it the opportunity it to do what it does best.

Obviously, you'll want to "see your lawyer" before dispensing this kind of advice in a professional setting, but the point remains. If you really want to sustain your health, the fundamental art lies in fighting the fight with your intrinsic powers first. This means demedicalizing your life as much as you possibly can. Not only should we cut back on excessive use of medical care, but we should also stop thinking of our bodies and our lives in medical terms. Do we really need medical supervision to tell us what to eat and how to exercise? Do we really see ourselves as chronically sick and in constant need of medical expertise? What happens to the human experience when we start from an assumption of illness?

Not only will this approach benefit your body and your resilience, but it will also benefit society as a whole. By using less medicine, we reduce the load on our already overburdened health care system. If everyone leaned a little more toward their own powers of adaptation, the entire health and medical system would work a lot better. This would be a dramatic win–win.

TRUST YOUR BODY

One of the greatest tragedies of medicalization is that people have lost faith in their powers of adaptation, and it may not even cross our minds that we're capable of solving physical problems on our own. But this failure of trust has severe consequences, not just for our ability to heal as individuals, but also for large-scale social and cultural beliefs about what's possible in the face of our environmental and social crisis. For example, any suggestion that we might be able to make do with less energy-intensive technology is often rejected out of hand. We simply assume cars, refrigerators, air conditioning, and computers are essential for survival. We can scarcely even entertain the idea that a simpler, more physical life is even possible. Our imagination is impoverished by our sedentary lifestyles and our lack of robust physical experience.

But of course our bodies could find ways to survive and even thrive in simpler, more physical circumstances. The trick is to trust our history and our almost unlimited powers of adaptation. In fact, our bodies are far more powerful and creative than we've been led to believe. If we're going to create a functional future, it's essential we stop thinking of ourselves as perpetual patients. Stop interpreting every sensation and experience in medical terms. Above all, trust your body to adapt. It's done it before, and it can do it again.

TO US, BY US

Medicalization also forces us to ask some fundamental questions about the nature of medicine itself. Given the complexity of human physiology and the myriad ways that our bodies relate to the world, this may not be entirely obvious. We think we know what medicine is, but our ideas are inevitably shaped by history and culture. And in our New Way world, medicine is generally defined as something done *to us*, not something done *by us*.

This distinction was first proposed by Dr. Herbert Benson in his 1979 book *The Relaxation Response*. As a pioneer in mind–body medicine, Benson was forced to wrestle with typical the "conventional-alternative" classification system. His research demonstrated conclusively that meditative practices produce measurable and substantial benefits, but these practices didn't fall neatly into popular pigeon holes. Instead, Benson proposed a different taxonomy: The practices he described weren't things done *to us*, but rather *by us*.

This great thing about this distinction is that it gives us a completely new picture of medical practice. Things done *to us* include surgery, drugs, acupuncture, massage, chiropractic, herbal treatments, nutritional supplements, and homeopathy. Things done *by us* include exercise, meditation and related stress-relief practices, cognitive training, food choices, and lifestyle modifications such as changes to social life and work-task management. (And yes, there are some practices that include a mix of both *to us* and *by us* methods.)

The distinction is exciting because it generates a host of surprises and strange bedfellows. Suddenly, our minds are forced out of traditional ruts and new ideas are free to emerge. When we think about things done to us, we find that surgery, acupuncture, root canals, and massage all belong in the same category. If, on the other hand, you change your behavior with exercise, food, behavior, meditation, or social affiliation, you are the author of your treatment and your process. Even if that behavior is inspired or informed by a coach, therapist, trainer, or teacher, the operative agent is you.

This gives us another way to think about medicalization. That is, our problem isn't just medicine itself, but our over-reliance on *to us* methods, treatments, and substances. In a medicalized society, we're always looking for someone to do something to us to ease our suffering. We want to be rescued from our pain and dysfunction. Intoxicated by the awesome power of antibiotics, surgery, and similar methods, we tend to overlook and devalue an entire class of methods that can make a big difference in our health and happiness.

To be sure, the *to us* methods have their place, and we can be grateful to have them available, but it's the *by us* methods that really hold the key to reinhabiting our bodies and creating a functional future. This is especially the case in the world of lifestyle disease, where *to us* treatments are notoriously ineffective. When it comes to tackling the challenges of obesity, diabetes, and other "diseases of civilization," the real promise lies in behavioral change, which is to say, *by us* methods.

This distinction also gives us some guidance in the world of health and medical education. As it stands, the vast majority of our health and medical professionals are trained to work as technicians and to deliver the finest *to us* procedures they possibly can. This kind of service is extremely valuable in the treatment of acute conditions, but it fails to deliver in the age of lifestyle disease. To succeed in this domain, what we really need are teachers who can guide us in creating and maintaining our own *by us* behaviors.[126] Technicians will always have a role to play, but at this point in history, what we really need are more lifestyle leaders who say, "Do this," not just, "Take this."

INTEGRATION

> Wholeness is not achieved by cutting off a portion of one's being, but by integration of the contraries.
>
> —C.G. Jung

Everyone wants to be healthy, but medicalization has left many of us in a state of dependency and confusion. Common conversations about health and disease often sound like a "this for that" formula, not unlike the advice dispensed at the supermarket checkout stand.

There's a treatment for this illness, a medication for that symptom, a food for this condition, and an exercise for that injury. Health begins to sound like a box of arbitrary, disconnected fragments, and we can go crazy trying to track it all. But what if health were actually one thing? What if we could integrate all the various elements of our bodies and our lives into a single unifying experience? Wouldn't this be a more satisfying and powerful way to live?

To grasp the depth and potential of this idea, it's essential to realize that the human body—all animal bodies, in fact—are not unitary structures. Rather, we are collections of component parts, layered together by evolution over the course of millions of years and untold thousands of generations. As French biologist Francois Jacob put it: "Living organisms are historical structures; literally creations of history. They represent not a perfect product of engineering, but a patchwork of odd sets pieced together when and where opportunities arose."

For many, this is a surprising way to think about ourselves. After all, we look and generally feel like singular entities. The human body seems like one thing, not many things. But in fact, our bodies and brains are best described as kludges (sometimes spelled kluge). The word comes from the world of engineering, where a kludge is known as a workaround or quick-and-dirty solution that's sometimes dismissed as clumsy, inelegant, inefficient, and hard to maintain. One definition tells us that a kludge is "an ill-assorted collection of poorly-matching parts, forming a distressing whole." [127]

We see examples of kludges everywhere in the modern world. The typical city is improvised over the course of hundreds or thousands of years as new neighborhoods are tacked on to the old. Buildings, roads, and bridges are layered in as needed, building on what's already in place. Likewise, homeowners often remodel their houses in a kludge-like way. They don't demolish the entire house, but add on to the existing structure as desired.

Our bodies are not so different. The timespan is far greater, of course, but the process is much the same. Take a simple life form, add a new feature or symbiotic relationship, and expose the resulting kludge to the world. If the new combination succeeds, it will replicate and pass on its code into the future. Repeat this process over the course of billions of years, and you'll wind up with some astonishing and magnificent plants, animals, and ecosystems. We may not like it when biologists describe our bodies as "ill-assorted collections of poorly matching parts," but this is the legacy of evolution operating over vast reaches of time. The body is many, trying to make its way as one. And most of the time, the totality works incredibly well.

In the body, kludges are everywhere. Every cell contains organelles and structures that have come together over time, not by intentional forethought or design, but by trial and error. Mitochondria, the cellular powerhouses inside every cell, were once free-living organisms that entered ancient cells more than a billion years ago. Likewise, our genomes are riddled with fragments of ancient viruses, and even entire organ systems look like workarounds. For example, the stress response system is a classic kludge: the hypothalamus talks to the pituitary gland, which talks to the distant adrenal glands which in turn release hormones into the bloodstream. From a structural point of view, it looks like an incredibly inefficient and ad hoc system, surely not the work of a sober designer. But it works pretty well for mobilizing the body to action and defense.

Kludges are also common in the human brain: a primitive brainstem, layered with a limbic system, layered with a sensory–motor cortex and a prefrontal cortex. Likewise, our bodies contain thousands, if not millions, of molecular "clocks" that carefully orchestrate the functioning of our tissues and organs, from the heart to the lungs to the liver.[128]

But it's not just tissues, organs, and brains. As Gary Marcus points out in *Kluge: The Haphazard Evolution of the Human Mind*, "the human mind is no less a kluge than the body." As we all know, our thoughts and emotions rarely come to us in linear, coherent forms. We feel internal diversity and competing influences within, driven by a patchwork of layered structures, circuits, and hormones. The end result is a mind that's swarming with ideas, voices, and inclinations. As the British novelist Lawrence Durrell put it, "Each psyche is really an anthill of opposing predispositions. Personality as something with fixed attributes is an illusion." To paraphrase Walt Whitman, "we are large, we contain multitudes."

There are some powerful life lessons here. As kludges, all of us are working with competing impulses and dispositions. Every one of us is a collection of inclinations, all overlapping and operating more or less simultaneously. All of us are vulnerable to feelings of disconnection and internal conflict. It's no wonder we behave in ways that are inconsistent and even hypocritical; this is part of our historical legacy. It shouldn't surprise us in the least when people do and say things that are contradictory. Of course people zig and zag through life; it's amazing we're as consistent as we are. Our internal diversity is a bug in the human system, but sometimes it's a wonderful feature.

HISTORY

For most of our time on the planet, integration of the body, mind, and spirit has mostly taken care of itself. Exposure to heat, cold, rough terrain, and long distances concentrated our energies and drove our performance. When the animal body is forced to be strong or endurant in the face of intense survival challenges, it responds by pooling its resources in concentrated efforts. Muscles, digestion, sensation, immunity, attention, and spirit come together in singular acts. When life is threatened, the animal body does everything possible to unify its forces and do what needs to be done. Physical adversity focuses the mind–body to become one.

Not only did this integrative pressure promote our survival, we can also be sure it maximized our ability to heal. When the body's systems are driven to work in harmony, the organism becomes more efficient at managing trauma, injury, and stress. In our popular, modern imagination, nature heals because it's magnificent, comforting, and nurturing. But in the Paleo, nature "healed" us by being physically demanding and even life-threatening. Scarce food, wildfires, predator attacks, and temperature extremes forced us to rally our internal forces into cohesive acts of physicality and powerful movement. In this sense, habitat was both a teacher and a physician. By driving our energies together, it made us strong and resilient.

Unfortunately, the modern world sabotages our integrative efforts with an excess of comfort and ease. As physical challenge declines, the body's systems tend to drift apart as each begins marching to the beat of its own drummer. Spend a few decades sitting in cars, on couches, and in front of computers and your body's systems will no longer have an incentive to work together. In this sense, sedentary living is far more than just a problem of muscular atrophy and adipose tissue; it's a problem that strikes right at the heart of our body's ability to function.

Even worse, we're now subjected to a punishing array of *dis*integrating forces: distraction, noise, isolation from the natural world, artificial light, chaotic occupations, random food intervals, multitasking, and cognitive overload. We're always being chopped into bits, our attention pulled in every direction, our beings fragmented. From this perspective, it's easy to see how disease can creep into our bodies. When our various psycho-physical systems pull in different directions or work at different speeds, friction and inefficiencies drag down the performance of the whole. If the muscular system is going one way while digestion goes another and immunity goes still another, you're going to feel terrible. Your body will fight for synchronization with some incredibly sophisticated workarounds and compensations, but it can only do so much.

Over time, disintegration weakens us and makes us more vulnerable to a range of challenges: microbial, chemical, physical, social, emotional, and psycho-spiritual. Today's epidemic of lifestyle disease is surely exacerbated by our widespread disintegration, forced upon us by a stressful and alien environment. Disintegration doesn't just leave us more vulnerable to physical diseases; it also lies at the heart of our mental and psychological anguish. If we don't feel whole, we're more likely to suffer anxiety, depression, and turmoil.

We crave integration, but New Way culture, with its inclination toward reductionism and specialization, leads us in the opposite direction. It teaches us how to break things apart and study them in depth, but rarely does it tell us how to put our lives together in a meaningful, functional unity. And it's hard to feel whole when your culture tells you mind and body are separate entities. It's hard to feel integrated when your culture tells you your body is one thing and "the environment" is something else. It's hard to have a sense of unity when your culture insists humans are the supreme organism, separate from and superior to every other creature on the planet.

Things would be far different if we moved toward a circular, Old Way orientation where interdependence is assumed. This narrative begins with unity and returns to unity. The human species is *one* animal, not *the* animal. The human mind and body are reflections of one another, bonded together by the nervous system and informational substances that flow through the body. Body–nature–tribe–cosmos is thought of as a single, unbroken entity. In this kind of culture, psycho-physical integration comes easily. When everybody in your tribe is living with a circular sense of wholeness, you're far more likely to see the world as a single unity. In turn, your body–mind–spirit is likely to feel connected, comfortable, and powerful.

INTEGRATIVE PRACTICES AND THE DRIVE TO UNITY

The good news is human beings have an instinctive drive toward integration, a process famously described by Carl Jung. We suffer and take hits in life, but we're always craving wholeness and looking for ways to put our minds, spirits, and lives together. This is one of the most powerful of all human motivations.

The drive is particularly evident in our universal interest in circles, mandalas, and other symbols of unity. Even today, the internet is packed with circular models that attempt to capture the basic elements of health into a single unity. Some are three-part models based on "mind, body, and spirit" or "bio–psycho–social."[129] Some have four parts, such as the 4-H Club's circle of "health, hands, heart, head." Some include food, sleep, emotions, relationships, education, and even financial health. But while the details can be interesting, it's the drive toward integration that really moves us. The body and the psyche want to be whole.

And so we practice. We dive into various arts and disciplines, always looking for ways to become one with ourselves and the world. In this sense, it's all yoga. We may or may not do the postures and poses we see in a conventional yoga class, but the objective is the same: put the pieces together, create a union with our bodies, minds, tribe, and habitat. The whole idea, you might say, is to be whole.

We see the quest in all manner of practices and disciplines. Teachers and coaches in almost every sport, art, craft, and musical practice advise students to bring the totality of their bodies, mind, and spirit to the execution of their skill. We see it in the world of physical therapy and athletic training where teachers and coaches help clients and athletes synchronize the action of muscular or kinetic chains. In this context, the aim is to generate smooth, athletic movement by training individual muscles to fire in the right sequence, in the right intensity. Failure to integrate the chain leads to weaker movements and a greater chance of injury. That's why we sometimes hear strength coaches yelling, "Lift the weight with your whole body!" The more integrated the chain, the more powerful the movement. Bruce Lee knew it too: "Coordination is the quality which enables the individual to integrate all the powers and capabilities of his whole organism into an effective doing of an act."

Naturally, integration is a common theme in the world of therapy. When a patient is traumatized, mind, spirit, and identity begin to fragment and the patient may disassociate certain parts of her experience or life story. In effect, traumatic memories become walled off from consciousness and may even become inaccessible. As long as this separation continues, the patient will continue to feel anxiety, anger, or hostility and struggle with adaptation. The therapist's job is to help her process or metabolize the trauma and bring it back into connection and conversation with the rest of her mind and life. In other words, the goal is always integration.

As we've seen, the intense physical demands of prehistory were powerful drivers of integration, but physical adversity is not the only force that moves us toward mind–body–spirit unity. All of our familiar lifestyle practices—vigorous movement, sound sleep, meditation, contact with natural habitat, social support, and love—move us toward integration and in turn, personal health.

Of course, it's impossible to know precisely which experiences are integrative for any individual. Because our experience is so wrapped up in personal meaning and story, what's integrative will vary from person to person and even over the course of a person's lifetime. However, we can take some guidance from our experience and the experience of others. Does an activity make us feel whole and complete, or does it fragment us into pieces? In particular, look for a sense of immersion and the "flow state" that's often reported by athletes, artists, and musicians. If you're feeling completely engaged and immersed in an activity, there's a good chance the various systems of your mind and body are working together.

Whenever possible, select integrative experiences—IEs—in your daily life. Classic IEs include childhood play, sports (especially

MEDICINE   243

outdoor athletics), yoga, music, art, meals with loved ones, and of course, love-making itself. Naturally, your selection will be your own, but the most powerful IEs include at least some physicality, natural light and sensation, high engagement, passion, desire, risk, and effort. In particular, intense curiosity and the rage to mastery move the mind–body–spirit toward coherence. Likewise, a sense of meaning and purpose has a clarifying, integrating effect. When we know exactly what we're trying to do in the world, all the body's systems tend to get on board with an "all for one" effort.

But no matter your choice, stay alert for the integrating and disintegrating forces in your life. Become a connoisseur of integration. Ask yourself, Is this activity pulling me together or breaking me into pieces? What activity can I practice right now that will help me integrate my energies? Along the way, be alert for signs of disintegration: anxiety, distraction, ineffectiveness, apathy, or confusion. There's a weakness somewhere, and you've got to bring it back into harmony with the rest. In other words, treat your life like a wheel. Take care of all the spokes and adjust continuously. If something's short, lengthen it. If something's weak, strengthen it. If something's dormant, wake it up. If something's hyperactive, calm it down. And whatever you do, keep your eye on the whole.

SCOPE OF PRACTICE

To really understand the challenge of health and medicine in the modern world, it's essential that we consider the breadth and depth of the enterprise, something professionals call "scope of practice." What's the domain of the physician's art? What kind of patients is he or she qualified to work with? What kind of afflictions can he or she treat?

Historically, this was never much of an issue. Shamans, healers, and herbalists worked with whoever was sick, and there were no legal limits on what they were permitted to do. A tribal shaman could do almost anything in the service of healing, and since all things were considered to be intimately connected, his scope of practice effectively included the entire cosmos.

But for modern medicine, scope of practice is a complex and often thorny issue. Every medical art has its domain, and woe to those who go outside the limits. In practical terms, this makes sense. In a world that includes millions of practitioners and thousands of possible treatments, some limits are necessary. You wouldn't want your optometrist operating on your heart, or your massage therapist managing your chemotherapy treatments. Professional associations expect practitioners to stay within established legal boundaries, and if they stray, they're subject to legal action or even expulsion.

Nevertheless, there's a substantial downside to this specialization of medical labor. The problem is that it severely limits the scope of our imagination. As we've seen, our bodies are massively interconnected with the so-called "external world." As soon as we set up specialties, we run the risk of violating this basic principle. To be sure, there are some perfectly valid reasons to focus on specific diseases and body parts, but there's a price to be paid. By viewing and treating the body in isolation, we cut ourselves off from the life support systems that keep us alive, healthy, and whole.

The problem with a narrow scope of practice is that it reinforces the myth that the human body is an isolated organism. Far from being an abstract philosophy, this orientation has very real consequences for the ways people relate to their bodies, their lives, and the world at large. If we believe the human body is a stand-alone organism, we're far less likely to look at our relationships with the world. We're unlikely to look at our history or the life-support systems that nourish us.

In short, we might well say that the medical profession itself is afflicted with a dangerous form of "narrowitis," a myopic vision that refuses to examine or act on matters that lie outside a patient's skin. We might even go so far as to describe modern, context-free medicine as a kind of institutionalized, culturally driven malpractice. Ivan Illich would have called it "iatrogenesis," harm caused to a patient by medical care.

The good news is some observers have proposed a more inclusive approach. In a landmark 1977 article in the journal *Science*, psychiatrist George L. Engel called for a new medical model.[130] Engel was disenchanted with the limitations of analytical biomedicine and believed that physicians must attend to the biological, psychological, and social dimensions of illness. Engel challenged reigning medical orthodoxy and called for the adoption of a more inclusive, systems-based approach.

For Engel, the problem with the biomedical model is that it "assumes disease to be fully accounted for by deviations from the norm of measurable biological variables. It leaves no room within its framework for the social, psychological, and behavioral dimensions of illness." Even worse, the biomedical model has been fully absorbed into modern culture and imagination. "The biomedical model has thus become a cultural imperative, its limitations easily overlooked. In brief, it has now acquired the status of *dogma*."[131]

Engel's holistic vision was an essential step forward, but as we can now see, even his perspective was incomplete, something native people would recognize immediately. Yes, the bio, psycho, and social elements are all well and good, but where is the habitat that sustains us? For indigenous people, this would be seen as a glaring omission, a rookie mistake. Yes, it's laudable that some segments of medical culture have moved beyond the mechanistic view of the body to include mind and society, but if you're really serious about bringing together all the influences on human health into a single practice and philosophy of care, you have to include the land. To do anything less is to treat a fraction of a person.

This brings us to a new, unified sense of health and medicine, what we might call a big health perspective. In conventional settings, environmental activism and health care are said to exist in entirely different pigeonholes, separated by miles of empty space. Nonprofit organizations attempt to save habitat and species while hospitals attempt to save human lives, but almost never do these two sectors work together. It is almost unheard of, for example, for a hospital chain or physician's organization to endorse habitat protection as a health policy objective. But when we get serious about the link between human health and habitat, we come to the inevitable conclusion that environmentalism must be seen as a form of health care in its own right. Human health and habitat protection are not separate disciplines; they are part of a single whole and must remain connected. Saving habitat is synonymous with saving health.

Fortunately, the tide is turning. In 2007, activists in the American Veterinary Medical Association established a One Health Initiative Task Force dedicated to the linkage of human, animal, and ecosystem health. A journal review described the perspective this way:

> The current fragmented framework of health governance for humans, animals, and environment, together with the conventional linear approach to solving current health problems, is failing to meet today's health challenges...Deterioration in biodiversity and ecosystem services threatens to reverse the health gains of the last century. A paradigm shift is urgently required to de-sectoralize human, animal, plant and ecosystem health and to take a more integrated approach to health, One Health.[132]

Likewise, inVIVO Planetary Health is a collaborative network of scientists, clinicians, and educators that's taking a leadership role in this new paradigm. As they see it,

The concept of planetary health emphasizes that human health is intricately connected to the health of natural systems within the Earth's biosphere—and that the health of all species depends on the health, biodiversity and stability of whole systems.[133,134]

The Planetary Health Alliance, a consortium of over seventy universities, NGOs, government entities, and research institutes, also advocates for a "planetary health lens" and works to "decipher the links between accelerating global environmental change and human health." Even the Centers for Disease Control has adopted its own One Health approach. A promotional video leads with a simple statement: "A healthy individual does not exist in isolation." The organization calls for a new focus on "environmental health" and seeks to promote interdisciplinary collaboration.

A CALL TO LEADERSHIP

Today, the writing is on the wall. Interdependence is not only real—it's an essential, unifying concept in our effort to create personal health and a functional future. The time has come for medical organizations, colleges, and institutions to expand their scope of practice. It's not enough for practitioners to be competent in some narrow sliver of physiology, biochemistry, or anatomy. We need an explicit acknowledgment of the human–habitat connection. In short, medicine needs to be bigger.

But to achieve this, leadership is sorely needed. As it stands, most advocacy in the medical field is restricted to narrow policy debates. Is a particular drug effective? Does this particular test work? How can we reduce costs? These questions deserve attention, but far more important are the big-picture views. Physicians should be standing up, hair on fire, speaking out on behalf of the life support system that sustains all their patients. Likewise, health care professionals should be calling for more spending and action on public health, habitat health, social health, and prevention.[135] After all, most people trust their health care professionals, most of the time. If physicians were more outspoken about the totality of health, the world would listen.

This is where things get really interesting. In conventional conversation, health sounds like one of the safest, least controversial topics under the sun, something everyone should be able to agree on. But once we get serious about preserving the continuities between our bodies and the world, we find ourselves forced to consider the welfare of the biosphere as well as human communities. And in this sense, health becomes a revolutionary idea.

By definition, health means a whole life, in context. When we expand our thinking to include the reality of interdependence, we begin to realize that the very things that sustain human life are under direct, imminent threat. This is what makes the word *health* so inconvenient. It widens our scope of attention and in the process, disrupts a host of cultural assumptions about who we are and how we ought to behave in the world. It demands that we question entrenched attitudes, narratives, rituals, and institutions. It compels us to take a hard look at things like capitalism, corporate dominance, perpetual growth, affluence, technology, social hierarchy, work, and governance. Most importantly, it demands that we examine our relationships to the Earth and each other. In short, it calls into question just about everything we've created since the dawn of agriculture, some ten thousand years ago. In this respect, the pursuit of health can be a profoundly subversive activity.

If we're going to be whole, we've got to be engaged in the world. And that means acting in defense of the processes that keep us alive, especially our habitats and our communities. Activism is just as vital to our health as exercise and good eating. There can be no hiding out in our specializations or personal welfare. To be whole and complete, we've got to preserve the integrity of the entire biosphere. For our bodies to be healthy, the whole must be healthy.

HEALING FORWARD

These days, resilience is all the rage. After 9/11, the financial crisis of 2008, and the catastrophic election result of 2016, people are feeling bruised and battered. Traumas big and small have come into our lives, and we're longing to regain a sense of control, predictability, and wholeness. We dream about bouncing back to our former state of integration, so it's no wonder we see a growing industry of resilience training in education, business, community, and leadership. Some cities have even hired Chief Resilience Officers who're in charge of getting urban areas back on their feet after a major disruption.

It's all well and good, but there's a misunderstanding at the root. The popular vision is that resilience is all about bouncing *back* to some original, healthy state. We patch up the flaws, repair the damage, and go back to our former condition of function and happiness. We imagine our bodies and spirits returning to youthful vigor and exuberance. We imagine degraded ecosystems bouncing back to their original glory after being raped by strip mining, clear cutting, and development.

But our thinking is flawed. Strictly speaking, there can be no bouncing back for any living systems, bodies, or habitats. Physiologies and ecosystems only run forward in time. Healing does occur, but when it does, it's always to some new state of integration. The thing we call resilience is really a process of bouncing forward.

Suppose you hurt your knee in a basketball game. With some rest and treatment, you usually get over it, but the tissue in question is slightly different than before. Your body has engineered a workaround and some compensations—there's some scar tissue on your ligaments, some thickening of fibers, maybe some new neural stimulation to the kinetic chain. Your knee works well enough now, and it no longer gives you pain, but it's really a different knee. You haven't bounced back; you've bounced forward.

The same holds true at the level of habitat. When a forest ecosystem burns or is clear cut, it eventually transforms to a new state of function and health. We might say it "heals," but conditions are not precisely the same. Some species have disappeared, and new ones have taken hold. The forest grows back and may even appear to have recovered, but there are subtle new relationships between plants, animals, and microorganisms.

The problem with our popular image of resilience is that it offers false hope of return. We lead ourselves to believe we can rebound to a golden age when everything was working "as nature intended." And if we believe in this kind of resilience, it can blind us to the very transformations we need to move forward. In this way, our belief in resilience can even be a kind of denial.

All the "re" words suffer a similar flaw: *return, restore, rebound, regenerate, recuperate.* It's a common and thoroughly understandable human desire, but it's a mistake that can actually interfere with the healing process. The belief is seductive: With good luck and hard work, we can return our bodies and our ecosystems to their original golden age. We'll take all the broken pieces, repair them, and put them back into their original order and everything will be as good as new. But this kind of fantasy resilience is simply impossible. The river of ecosystem function, physiology, and life only flows forward. And it's never the same river twice.

We see similarly flawed reasoning in discussions of culture and where society ought to be headed. Distressed about the many challenges of the modern world, commentators often call for some kind of return. Islamist extremists call for a return to a premodern world of strict religious discipline. American conservatives call for a return to the Reagan era or the simplicities of the 1950s. Some prefer the age of Mark Twain's Missouri while others long for the enchantment of the Middle Ages or the sophistication of Ancient Greece. And some of us dream of the deep Paleo, the age of primal contact and integration with nature.

But we're all fools. There can be no backward motion to a golden age of social or ecological harmony, any more than there can be a return to childhood or an age of lost athleticism. The arrow of time goes one way. We aren't going to put North America back together again into some kind of pre-Columbian utopia. There's been too much change. Likewise, we can't put the Colorado river back into its original state, even if we removed the dams. Or the Amazon rainforest, or the oceans, or the atmosphere.

Many people have taken to describing the biosphere as resilient, but taking the long view, we can see that life has really been surging and healing forward for hundreds of millions of years. Mother Earth has weathered asteroid strikes, oxygen holocausts, shifting tectonic plates and radical changes in sea levels. Massive extinction events have traumatized her, but she doesn't rebound—she creates new forms and relationships. So too for our bodies. Every day, millions of human bodies are bouncing forward from injury and illness. Nervous systems are constantly performing intricate workarounds to compensate for damaged tissues. Like ecosystems, people create their way to new states of health.

From one point of view, history is a vital study. Bodies, ecosystems, and cultures are all creations of history, and if we really want to understand our world, we must examine the past. And as we've seen, historical illiteracy is a very real problem in modern New Way culture. But seen from another angle, history is irrelevant and a distraction from the challenge at hand. If we want to get better, it simply doesn't matter how we got here. We've got to work with what we've got right now. Once again, this calls for the art of bricolage: take the broken pieces of mind, body, society, and habitat and put them together in some new combination that's functional and whole.

Healing forward may sound like a strategy for occasional use, especially in the wake of trauma, injury, or disease, but when we take the lesson to heart, we start looking at our lives from a whole new perspective. In this, healing forward becomes a fundamental skill in its own right. It's not just something we do in the aftermath of an adverse event; it's something we can practice every day, always working with what we've got on hand, always putting together new combinations that move us ahead. In this practice, healing forward is a muscle that gets stronger with use. The more we create with existing conditions, the better we get.

So forget about getting back in shape or going back to the Pleistocene; it's not going to happen. Give up the nostalgia for a lost age; it's gone. Instead, create forward, train forward, and heal forward. Take the existing state of body, habitat, or culture and create something that works. Work with what you've got, and keep moving. The present moment is the raw material for your art.

STORY

There's more to biology than biology.

—Daniel Moerman
Meaning, Medicine and the 'Placebo Effect'

Imagine once again you're a child in prehistory, living a wild life among a band of hunter–gatherers somewhere in the rolling hills of East Africa. You're mostly naked, but you're highly intelligent and living an active, physical life of outdoor survival and adventure. You know your habitat by heart and the faces of everyone in your tribe. Your fondest wish is to grow up and go hunting with the elders one day.

One fine evening, you're squatting around the campfire with your tribe, your belly full of meat from the day's kill. It's some seventy thousand years before the present day, thunderstorms are dancing on the distant hills, and you can hear the lions roaring in the distance. Your tribe has been using gesture and spoken words for generations, but tonight is special. Something clicks into place, and incredibly, stories come forth. The hunters share vivid images of the day's events: the tracking through the bush, the smell on the wind, the river crossing, the carnivores in the distance, the sighting of the prey, and the moment of truth. You listen transfixed, captivated by the images that form in your mind. You can't wait to go and experience it yourself and even better, tell a story of your own.

In the generations to come, the stories will grow more vibrant and sophisticated. The elders will speak of not only the hunt but of great cosmic mysteries and the origins of Earth, plants, animals, and humans. Everything is a candidate for story. The floodgates are open.

In his landmark book *Sapiens: A Brief History of Humankind*, Yuval Noah Harari tells the story of story, our cognitive revolution, and the sweeping transformation of human communication that changed everything, including the trajectory of human life. As Harari put it,

> Myths and fictions accustomed people, nearly from the moment of birth, to think in certain ways, to want certain things, and to observe certain rules. They thereby created artificial instincts that enabled millions of strangers to cooperate effectively. This network of artificial instincts is called 'culture.'

As stories spread and coalesced, humans would later come to rough consensus around the meaning and purpose of nation states, religion, democracy, money, and government. Story didn't just entertain our ancestors; it completely reorganized human society and the fabric of human experience. It undoubtedly sculpted the structure of our brains as well.

Modern science confirms the power of story in tribal cohesion and survival. Working with a Filipino hunter–gatherer population known as the Agta, researchers explored the impact of storytelling on hunter–gatherer cooperative behavior. Reporting in Nature Communications,[136] the authors showed that the presence of good storytellers is associated with increased cooperation. In turn, skilled storytellers are preferred social partners and have greater reproductive success, providing a pathway by which group-beneficial behaviors, such as storytelling, can evolve via individual-level selection.

As is typical among foragers, Agta stories emphasize the values of gender equality, friendship, and the social acceptance of difference.

For example, "There is a dispute between the sun (male) and the moon (female) to illuminate the sky. After a fight, where the moon proves to be as strong as the sun, they agree in sharing the duty—one during the day and the other during the night." Researchers found that individuals who live in camps with a greater proportion of skilled storytellers cooperate more readily with one another and are therefore more successful in their foraging. Stories bind our imaginations and our behavior together.

THE POWER OF STORY

Story is the sculptor of human life, health, and spirit. One way or another, we're always involved in the process. We may not think of ourselves as "storytellers," but we're creating constantly, telling stories to others or to ourselves. Every gesture, every word, every decision, every action; it all creates story, and we're under the influence every minute of every day.

Stories take our vast, mysterious, and often incomprehensible life experience and condense it down into handy narratives we use to navigate, explain and explore our world. They tell us how to organize our experience and our emotions, navigate complex realities, and make decisions. Stories give us a sense of identity, and when all goes well, they give our lives meaning.

There's more to this process than we might think. It's easy to understand that the stories we tell are reflections of the state of our body and spirit. If our bodies feel angry, we tell angry stories. If our bodies feel amorous, we tell amorous stories. Our choice of tone, plot, and characters come from emotion, which is to say, from the body. In this sense, all our stories have physical origins.

But the stories we tell are also drivers of physiology, spirit, and imagination. Story stimulates the flow of informational substances in the body, especially hormones and neurotransmitters, and in turn, these changes produce actual transformations in the function of tissues and organs. The effects may be subtle or pronounced, but over the years, the process adds up to some very real physical consequences. In this way, story can drive us toward or away from health and sapience.

Stories literally change the tissue of our brains and bodies; we become what we read and listen to. Stories turn our stress response on and off and help us answer the body's primal question: "Is the Universe friendly?" Story shapes mind, and mind shapes body. The story–body connection is not only real; it's one of the most powerful forces on the planet.

No research is required. Just imagine two sets of children: One set grows up hearing only stories of wholeness, love, friendship, compassion, and kindness. The other set hears only stories of danger, threat, violence, selfishness, and ego. You don't have to be a neurobiologist to know that by the time these children become adults, their brains will be different. And when brains change, so does behavior, health, and life trajectory. Story lies at the ridge of life's watercourse. Stories carve grooves into our minds and bodies, and once those ruts and valleys are established, the rest of life's experiences tend to flow along the same channels.

The power of story has been famously demonstrated by Carol Dweck in her landmark work on the psychology of growth. In *Mindset: The New Psychology of Success*, Dweck begins with a simple question: "What are the consequences of thinking that your intelligence or personality is something that you can develop, as opposed to something that is a fixed, deep-seated trait?"

In her research, Dweck primed groups of students with either fixed or growth narratives and compared the outcomes. Those who were told their capabilities were static tended to perform poorly when faced with novel challenges, but those who heard about their ability to grow were far more resilient and creative. Story made the difference. Students who saw themselves as living, growing creators were far more adept at adapting to new conditions. Those with a fixed mindset were more susceptible to frustration and eventually, depression.

In retrospect, these findings may not be surprising, but they are vitally important because they sharpen our appreciation for the power of story. As Dweck points out, our mindsets change the very meaning of adversity, challenge, and failure. "Believing that your qualities are carved in stone—the fixed mindset—creates an urgency to prove yourself over and over." On the other hand, "the growth mindset is based on the belief that your basic qualities are things you can cultivate through your efforts."

Not surprisingly, we see similar story–body effects in our response to stress. Researchers primed subjects with narratives that described the effects of stress as either "enhancing" or "debilitating." Naturally, those in the stress-is-enhancing group did better on follow-up tests than those in the stress-is-debilitating group. In other words, the story we tell ourselves about stress has measurable physical and psychological consequences.[137]

The power of story is also revealed in therapy, most notably in the discipline known as cognitive behavioral therapy or CBT. CBT attempts to change dysfunctional patterns in cognition, a process known as "cognitive restructuring." Therapists work to replace distortions such as overgeneralizing, magnifying negatives, minimizing positives, and catastrophizing with more realistic and effective narratives. The methodology varies, but in essence it's all about changing the patient's storytelling habits and in turn, relieving their suffering. CBT has been shown to be effective across a range of disorders including anxiety, depression, and other afflictions of the modern world.

The story–body connection even shows up in the way the body responds to the aging process. Researchers compared groups who held different narratives about growing older. The findings showed that "individuals who held more negative views toward aging showed a steeper decline in hippocampal volume and greater accumulation of amyloid plaques associated with Alzheimer's Disease than their peers who held more positive views toward aging." [138] In other words, the stories we tell ourselves about aging have an actual, physical effect on the brain itself.

The power of story is also revealed in the way supposedly inert substances—placebos—can alter our bodies and the trajectory of our health. Placebos can improve just about any dimension of human experience and capability: athletic performance, intelligence, creativity, memory, compassion, gratitude, and happiness. And of course, nocebos—substances or experiences coupled with a negative expectation—take us in the other direction entirely. The power of expectation and belief is almost boundless.

When we think about placebos, most of us are quick to imagine inert sugar pills given to unwitting test subjects in medical trials, but our popular view is far too narrow. In fact, *every* health and medical procedure carries a placebo effect. Surgery, physical therapy, orthotics, even stents, the mesh devices placed in coronary arteries to relieve chest pain in heart disease, may work by way of mind–body influence. [139] Even the most disciplined, scientific, evidence-based treatments bring powerful meanings along for the ride. There's meaning in the stethoscope, the white lab coat, the MRI machine, and the framed diplomas hanging on the wall.

Even our beliefs about exercise are influential. Alia Crum, the head of the Mind & Body Lab at Stanford University, studied hotel workers and primed them with story. Some were told that housekeeping is exercise—this group went on to show statistically significant improvements in their biomedical profile. [140] In a similar study, Crum's team examined a database that tracked people's beliefs about how much they exercised and how long they lived. They found a strong correlation between people's dying early and their belief that they were relatively inactive, even if they were getting as much exercise as others their age in this group.[141]

As vulnerable humans in an uncertain world, we're always on the alert for signals that might give us a hint of where our lives are headed. Placebos and nocebos live in relationships, experiences, technologies, and casual conversation. Every time we turn around, our bodies are scanning the world for clues that might tell us about the nature of our lives and how we might fit in. We're hungry for meaning, and we'll take it wherever we can get it. Anything that has a story attached to it can influence our bodies and minds, for better or worse.

In fact, some observers have suggested we need to refine our definitions. In *Meaning, Medicine and the 'Placebo Effect'*, Daniel Moerman suggests that it's time to abandon the term "placebo effect" and replace it with the more accurate "meaning effect." From this perspective, we're no longer limited to studying the mind–body effects of inert sugar pills. We can start looking for placebos and nocebos across the entire scope of human life.

NARRATIVE HEALTH

Faced with the epic challenges of mismatch, environmental degradation, and social chaos, we're struggling to find our way in an unfamiliar landscape, and to make matters worse, we've got no master narrative to guide us. The dominant New Way narrative of progress and infinite growth lives on, but many of us no longer believe its promise. Likewise, religious narratives no longer carry the influence they once did; an increasing number of young people identify themselves as "nones," which is to say, they have no affiliation or interest in the subject.[142] Futurists try to whip up enthusiasm for a technological utopia, but many of us remain skeptical of this narrative as well. We are, as theologian Thomas Berry put it, "between stories."

To put it another way, author Alex Evans says we're experiencing a "myth gap."[143] As a former political adviser with the British government and at the United Nations, Evans counsels scientists to be better storytellers and myth makers:

> In this time of global crisis and transition—mass migration, inequality, resource scarcity and climate change—it is only by finding new myths, those that speak to us of renewal and restoration, that we will navigate our way to a better future. It is stories, rather than facts and pie-charts, that have the power to animate us and bring us together to change the world.

The problem with the myth gap is that it leaves us exposed to distraction, division, and toxic myths that erode our health, our lives, and our future. Without a functional story, we become vulnerable to whatever story happens to be making the rounds at the moment and puts us at the mercy of whoever's got the biggest megaphone. A culture without a unifying narrative is in big trouble.

Sadly, many of the narratives that circulate through modern culture take us in the wrong direction entirely. Action adventure movies are often built around themes of revenge, conflict, and life in a zero-sum, post-apocalyptic world: the *Terminator* series, *Interstellar*, *Elysium*, *Snowpiercer*, *Planet of the Apes*, *Hunger Games*, *World War Z*, and *WALL·E*. This disturbing genre of "apocalypse porn" paints a vivid picture of a dying earth and humanity in crisis. As these stories tell it, our condition is beyond hope, and the only recourse lies in the ultimate, violent defeat of some horrifying enemy.

At the same time, many of our traditional, guiding narratives have been replaced by synthetic commercial narratives that have come to dominate modern consciousness. Today we no longer talk about Paleo themes of habitat, hunting, or the spirits that inhabit the world; instead, we talk about brands. We design stories to sell lifestyles to sell stuff. And in the context of human history, this behavior is profoundly abnormal.

In fact, today's synthetic narratives are so far removed from their original, organic form that they're best described as "plastic narratives" or "narrative products." Like food products, these narratives are refined, distilled, and stripped of their original nutrients and meaning. They're intentionally produced, not to reveal, express, or enlighten, but to manipulate and exploit. The objective is to produce a certain kind of behavior in the consumer, usually in the form of clicking the "buy now" button.

But synthetic narratives don't just lure us into buying particular things; they also manipulate us into living in particular ways. Lifestyle brands are everywhere now, powered by narratives that tell us what to eat, what to aspire to, and how to succeed in life. And above it all is the master commercial narrative that tells us that we can buy our way to beauty, happiness, power, and control. All things are possible if you just spend enough. Health, adventure, romance, and transcendence can all be yours on an easy payment plan.

In the Old Way, tribal elders told us what was important and how to live, but in the New Way, it's logos, tag lines, and branded content that drive our consciousness and our behavior. This is a drastic, radical change in the human experience and the human imagination. There's a world of difference between narratives that come from the heart of a tribal elder and those that come from a conference room in a marketing department. One is sincere, authentic, and based on a lifetime of valuable human experience in a challenging, natural habitat; the other is calculated, plastic, and in many cases, nakedly cynical.

Just as excess consumption of food products eventually compromises our health, the chronic consumption of synthetic narratives ultimately degrades our ability to think clearly and exercise our own judgment. The threat is subtle and insidious–narrative products sound like real stories and are highly palatable, maybe even tastier than the real thing, but the danger is real, to individuals and to our culture as a whole. Try to get by on a diet of synthetic narratives and you'll eventually lose contact with your identity, your history, and your purpose. You'll simply exist as a character in someone else's story. In the process, you'll degrade your personal health and your chance for an authentic human future.

So what kind of stories should we be telling ourselves about our moment on Earth? What narratives will lead us out of the myth gap and into a functional future? Can we make our narratives healthier in the same way we make our bodies healthier?

Narrative health may well sound like a new thing. In the modern world, our tendency is to listen to stories and rate them for something we call "entertainment value." Most of us either like or dislike stories, and rarely do we hear a movie reviewer claim that a film was a "healthy narrative" or a "diseased narrative." But given the power of the story–body connection and the ability of narrative to shape our culture and our future, this orientation makes perfect sense. If we can make our stories healthier, we can make our lives and our culture stronger. In fact, given what we know about the power of language to shape our sense of reality and the function of our bodies, narrative hygiene is probably just as important to our health as our more familiar practices of diet and exercise. Get the story right, and your body will flourish. Get the story wrong, and no amount of cardio, strength training, or vegetables will save you.

BIG, HEALTHY NARRATIVES

The contrast is clear: Healthy narratives bring us closer to the wellsprings of life: our habitat, our bodies, our imagination, and one another. Diseased narratives move us further away from the things that sustain us. Healthy narratives move us toward unity and integration with the biosphere and one another; diseased narratives move us toward division, fragmentation, fear, and chaos. Healthy narratives show us a path to a meaningful future, but diseased narratives drag our spirits and our bodies down. They sap our sense of meaning and leave us empty, unable to take the next step into a functional future. Healthy narratives emphasize continuity, connection, and courage in the face of ambiguity and uncertainty. Diseased narratives leave us stranded and disconnected or worse, put us on a path to polarization, cynicism, nihilism, and destruction.

Throughout history, our great spiritual leaders have given us healthy, integrating narratives that stressed the unity of humankind and the universe, but biology tells a similar story. Many of us have come to believe science and religion are mutually exclusive domains and that it's necessary to choose up sides, but from this perspective, the two are natural allies. Fundamentally, the core message of LUCA, deep ecology, and planetary health is no different from the teachings of Jesus, Buddha, Mohammed, or any of the Old Way elders. It's all one thing. We all breathe the same air and share the same ancestry. We're united by DNA, human universals, a collective unconscious, and now, a shared planetary fate. The whole world is kin, and the time has come to start acting like it.

NARRATIVE ACTIVISM

At this moment in history, narrative health is essential, but when it comes to choosing and sharing meaningful stories with one another, most of us are slop artists. We speak impulsively and choose our words with little regard to their systemic consequences. Many of our utterances are simply news reports, statements of emotion, complaints, or random observations about people and the world. We talk and talk, but rarely do we stop to consider the full potential of our narratives and what effect they might have in the bodies and minds of our listeners.

What we really need is a sense of narrative activism, a conscious, intentional telling of stories that pull us toward a functional future and a long-term relationship with the planet. The beauty of this approach is that it's available to anyone and requires no special credential or position in life. Not everyone can be a political mover and shaker, and few of us have access to big media megaphones, but we all tell stories—and those stories have the potential to travel far and wide. When you speak, you're not just talking to your friends. You're also speaking to your friends' friends' friends.

BEHAVIORAL STORYTELLING

A good place to begin this art is with an expanded sense of what constitutes a story. For most of us, stories are self-contained, stand-alone journeys of the imagination that take us from "once upon a time" to "happily ever after." Movies last several hours, and novels span a few hundred pages. But story is always in progress, always emerging and unfolding out of our lives and behavior. Sometimes our stories span just a few words, and even our posture, our tone of voice, and our silence can tell a tale. People say "every picture tells a story," but even more to the point, every behavior tells a story. A nod of the head, a gesture, even the very act of paying attention can give life to a story. A few words here tell a tale of victimhood, a few words there shift our attention to an act of courage and resolve. By our slightest actions, we give stories power, diminish them, or reframe them. It's one big act of continuous social creation. Even if you never open your mouth, you're still the author of something.

This adds up to a challenge for our awareness and motivates us to be more alert to the narrative consequences of casual speech and social engagement. What am I doing right now to advance, retard, or reframe the narrative of our day? What kind of story is my behavior telling about the world? If an observer witnessed my behavior from afar, what would he say about the story it tells?

KNOW YOUR WINDOW

To be effective as narrative activists, it's essential that we pitch our stories at the sweet spot of the listener's mind, experience, and belief system. To put it another way, the story has to fit within certain boundaries of discourse, sometimes described as the "Overton window." The original term comes from the world of politics, but we can see the same idea in any domain of discourse, from the intimate conversation of couples, to friendships, families, workplaces, and communities. If you're inside the window, you've got a chance of having an impact, but if you're outside, your pitch will be dismissed as crazy, deviant, or irrelevant. Inside the window, it's business and culture as usual, and certain topics are considered sensible, acceptable, comfortable, and normal. But outside the window, things are deemed radical, even unthinkable.

The trick is to know the disposition and values of your audience and to pitch your story at the right level. If you're too close to the center, you'll simply reaffirm the status quo and nothing meaningful will be accomplished. Your presentation may be boring, but it won't send anyone into a panic. But if you go too far outside the window, your ideas will be rejected as irrelevant and your efforts may be wasted. This, at least, is the conventional view of the art of politics.

But things are not always what they seem, and sometimes it makes sense to work the edges. For example, a 2017 book by biologist E.O. Wilson argued for setting aside half the terrestrial surface of the earth to preserve what's left of biodiversity.[144] It's a great idea and almost certainly necessary, but it's so far beyond the bounds of our cultural imagination that it can't get traction, for the moment at least. As always, it's about context and relationship to other stories in circulation. A single, wildly radical idea is easily rejected, but when enough of these ideas get exposure, they can actually move the center and the range of discourse. Over time, slightly radical ideas can make less radical ideas seem more palatable. When a highly respected scientist like E.O. Wilson calls for setting aside half the planet for preservation, stopping the construction of new oil pipelines or shutting down fracking operations suddenly doesn't seem so unreasonable.

For the activist, the trick is to know your window and to pitch your ideas with precision. If you make your pitch at the center, you'll have a willing audience, and your proposals will be deemed practical and reasonable. There's almost no risk here, which is precisely why so many people seek the center. But curiously, it's also easy to make a pitch way outside the window. Your radical ideas will quickly be dismissed, and you won't have to face the messy, difficult work of following through on your vision. What takes real courage is to make a stand at the perimeter, make your case, and keep making it. Stretch the elasticity of your audience as far as you can without breaking their imagination. Encourage them to broaden their attention and accept new ideas into their conventional discourse. Help them feel safe, but feed their appetite for transformation. Be the guide.

THE ART OF THE REFRAME

For the narrative activist, a closely related skill is the ability to reframe ideas and issues to lead your audience where you want them to go. When we reframe an issue or perspective, we open up new possibilities for awareness, action, health, and even sapience.

Of course, reframing is as old as storytelling itself and can be used by anyone, for any purpose. Marketing, public persuasion, courtroom presentations, and political campaigning are all about framing. Most of our difficult conversations and arguments in daily life, romance, and family are about where to put the frame. All of us are reframers to some degree, although some of us are better at it than others.

The beauty of reframes is that, used wisely, they can move us in positive directions toward a functional future. For example, when we reframe lifestyle behaviors like sleep and exercise as pro-social and pro-future, we promote personal and public welfare simultaneously. Likewise, when we reframe a crisis as an opportunity, we change our experience in a fundamental way. Suddenly, our stress and fear feel less overwhelming and our minds are free to pursue the possibility for growth. Instead of thinking, "Adversity is a stressor," we can reframe the situation and say, "Adversity is a stimulus for adaptation." We can even reframe our injuries as opportunities to live and move our bodies in new ways. Pain is unpleasant, but it's valuable information that can lead us in new directions.

On a larger scale, "environmentalism is health care" is an extremely powerful reframe because it shifts our attention to the human–habitat connection and illuminates our continuity with nature. Suddenly, we see the link between our bodies and the world.

In the world of activism, reframes can be particularly powerful. In 2016, activists at Standing Rock declared, "We are protectors, not protestors." This kind of reframe moves the focus away from militancy and toward the preservation of something universally valuable.

Bioregionalism is another powerful reframe. It calls us to ask hard questions about the way we've been structuring our politics, our economy, our commerce, and even our relations with one another. It gets us out of the homosphere and forces us to look at the habitat and creatures that sustain us.

Equally powerful is the Rights of Nature movement. A small but growing number of governments are now granting rights to various ecosystems.[145] The first Rights of Nature lawsuit in the US was filed in 2017, seeking judicial recognition of the Colorado River as a person under the law, with the right to exist and flourish. This follows similar legal actions in India, Columbia, Ecuador, and New Zealand. And in July 2018, the High Court of Uttarakhand at Nainital in northern India issued a ruling declaring that "[e]very species has an inherent right to live and are required to be protected by law."[146] The beauty of this reframe is that it forces us to confront the contradiction that lies at the heart of our culture and our failure to give voice to the world that gives us life.

Another powerful reframe comes from the world of neurobiology and brain science. For most of human history, we've been quick to condemn people with bad behavior as "evil" or "stupid" or of "poor character." We put them in jail, exile them from our communities, or kill them outright. But today we're beginning to understand and appreciate the biological effects of adverse childhood experiences, trauma, concussions, combat, and disease. In this light, people who behave badly almost certainly aren't bad people—they're people with neurological injuries, and they can be helped. Our reframe moves us away from retribution and toward compassionate treatment strategies.

Even the entire field of biology can be described as a reframe. Darwin's *Origin of Species* threw our entire identity into question, and suddenly, humans went from being the greatest creation the world had ever known to just another animal. For a modern New Way culture built on the assumption of human supremacy, biology is turning out to be one radically inconvenient idea—and one of the greatest stories every told.

These reframes are just a beginning. No matter the issue or challenge, there's always another perspective that we can bring. For the narrative activist, this is the essential skill. Stay fluid and alert for new visions of old problems. There's almost always another way to see it.

THE ART OF PRESENTATION

It's one thing to tell a story to your family and friends, but if you really want to have an impact in the wider world, you've got to stand up and deliver in front of an audience. Unfortunately, this aptitude has largely atrophied in modern culture. Most of us avoid speaking in public, and when we're forced into it, we often play it safe with dry, calculated presentations that fail to inspire. Listening to presentations at modern professional conferences, it soon becomes obvious that most of today's presenters fail to understand the power of story or the need to speak to the human experience. Constrained by rigorous academic training, presenters punish their audiences with detail, formulas, methodologies, and timid, watered-down calls for more research. It's no wonder most audiences reach for their phones.

The better approach is to think back to the campfire and the spirit of Old Way. Get back to emotion, humanity, and the body. Above all, take a risk and show some life. Practice, but don't memorize. Put your curiosity and passion on display. Stop hiding behind the podium or a digital format. And if you really want to connect with an audience, be careful with numbers. As some speaking consultants have pointed out, "Numbers numb. That's why they're called numbers." Or as the legendary psychologist Daniel Kahneman put it, "No one ever made a decision because of a number. They need a story."

For our presentations to be truly effective, we've got to develop a story sense, an ear for narrative patterns and the way they connect with human experiences, values, and emotions. Above all, we've got to be alert for a presentation's human significance. A good story isn't a bunch of facts or data; it tells us something important and revealing about the experience of being alive in this mysterious, ambiguous, and tenuous world. People with story sense know how to get to the essence with the fewest possible words.

In our nervousness about speaking in public, we tend to forget audiences are people too and that these people possess the universal human desire to feel felt. As a presenter, it's absolutely essential to spend some time imagining what your audiences' lives are like. Craft your story to speak to their needs, problems, desires, sufferings, and dreams. Don't just speak to the head. Speak to the whole body, the whole animal in context.

But what exactly do you want to say? When faced with the prospect of delivering a presentation in a public forum, many of us are inclined to panic and include as many ideas and facts as we can possibly can. Our enthusiasm gets out of control, and we wind up burying people under mountains of content. Once again, minimalism is the solution. In her book *Resonate*,[147] Nancy Duarte encourages presenters to focus on one Big Idea that drives the entire presentation. The Big Idea must articulate your point of view, convey what's at stake, and take the form of a complete sentence. It's not enough to say, "My presentation is about planetary health." Better to say, "My presentation is about ways the planetary health paradigm can help us create a functional future." If you can't articulate your presentation in a simple, coherent statement, you're not ready for prime time.

Then, when you do stand up to deliver, stick to the Big Idea. You'll be tempted to deliver as much content as possible, but the time goes by fast, and you'll end up racing to fit it all in. Better to say less. Give yourself a chance to breathe, and let the words bubble up from the deep body. You've done your practice. Now it's time to let go and let your story tell itself.

Story needs structure, and no matter your subject, a good place to begin is with a dilemma, mystery, or something that just doesn't add up. This is the hook, the idea or image that grabs your audience and sustains their attention. Don't just say, "My talk is about this subject, and here's my first slide." Tell a mini story about someone in trouble, something that's broken, something that feels wacky or out of place. The more vivid the contrast and the tension, the better. Once you've got the setup working, you can dig into the details, and people will listen.

Another powerful way to organize your ideas comes from Randy Olson in *Houston, We Have a Narrative: Why Science Needs Story*.[148] He calls it the ABT model:

Here's a fact AND another fact that add up to a situation, BUT there's an anomaly or a conflict; THEREFORE, this is what it means, and here's what we should do about it.

For example, "We've made tremendous strides in scientific discovery AND technological power, BUT we're inflicting massive destruction on the biosphere; THEREFORE, we need a revolution in culture and consciousness." If you can structure your presentation in this way, you've got a good chance of connecting with your audience.

As for the visual content of your presentation, it's essential to come to grips with the curse of slides. As technologically sophisticated New Way presenters, we assume PowerPoint and Keynote are essential to success, but are they really? At their best, visual graphics delight audiences and pull them deeper into the narrative, but at their worst, they simply serve as coffin nails for presentations that barely have a pulse. When templates rule the show, everyone knows it, and it's no wonder that "death by PowerPoint" has become such a popular meme in modern culture. We've slept through it a thousand times.

So remember, the slides aren't the show. The story is the show. Keep your master narrative front and center, and above all, don't read your bullet points out loud. Your audience knows how to read, and they can do it faster than you can speak. Reading your slides to your audience is simply redundant and mostly goes to prove that you're either too nervous or don't really have anything interesting to say.

To clarify your thinking, imagine a complete technological meltdown on the morning of your big presentation. Your laptop dies, the internet is down, and you've lost your backup drive. Could you still give your presentation? If you have doubts on this score, you'll want to revisit your story idea, and remember the emotional forces that are driving your talk in the first place—curiosity, concern, passion, wonder. And of course, practice. Give your presentation to your dog or your garden, over and over until you get it right. Overprepare, and you'll be ready for any surprise.

Finally, give some thought to your final words. You've set things up with a conflict or a problem and taken your listeners on a journey into the details, but don't leave it hanging. As you reach the end of your talk, make a circle. Refer your audience back to your initial dilemma or mystery. This wraps up everything and conveys a sense of completeness. People may not remember the facts and details in the middle of your talk, but they'll remember the totality of the journey. By connecting your conclusion to your initial proposition, you'll make the experience whole.

STORIES ARE REPS

Story is the most underrated power on the planet today. Everyone loves to be entertained, but most of us believe stories are nothing more than fleeting collections of words and images that tickle our minds and emotions. But in fact, the story effect is just as physical as any other encounter with the world. Every time we hear or tell a story, our bodies are literally transformed. The effects are microscopic and subtle but immensely consequential. When synapses and circuits change under the influence of story, so too does the trajectory of our lives.

As we've seen, the human nervous system is constantly remodeling itself as it attempts to adapt to the world around it. In every moment, millions of synaptic membranes are becoming more or less permeable to stimulation, and millions of nerve fibers are becoming more or less insulated with myelin sheaths, making them faster or slower. The cortex of the brain is continually remapping itself to manage new sensory and motor demands.

Stories play right into this process. Every story we tell or hear—especially those with emotional impact—produces a distinct neuroendocrine response in the body and the brain. With every telling, the brain becomes more receptive to the meanings that come with the story, and this becomes the beginning of a watercourse. With each retelling or rereading, human attention becomes more likely to follow along and deepen those grooves, for better or for worse.

In this sense, repeated tellings and listenings are no different from the reps we perform with dumbbells in the gym. Listen to a story once and you might be momentarily moved, but listen to that story a hundred times and your body actually begins to change. In turn, your transformation will touch the bodies and minds of people around you and even be passed from one generation to the next. Stories don't just carve grooves in your body and brain; they also carve grooves in the future.

Even in folklore, we have an understanding of this process. We say, "The hand that rocks the cradle rules the world," but we might well put it in terms of story: "The voice that tells the earliest narratives rules the world." First stories are the most powerful. The narratives we share with our young people will shape not only their lives, but the lives of their children's children.

The implications go far beyond the lives of individuals; the effects are literally intergenerational. The attention we pay today may well be flowing along grooves and ruts laid down by storytellers in our distant past. Likewise, the stories we tell today are carving grooves in the nervous systems of our descendants. This means storytellers—all of us—have an immense responsibility. Every time we open our mouths or put our fingers to the keyboard, we're shaping people's bodies and yes, the future of the human race. Many of us complain about being voiceless and powerless, but if you can tell a meaningful story, you can make a difference.

SAPIENCE

Sapere aude

("Dare to be wise")

Dark clouds gather on the horizon, and the future looks bleak. Climate change nags at our minds, while the destruction of the natural world eats away at our spirits. Conventional prescriptions feel inadequate, and Mother Culture just isn't giving us the guidance we so desperately need. Our lives are saturated with data and information, but we still feel lost. Catastrophe looms, and the biosphere hangs in the balance. If there were ever a time to wise up, this is it.

Unfortunately, sapience (aka wisdom) seems to have largely disappeared from our cultural radar in recent years. In the Old Way, wisdom was a central organizing theme of human life, but in today's world, we rarely hear about it, nor do we teach it in any intentional manner. It's perfectly possible to go through an entire educational career, all the way to a PhD and beyond, and never be exposed to the study of sapience. So where has wisdom gone?

The short answer is it's been eclipsed by practical, utilitarian, and commercial concerns and our modern love affair with intelligence. Wisdom is considered old school and even irrelevant, but intelligence is sleek and sexy. Intelligence gives us quick, tangible rewards, so we promote it at every opportunity. We do everything possible to define it, measure it, and reward it. We worship processing power, both human and artificial, and create vast industries to build intelligent machines. We train our children to be more intelligent, and some of us even aspire to be more like the computing machines we slave over each day.

There's no real mystery here. We worship intelligence because it promises to give us ever-greater levels of power, control, and predictability. In this paradigm, everything becomes a puzzle to be solved, a code to be cracked. Once we've mastered the algorithms, we can become masters and possessors of Nature. We can become the alpha animal. This is the promise of the New Way.

To be sure, intelligence has its uses, but as a standalone quality for creating a healthier world, it's wildly overrated. In the first place, it fails to honor context. It tells us how to solve problems, but doesn't tell us whether those problems ought to be solved in the first place. It tells us how to hack the human genome and send people to Mars, but it doesn't tell us why we should do it. It tells us how to build wickedly fast machines that will disrupt and revolutionize modern life, but it doesn't tell us about the human and ecological consequences. It tells us how to dominate the world, but it doesn't have anything to say about how we might relate to what's left.

Of course, some would argue that a substantial percentage of modern culture has gone in the opposite direction entirely, rejecting both wisdom *and* intelligence. With the election of 2016, American culture took a big step closer to the dystopian, anti-intellectual society depicted in the 2006 movie *Idiocracy*. In this Trumpian world, show biz is everything and reality is irrelevant. Rational, measured discourse is attacked as "fake news," and lies and truth are interchangeable. "Alternative facts" are just as good as actual facts, higher education is shunned as elitist, and science is rejected as a liberal conspiracy. Climate change is a hoax, impulse is plenty good enough, and sapience isn't even on the radar. Obviously, this is not a recipe for a functional future.

In any case, intelligence just isn't working for us in its current form.

Our problem, once again, is our failure to honor context and inter-dependence. In the New Way, we cast intelligence as a free-floating capability, independent of the world at large. We distill and refine it out of its normal setting, much the same way we refine certain elements from wheat, corn, and rice. Just as we talk about white bread, we might also talk about "white intelligence." Like white food, white intelligence can give us a quick reward, but it's not real nourishment. And when consumed in large quantities, it ultimately makes us sick.

Historically speaking, this abstracted, white intelligence is profoundly abnormal. In a normal, indigenous human culture, intelligence is first and foremost relational. If you're going to succeed as a hunter or even as a gatherer, you've got to see the totality of your habitat. The very act of isolating things from context is viewed with deep suspicion and might even be considered the opposite of intelligence. If you take a thing or process out of its natural setting, you end up with something irrelevant, misleading, or dead. Solving an abstract puzzle might be a good trick, but the most vital challenge lies in understanding and working with relationships in the real world, *in vivo*.

Our love affair with the head and intelligence is reflected in an increased focus on the STEM curriculum in schools across the modern world. That is, science, technology, engineering and math are now presented to young people as the only viable formula for success in life. In this process, we push the humanities aside as quaint, outdated, and romantic pursuits. We snicker at those who study language, music, dance, art, and drama, then joke about their dismal job prospects. "Do you want fries with that major?"

But this is a perilous and ultimately self-defeating move. STEM might well solve some of our practical problems, but by itself, it only digs our hole deeper. Now more than ever, we need the humanities to tell us about our psycho-spiritual relationships with the world, one another, and the experience of being alive. STEM teaches us almost nothing about these things. Science speaks volumes about the mechanics of cause and effect and tells us a great deal about the specific consequences of particular actions, but it tells us almost nothing about the spiritual qualities of our experience or how to create healthier relationships with the world at large.

Science tells us about actions, not attitudes or values. It tells us in no uncertain terms that we are destroying our future and suggests specific prescriptions about how to reduce our impact, but it offers little guidance in how to transform our culture or our consciousness. In one sense, science is absolutely essential to creating a functional future, but in another it is very close to being worthless. If I'm suffering from a case of ecological angst, depression, and existential dread about the future, all the research articles in the world are unlikely to help me. But the humanities, with its deep history of reflection on the human encounter with life, might show me a way toward wholeness.

WHAT WOULD WISDOM DO?

If we think about wisdom at all, most of us imagine it's something for long-dead Greek philosophers or monks in monasteries, not for real, busy people in a complex world. Intelligence offers the lure of power, control, and lately, incredible wealth through disruptive technologies and internet startups. In comparison, wisdom appears to offer little more than contentment and a sense of equanimity. Even worse, wisdom sounds like a long, hard road that requires a lifetime apprenticeship and a life of deprivation and austerity—not an easy sell in today's marketplace. Wisdom, we might say, has a branding problem.

But what if we're wrong about all of this? What if sapience is not only possible for the average human, but something that's lingering just below the surface of our lives, ready to be revealed with a shift in perspective? What if sapience is actually a normal human characteristic that's teachable and learnable? What if wisdom were held as an integral, essential part of our culture?

Maybe developing wisdom isn't such a stretch. After all, the pursuit of wisdom was a common, even universal, feature of the Old Way. To be sure, the Paleo must have had its share of impulsive, foolish behavior, but across a wide range of human native cultures, the quest for wisdom has long been considered normal and even unremarkable. So maybe Linnaeus—the 18th century taxonomist who coined the term *Homo sapiens* in the first place—was right all along. Maybe sapience is a normal human characteristic that's simply been forgotten in the madness of modernity.

So what exactly is wisdom? Philosophers will argue about definitions, and even whether a definition is possible, but it's easy to see consistent themes in Old Way traditions across the planet. If pressed, most of us could point to qualities that would be considered "wise." Even children have some sense of how a wise person might behave. Details will vary, but if we stopped to think about it, most would agree that wisdom has a distinctive set of characteristics:

Above all, wisdom is about context and the art of "seeing whole." Always suspicious of disconnected fragments, it assumes interdependence. How does a thing or process relate to everything around it? Component parts may be interesting, but it's the big picture that really matters.

Wisdom also has a powerful sense of proportion and an appreciation for the middle way. It understands that almost everything in the biosphere follows the famous inverted-U-shaped curve. There's a sweet spot for every process, an ideal level for every substance and effort: a hypo, a hyper, and an optima. Wisdom is suspicious of extremity, a theme we see repeated in cultures all over the world. In the East, the Buddha described the Noble Eightfold Path as the middle way between the extremes of sensual indulgence and self-mortification. In Sweden, people speak of "lagom," meaning "just enough," "a fair share," or "a sufficient amount." In ancient Greece, philosophers spoke of the "golden mean," and in popular culture, we tell stories about Goldilocks and the Three Bears.

Sapience is modest and lives from a stance of humility, a natural consequence of generations of survival on the grasslands of Africa, where life was fragile and people were vulnerable. When you're surrounded by predators and natural forces you can't possibly control, it doesn't make much sense to play it any other way. In this kind of world, modesty and humility are considered, not as signs of weakness but as essential qualities for learning and integrating with the world. They're practical, proven concepts.

We see this understanding reflected at every level of the Old Way. Individual displays of stardom and self-aggrandizement are discouraged. As astute observers of the natural world, our ancestors knew full well no one gets to be alpha, at least not for long. Life in the wild is a game of rock–paper–scissors. When you violate the circular, interdependent nature of nature, something is bound to break. Pride goeth before the fall, and a haughty spirit is a recipe for disaster.

Sapience honors an ethic of living lightly and respectfully. Old Way cultures never presumed to own their habitat and saw themselves as guests, invited to this Earth and given an opportunity to experience its comforts and its wonders. In *The Fine Art of the Good Guest*, Jeffrey Lockwood describes the practice and the attitude:

> One begins by demanding nothing more than the bare elements of life and dignity, which every host is more than delighted to exceed. The good guest then simply allows the other person to be a good host—to share his gifts, to play her music, to tell his stories, to show her places, and to serve his foods. Finally, a guest should cultivate and express genuine gratitude. It need not be effusive or exorbitant, only sincere. We might also think of ourselves as uninvited, but not

unwelcome, guests of the planet. And I think the rules for being a good guest of the world are just the same: Ask little, accept what is offered, and give thanks.

Sapience knows that behaviors tend to circle back on themselves. Any time we act, we are acting on the whole, and since we're part of the whole, our actions always return in one form or another. Whatever we do to the world, as individuals or as a species, we do to ourselves. All behaviors, we might say, are boomerangs.

Examples of this worldview are everywhere in the indigenous tradition. We recall the legendary words of Chief Seattle: "What we do to the earth, we do to ourselves." In the Eastern tradition, the Sanskrit word *karma* refers to the spiritual principle of cause and effect; the intent and actions of an individual influence the future of that individual. In popular conversation we say, "What goes around comes around." Every religious tradition shares a similar "golden rule." Christianity teaches us that "We reap what we sow," and "Live by the sword, die by the sword." Likewise, "Do unto others as you would have them do unto you."

Of course, we are accustomed to thinking of karma and golden rules in exclusively human terms, but the time has come to update our notion of "others" to include habitat—plants, animals, soils, water, and atmosphere: "Do unto the Earth as you would have the Earth do unto you." Or, as Wendell Berry put it, "Do unto those downstream as you would have those upstream do unto you."

Sapience is also patient. Intelligence is relentless in its quest for power and control, but wisdom takes all the time it needs. Sapience understands the value of restraint, persistence, and the long game. Never impulsive, never hurried, wisdom understands that ambiguity is our constant companion. There's no need to rush after certainty; when faced with a marshmallow and the promise of more to come after a wait, wisdom takes its time. The marshmallow will come in due course, and if not, that's okay too.

While intelligence strives inexorably toward its chosen end, wisdom honors means. The quality of the journey shapes the destination; the *how* is vital. As Mahatma Gandhi put it, ends and means are inseparable: "Realization of the goal is in exact proportion to that of the means... As the means, so the end." Likewise, Aldous Huxley: "Good ends, as I have frequently to point out, can be achieved only by the employment of appropriate means. The end cannot justify the means, for the simple and obvious reason that the means employed determine the nature of the ends produced."

Finally, wisdom is inclusive. Conservationist Aldo Leopold suggested that the maturity of humanity would be marked by an expansion of the sphere of our moral concern. The process begins by including all people, then extends to nonhuman animals, habitat, and so on. Naturally, this widening circle of inclusion leads to a sense of compassion for all. We're all in this mismatched predicament together. We all came from LUCA, the same common ancestor. Everyone's body is ancient, and everyone is struggling to adapt. No one really knows how to manage this strange and unprecedented world, so have patience with yourself and those around you. Be kind to your kind, which is to say, all living things.

All of these qualities may sound exotic or unattainable, but in another sense, they're really quite familiar and not at all beyond our grasp. Every day, we stumble and adjust, learn life's lessons, and move, sometimes with barely perceptible progress, toward a wiser, more mature way of being in the world. The path lies in experience, especially by way of our errors, our awkwardness, our disasters, and our suffering. As with every human aptitude, we get better with practice. We get better at sapience by practicing the very qualities that define it: interdependence, proportion, modesty, humility, patience, kindness, and compassion. Like every art, sport, and discipline, the "secret" is no secret at all. Practice is perfect.

BIG IMPERMANENCE

Ultimately, our quest for sapience brings us face-to-face with the elephant in our lives: impermanence. All things come and go; everything arises and fades away. Just when life starts to make sense, everything changes. We are fragile beings in a temporary world.

Naturally, we try to paper over this reality with all manner of cognitive gymnastics, ideologies, achievements, and possessions that promise to give us the permanence we seek. But in times of crisis, we're confronted by the fleeting nature of our lives, our health, our loved ones, and our work. And in these times, some of us find solace in the teachings of the Buddha, and in particular, the first Noble Truth.

Sometimes translated as "All life is suffering," it's better understood as "All is impermanent and therefore unsatisfactory." No matter what we do, we'll eventually lose our possessions, our friends, our families, and our health. It's all going away. As the Buddhist writer Pico Iyer put it, "loss is the law of life." In this sense, the path to peace lies in honoring and respecting impermanence and relinquishing our attachment. If we can let go, we can transcend our suffering.

This sounds right, and yes, with reflection we can even manage it on good days. Yes, we'll admit, our bodies will break down, our loved ones will pass away, and death is on the calendar. With some practice, we can breathe, relax, and come to peace with our inevitable demise. But there's another layer to our suffering that seems more problematic. It's one thing to accept our personal impermanence, but the death of the biosphere and the human species feels like an entirely different proposition. The looming destruction of species, ecosystems, and entire populations haunts us at a whole new level. It's not just our personal suffering and death anymore; it's the very fabric of life that's at stake. We may well be living on a planet without a habitable future.

The Buddha was a supremely astute observer of the human condition, but even he would have been shocked to learn the magnitude and pace of modern ecological collapse. He would have been taken aback by reports of climate change, hothouse Earth, ecological overshoot, and the sixth extinction. But then, after a period of reflection, he would have nodded with equanimity. "Yes, of course it would be so. All that striving for permanence could only lead to a deeper and more profound predicament. Are you not surprised? It's your fear and your continual striving for permanence that is making your world ever more insecure."

Which brings us around again to the crux of the matter—our insistent, fearful, and often compulsive drive for security, especially in the New Way. If we're ever to become sapient, we must understand the seductions of security and honor the fact that impermanence is woven into the fabric of biology and even the cosmos at large. Attempts to achieve ultimate security always backfire.

In the Old Way, impermanence is considered obvious and even unremarkable. Paleolithic people saw the waxing and waning of human and animal life right out in the open every day. But in the New Way, death is scarcely observed and often denied. It's hidden away in hospitals and rarely talked about. It's no wonder many of us suppose we can beat the game.

The foundational mistake of Western culture is to believe ambiguity is a solvable problem that can and should be fixed. Just get the right education, the good job, and a great partner, and all will be well. Exercise really hard and eat all the right foods and you'll never succumb to disease or aging. But it's all delusion. No amount of education, technology, wealth, exercise, or social status will insulate us from the uncertainty that's woven into life. Insecurity is our reality, and there can be no escape. Nothing is truly sustainable. Impermanence, in other words, is permanent.

Zen philosopher Alan Watts understood this clearly:

There is a contradiction in our desire to be secure in a universe whose very nature is fluidity and movement … If I want to be secure, that is, protected from the flux of life, I am wanting to be separate from life. Yet, it is this very sense of separateness that makes me feel insecure. In other words, the more security I can get, the more I shall want …

Sapience lies in embracing the tenuous quality of all life. Even planets and stars have a lifespan, and for all we know, the Universe itself may have its own kind of birth and death. In this, wisdom calls us to a deeper level of acceptance. Yes, let's relinquish our personal attachments and get comfortable with our losses and inevitable death, but don't stop there. Our species and life as we know it might well be in the process of decline, even death. All those magnificent creatures and glorious habitats that have inspired us to wonder, they're just as impermanent as our own bodies. It's a painful realization, and we are right to fight it, but sapience calls us to understanding as well. We will fight this fight, and we may well lose. The biosphere and even the earth itself is impermanent. Take a breath. This is our reality.

LEADERSHIP AND ELDERSHIP

The eyes of the future are looking back at us and they are praying for us to see beyond our own time.

—Terry Tempest Williams

Sapience does not arise from a vacuum. It's a product of our history, our culture, our failures, and the leadership of our elders. In traditional cultures, this much is taken as obvious, but in the modern world, there's something seriously amiss with our narrative about aging and seniority. Everyone knows the prevailing narrative–aging is one long, depressing decline into degeneration, illness, and loneliness. Certain events are said to be inevitable: decreased physical and cognitive function, massive medical bills and possible bankruptcy, neurological meltdown, and perhaps worst of all, social and cultural irrelevance. In short, getting older is a disaster to be avoided by any means possible.

The outlook is grim, so we medicalize the process. We treat aging like a disease and conjure up all manner of treatments to slow, stop, or reverse the process. Gripped by anxiety, we promote the virtues of "healthy aging." Experts tell us how to stop the clock, reverse the damage, delay the onset, and dampen the symptoms. In short, aging is a disaster to be avoided at all costs. In the process, time becomes our enemy.

But the personal, social, and cultural consequences of this narrative are catastrophic. Not only does it make us increasingly miserable and fearful as time goes by, it also drives the widespread practice of ageism. We begin to see seniors as nothing more than a drag on society and the economy. Old people are a burden and an inconvenience; they become progressively less valuable to us with every passing moment. Human value, in other words, decreases over time.

Not only does this narrative devalue great swaths of human life, but it also puts us under an insane level of stress. If you believe your best years are your thirties and forties, followed by a progressive decline into illness and irrelevance, the clock is going to be ticking loud and hard. You've got to hurry up and make something happen, because once your body starts slowing down, it's game over. Even worse, you've got to make yourself a pile of money, because once you hit fifty, the medical–industrial complex is going to step in and take most of it away.

Sadly, the modern health and wellness industry is a powerful enabler of this narrative. For every age-related insult to the human body, someone claims to have a solution. Diets and substances galore, exercise programs for every ailment, exotic treatments of every description—the list is endless. Magazine covers and websites glorify youth and sell us the promise of eternal life. According to the marketing pitch, aging is not inevitable; it's simply the failure to buy the right products and services.

But in the context of human history, today's narrative is profoundly abnormal. In the Paleolithic, tribal survival was highly dependent on the experience, knowledge, and wisdom of the elders. The old ones had participated in many hunts and observed the waxing and waning of animal life; they'd seen the tribe suffer and flourish through good times and bad. In this precarious world, their words carried enormous weight. As keepers of vital knowledge, they were the most valuable and respected members of the community. In the Paleolithic world, human value actually increased over time. This is why Native Americans still say, "When an elder dies, a library burns."

Tragically, we are the first culture in human history to devalue its elders, the first culture in history to reject the very people who might help us choose the best path forward. To make progress, it's essential to turn this narrative around, but where shall we begin?

An obvious first step would be to give up our obsession with youth and start taking responsibility for our role as elders-in-training. This means learning the ways of the world and sharing our knowledge with those within our reach. It is not acceptable to simply long for an easy retirement on the golf course. We must step up.

In the Old Way, the elders were fully aware of their role. Experience in wild outdoor environments made it clear: the primary why of the elder was to act on behalf of the tribe, to share their knowledge, to give away their insights so the tribe could live another day, another year. There would have been no thought of retirement, no notion of self-pampering or hoarding. For the Paleolithic senior citizen, the primal directive was simple: give away your knowledge so the tribe can live.

Seen in this light, our modern practice of hoarding and mone-tizing knowledge seems particularly perverse. Instead of giving our knowledge away to help the next generation survive, we do what-ever we can to profit by it. In a Paleo society, such a practice would be considered profoundly antisocial and even immoral. To hoard knowledge when the tribe might benefit from it is very close to be-ing criminal.

In this respect, the tribal elder is the ultimate servant leader. As she looks out at the grassland, she sees the immensity of her habitat. She feels the exposure and knows how hard it is just to stay alive. She worries about the state of her people and what it will take to keep them happy. Has she done all she can to help them navigate the world? Do the young hunters know all they need to know about the ways of the animals, the weather, and the threats from neighboring tribes? What else must she teach before she makes the great journey?

As a servant leader, the tribal elder understands her health in a unique way, one that may come as a surprise to modern ears. In to-day's youth-oriented culture, we're constantly bombarded with mes-sages, products, and services designed to keep us forever young. Heeding this call, we begin to do everything possible to maximize our individual health. We focus on ourselves, our training, our prac-tices, our bodies. We hoard our health, intent on keeping it as long as humanly possible.

But this strikes the tribal elder as a step in the wrong direction. Instead, the real purpose of health is to give it away. Give it away to the tribe and your loved ones so they can carry on. Give it away so that the people might thrive. Of course your body will start to decay. Of course you will die. But by giving her health to the world, the el-der fulfills her role and her purpose. What else is health for, if not to spend it on the people and causes that need it? Hoarding one's health is the ultimate foolishness.

Being a tribal elder is no easy path, of course. The problem is that

you're not going to be rewarded for your efforts, not in a conventional sense, and almost certainly not in your lifetime. The events you set
in motion today might take a long time to play out, and successful
outcomes won't materialize for years, decades, or maybe even centuries. In this sense, you're working for people who aren't even alive yet.
The seeds you plant today may not germinate for a hundred years.
Your seventh-generation descendants may ultimately celebrate your
efforts, but you won't be around to enjoy the rewards.

Obviously, this is a perspective that will take some getting used to.
In our conventional, modern lives, we expect to receive our rewards
in what might be called "a timely manner." After all, we've been
raised in a culture that's saturated with carrots and sticks, a point
made famous by educator Alfie Kohn in *Punished by Rewards*. As
Kohn tells it, most of us have been trained not just *for* rewards, but *by*
rewards. In other words, we've been conditioned first and foremost
to chase incentives and avoid punishments. In almost every setting,
from grade school to the corporate workplace, the basic instruction
is always the same: "Do this and you'll get that." If we adopt this as
our governing principle for living, life becomes little more than a
mindless exercise in stimulus-response.

But things are different when you're working for the seventh generation. You're working hard to sustain the tribe and the future of
our blue-green world, but you're almost certainly not going to be
rewarded in your lifetime. You're not going to earn a big salary, and
even more likely, you're going to be paying out of pocket for transportation, meals, lodging, and everything else that needs to happen.
If you're firmly attached to a big, immediate payoff, you're going to
be unhappy.

Environmental and social activism means sacrificing big chunks
of your life for people you will probably never meet, people who will
never be able to thank you. In other words, the activist's art is highly
speculative. In rational, economic terms, it is folly. Who would invest

in an outcome they will never see or experience?

But activism is not rational economics. It's something deeper and more powerful. And in this domain, sacrificing for a distant, tribal good isn't folly; it's an act of sapience. Giving one's life for downstream improvement not only feeds the greater good, it also makes us happier and healthier as individuals in this lifetime. The way to be healthier, in other words, is to give your health away.

If you're looking for a quick payoff, you're in the wrong line of work. If you're hoping for some kind of tangible reward in this lifetime, you're going to be disappointed. Instead, take your sense of satisfaction directly from the activity itself and from the meaning it holds. In other words, connect with the intrinsic pleasures that come with activism: working with people, organizing, creating curriculum, and crafting narratives. It's a tough gig, but that's just the way it is when you're working for the future. Big, audacious goals require a long view. As American theologian Reinhold Neibuhr put it, "Nothing that is worth doing can be achieved in our lifetime."

Ultimately, the effort is worth it. The beauty of getting older is that it gives us perspective. We give up some of our strength, endurance, and vitality, but we also begin to see the world with a far deeper clarity. In fact, growing older is not unlike the process by which our vision adapts to darkness. Think back to the last time you camped out in a remote area. You've probably noticed that, once you step out of your tent and into the night air, it usually takes some time to really see the stars. According to experienced star watchers and astronomers, the real clarity of vision doesn't come for an hour or more. But with this adaptation comes a better view, sharper detail, better focus, and above all, a greater appreciation of depth. Subtle features and relationships are revealed.

Turning to another metaphor, growing older is very much like climbing a mountain. With each passing day, the air gets thinner and the steps more difficult, but we're rewarded with a better view of our habitat and our lives. In time, higher altitude gives us vital perspective on our lives and the human predicament.

Nonetheless, being a tribal elder is no easy matter. Conditions are often wicked, and tough decisions and judgment calls must be made, usually with incomplete information. Along the way, you'll sometimes falter and mislead your people. You'll misjudge your habitat and the capabilities of your hunters. You'll be strong when you should have been adaptable. You'll be flexible when you should have been assertive. On occasion, you'll communicate poorly and mix your messages. New information might even reveal you've been moving in the wrong direction entirely. All of this is quite inevitable, but no matter how difficult the situation, you can lead with a spirit that's sincere, curious, and compassionate. You can maintain your focus on health, sapience, and a blue-green future. The seventh generation will forgive your screw-ups, your missteps, and your awkwardness, and they'll remember the dignity, effort, and sincerity you brought to the process.

FIGHT FOR LIFE

In the end, we stand on the brink, face to face with the epic challenges of mismatch and the looming prospect of radically disruptive change. We'd like to be good ancestors, but darkness is gathering and it's becoming increasingly difficult to know what's right. Our future is uncertain, and it's impossible to say with any confidence how our lives will play out. Very soon, we'll be called upon to live in new ways and dig deep for capabilities we may well have forgotten. Our bodies, our spirits, and our culture are going to be challenged in ways we can scarcely imagine.

In this new world, we'll be pulled in many directions simultaneously. We may find ourselves leaning toward intense engagement, inspired by a sense of frustration and outrage over what we're doing to this beautiful world. Or, we may be tempted to withdraw into a personal quest for peace, calm, and integration. But neither of these paths can work in isolation. In fact, it is precisely by holding both these potentials together that we will find a way forward.

In this sense, our predicament calls for a hybrid spirit, an ambidextrous style of living that's sometimes described as "equipoise." It's a common theme in the martial art world, where teachers speak of calm in the midst of chaos, of relaxation that actually deepens in the face of outrageous challenge. In the world of snowboarding and extreme sports, athletes describe this way of being as "tight–loose." Instead of leaning toward a single quality of spirit and action, we look for increased intensity on both sides. As the action becomes more challenging, we become even more relaxed.

This is a both–and approach to life and the world. Call it a spirit of focused equanimity or peaceful intensity. In this art, we become increasingly calm *and* powerful, receptive *and* active. With practice, we learn to rewire our minds, bodies, and spirits in a paradoxical way: as challenge threatens to divide us, we respond by becoming more focused and more peaceful.

The beauty of this equipoise model is that it shows us a way to be whole. For the beginner, fighting is stressful and disintegrating. Opponents attack our weaknesses and exploit our vulnerabilities, and the challenge drives us to pieces. But as we gain experience in the world, we learn to use the stress as an integrator and an asset. In this way, the fight becomes an essential, unifying experience and the enemy may even become an ally.

And so we fight. We fight for interdependence and planetary health. We fight for habitat and species that have no voice. We fight for our people, which is to say, all people. We fight for healthier narratives and the dignity and sapience of humanity. We fight for the welfare of the seventh generation.

Naturally, there will be days when the weight of reality will seem too onerous to bear and we'll be tempted to withdraw. These will be our moments of truth. Will we buckle in the face of looming climate catastrophe, sea level rise, and hothouse Earth? Will we revert to tribalism, xenophobia, selfishness, and antagonism? Sink into despair, denial, distraction, and depression? Or will we reach down into our reserves of courage and resolve and create something that works?

Whatever happens, go toward meaning and engagement. Look the predicament in the face and put your hope in the most powerful places you can find, especially the adaptability of our bodies, the resilience of the biosphere, and our endless capacity for cultural creativity. Take the broken pieces of our world—our traumas and illnesses, our mistakes and stupidities, the fragmented habitats of our biosphere, and the injustices we inflict upon one another—and create something better. Keep your strength up, heal forward, and keep your eye on the whole.

In this effort, you may lose individual battles, but in a spiritual sense, this is very much beside the point. The value lies not in the outcome, but in the struggle.

In the end, your efforts are sacred. And contagious.

ACKNOWLEDGEMENTS

Writing a book is a profoundly abnormal act. Seen from a Paleo or Old Way perspective, it's completely unnatural. The right hemisphere of the brain generates swarms of overlapping ideas, images, and mythologies, while the left hemisphere tries to beat them into neat, linear sequences. It can be a brutal affair. Long, sedentary hours on the computer, moving ghostly, abstract symbols around in a thousand combinations, all the while hoping one day those combinations will touch another human mind and maybe even transform an entire culture.

On hard days, I felt like I was alone on the edge of the world, typing into the abyss, my left and right hemispheres locked in a pitched battle for supremacy. And on really hard days, my body rebelled and demanded I abandon the keyboard and get back to some kind of authentic, ancestral lifestyle. It was all I could do to keep my butt in the chair.

The good news is that my effort has been amply nourished by a host of friends and allies who supported me in myriad ways and helped me pursue my *why*:

Sam, Beth, Alex, and Travis Forencich, Susan Fahringer, Ray Sylvester, Simeon Schatz, Michael Campi, Susan Prescott and Alan Logan, Pete Karabetis, Michael Zwack, Travis Janeway, Corey Jung, Seby Alary, Steve Myrland, Robert Sapolsky, James O'Keefe, Andrew Heffernan, Steve Laskevitch and Carla Fraga, Kay Turner, Dawni Rae and Alia Joy Shaw

READING

The Secret Life of Your Microbiome: Why Nature and Biodiversity are Essential to Health and Happiness by Susan Prescott and Alan Logan

No is Not Enough by Naomi Klein

The Patterning Instinct: A Cultural History of Humanity's Search for Meaning by Jeremy Lent

The Fall: The Insanity of the Ego in Human History and the Dawning of a New Era by Steve Taylor

The Parable of the Tribes: The Problem of Power in Social Evolution by Andrew Bard Schmookler

Affluence without Abundance: The Disappearing World of the Bushmen by James Suzman

The Story of the Human Body: Evolution, Health and Disease by Daniel Liberman

Punished by Rewards: The Trouble with Gold Stars, Incentive Plans, A's, Praise and Other Bribes by Alfie Kohn

The Earth Has a Soul: C.G. Jung on Nature, Technology and Modern Life, edited by Meredith Sabini

Surviving Survival: The Art and Science of Resilience by Laurence Gonzales

Beautiful Trouble: A Toolbox for Revolution, assembled by Andrew Boyd

The Monkeywrench Gang by Edward Abbey

Crazy Like Us: The Globalization of the American Psyche by Ethan Watters

Medical Nemesis by Ivan Illich

Narrative Medicine: The Use of History and Story in the Healing Process by Lewis Mehl–Madrona

Sapiens: A Brief History of Humankind by Yuval Noah Harari

The Upside of Stress: Why Stress Is Good For You And How To Get Good At It by Kelly McGonigal

Spark: The Revolutionary New Science of Exercise and the Brain by John Ratey

The Old Way: A Story of the First People by Elizabeth Marshall Thomas

Why Zebras Don't Get Ulcers: The Acclaimed Guide to Stress, Stress-Related Diseases and Coping, Third Edition by Robert Sapolsky

Ecopsychology: Restoring the Earth, Healing the Mind edited by Theodore Roszak

The Spirit Catches You and You Fall Down: A Hmong Child, Her American Doctors, and the Collision of Two Cultures by Anne Fadiman

When the Body Says No: The Cost of Hidden Stress by Gabor Maté

Man's Search for Meaning by Viktor Frankl

The Wisdom of Insecurity by Alan Watts

Being Wrong: Adventures in the Margin of Error by Kathryn Schulz

The Cure Within: A History of Mind–Body Medicine by Anne Harrington

The Aims of Education and other essays by Alfred North Whitehead

Curious: The Desire to Know and Why Your Future Depends on It by Ian Leslie

The Voice of the Earth: An Exploration of Ecopsychology by Theodore Roszak

Behave: The Biology of Humans at Our Best and Worst by Robert Sapolsky

The Rights of Nature: A History of Environmental Ethics by Roderick Frazier Nash

The Healing Path: A Soul Approach to Illness by Marc Ian Barasch

The Globalization of Addiction: A Study in Poverty of the Spirit by Bruce Alexander

A Sand County Almanac by Aldo Leopold

The Geography of Thought: How Asians and Westerners Think Differently ...and Why by Richard Nisbett

The World Until Yesterday: What Can We Learn from Traditional Societies? by Jared Diamond

Resonate: Present Visual Stories the Transform Audiences by Nancy Duarte

Shaman: A Novel of the Ice Age by Kim Stanley Robinson

Molecules of Emotion: The Science Behind Mind–Body Medicine by Candice Pert

The Wise Heart: A Guide to the Universal Teachings of Buddhist Psychology by Jack Kornfield

The Emotional Life of Your Brain by Richard Davidson

Lifting Depression by Kelly Lambert

The Plastic Mind by Sharon Begley

The Status Syndrome: How Social Standing Affects our Health and Longevity by Michael Marmot

A General Theory of Love by Thomas Lewis, Fari Amini and Richard Lannon

Winning the Story Wars by Jonah Sachs

Amusing Ourselves to Death by Neil Postman

The Wisdom of No Escape by Pema Chodron

In Search of Nature by E.O. Wilson

The Myth of Human Supremacy by Derrick Jensen

The End of Night by Paul Bogard

Ecotherapy: Healing with Nature in Mind edited by Linda Buzzell and Craig Chalquist

The Language of the Land: Living Among a Stone-Age People in Africa by James Stephenson

Ego is the Enemy by Ryan Holiday

The Hour Between Dog and Wolf by John Coates

Neither Wolf nor Dog: On Forgotten Roads with an Indian Elder by Kent Nerburn

The Brain that Changes Itself by Norman Doidge

Essentialism: The Disciplined Pursuit of Less by Greg McKeown

Original Wisdom: Stories of an Ancient Way of Knowing by Robert Wolff

Tao te Ching by Lao Tzu

Circle of Life: Traditional Teachings of Native American Elders by James David Audlin (Distant Eagle)

Black Elk Speaks by John Neihardt

The Youngest Science: Notes of a Medicine-Watcher by Lewis Thomas

Rhythms of Life: Biological Clocks that Control the Daily Lives of Every Living Thing by Russel Foster and Leo Kreitzman

Shop Class as Soulcraft: An Inquiry into the Value of Work by Matthew Crawford

The Revenge of the Analog: Real Things and Why They Matter by David Sax

Walking with Cavemen by John Lynch and Louise Barrett

Journey from the Dawn: Life with the World's First Family by Donald Johanson and Kevin O'Farrell

The Neuroscience of Human Relationships: Attachment and the Developing Social Brain by Louis Cozolino

Meaning, Medicine and the 'Placebo Effect' by Daniel Moerman

The Happiness Hypothesis: Finding Modern Truth in Ancient Wisdom by Jonathan Haidt

Flow: The Psychology of Optimal Experience by Mihaly Csikszentmihalyi

The Art of Worldly Wisdom by Baltasar Gracián

Lives of a Cell by Lewis Thomas

Wisdom of the Elders by David Suzuki and Peter Knudtsom

Chuang Tzu: basic writings by Burton Watson (translator)

The Omnivore's Dilemma: A Natural History of Four Meals by Michael Pollan

Counterclockwise: Mindful Health and the Power of Possibility by Ellen J. Langer

When Things Fall Apart: Heart Advice for Difficult Times by Pema Chodron

Our Inner Ape: A Leading Primatologist Explains Why We Are Who We Are by Frans de Waal

Ishi: In Two Worlds by Theodora Kroeber

Deep Survival: Who Lives, Who Dies, and Why by Laurence Gonzales

Mindset: The New Psychology of Success by Carol Dweck

Zoobiquity: What Animals Can Teach Us About Health and the Science of Healing by Barbara Patterson–Horowitz

The Powerful Placebo: From Ancient Priest to Modern Physician by Arthur Shapiro and Elaine Shapiro

The Placebo Effect: An Interdisciplinary Exploration edited by Anne Harrington

Placebo: Mind Over Matter in Modern Medicine by Dylan Evans

Original Instructions: Indigenous Teachings for a Sustainable Future edited by Melissa Nelson

The Practice of the Wild by Gary Snyder

The Power of Story by Jim Loehr

Rapt: Attention and the Focused Life by Winifred Gallagher

The Master and His Emissary: The Divided Brain and the Making of the Western World by Iain McGilchrist

Connected: How Your Friends' Friends' Friends Affect Everything You Feel, Think, and Do by Nicholas Christakis and James Fowler

The Power of Myth by Joseph Campbell

The Genius in All of Us: Why Everything You've Been Told About Genetics, Talent, and IQ is Wrong by David Shenk

The Last Hours of Ancient Sunlight: The Fate of the World and What We Can Do About It Before It's Too Late by Thom Hartmann

Dreamkeepers: A Spirit-Journey into Aboriginal Australia by Harvey Arden

Red Alert: Saving the Planet with Indigenous Knowledge by Daniel R. Wildcat

The Storytelling Animal: How Stories Make Us Human by Jonathan Gottschall

Descartes' Error: Emotion, Reason, and the Human Brain by Antonio Damasio

Mismatch: Why Our World No Longer Fits Our Bodies by Peter Gluckman and Mark Hanson

The Lab Rat Chronicles: A Neuroscientist Reveals Life Lessons from the Planet's Most Successful Mammals by Kelly Lambert

The Illness Narratives: Suffering, Healing and the Human Condition by Arthur Kleinman

Wisdomkeepers: Meetings With Native American Spiritual Elders by Steve Wall and Harvey Arden

A New Green History of the World: The Environment and the Collapse of Great Civilizations by Clive Ponting

My Name is Chellis and I'm in Recovery From Western Civilization by Chellis Glendinning

Ecological Intelligence: Rediscovering Ourselves in Nature by Ian McCallum

Full Catastrophe Living: Using the Wisdom of the Body and Mind to Face Stress, Pain, and Illness by Jon Kabat–Zinn

Go Wild: Free Your Body and Mind From the Afflictions of Civilization by John Ratey MD and Richard Manning

Ubuntu: I in You and You in Me by Michael Battle

RECOMMENDED AUDIO

Tribe: On Homecoming and Belonging by Sebastian Junger

Biology and Human Behavior: The Neurological Origins of Individuality, 2nd Edition by Robert Sapolsky

Big History: The Big Bang, Life on Earth, and the Rise of Humanity by David Christian

The Neurobiology of "We" by Daniel J. Siegel, M.D.

NOTABLE ORGANIZATIONS

American Public Health Association: https://apha.org

The Wildlands Network: https://wildlandsnetwork.org

Ancestral Health Society: https://ancestralhealth.org

The Yes Men: http://theyesmen.org

The Action Switchboard: https://actionswitchboard.net

Stand for Trees: https://standfortrees.org

Global Witness: https://www.globalwitness.org/en/

Center for Media and Social Impact: http://cmsimpact.org/program/comedy/

The Leap: https://theleap.org

The Liology Institute: http://www.liology.org

Idle No More: http://www.idlenomore.ca

Avaaz: https://secure.avaaz.org/page/en/

Artists Project Earth: http://apeuk.org/about-ape/

Center for Humans and Nature: https://www.humansandnature.org

Occupy: https://www.occupy.com

Survival International: https://www.survivalinternational.org

Global Alliance for the Rights of Nature: https://therightsofnature.org

International Center for the Rights of Nature: https://celdf.org/rights/rights-of-nature/

Fertile Ground Institute: http://www.fertilegroundinstitute.org

RAVEN: Respecting Aboriginal Values and Environmental Needs: https://raventrust.com

Art for the Sky: http://www.artforthesky.com

Oil Sands Truth: http://oilsandstruth.org

Stand: https://www.stand.earth

Global Health Institute: http://ghi.wisc.edu

Promise of Place: promoting place-based education: http://www.promiseofplace.org

Thomas Berry Foundation: http://thomasberry.org

Emerging Earth Community: http://emergingearthcommunity.org

Ashoka: https://www.ashoka.org

Local futures: https://www.localfutures.org

Actipedia: https://actipedia.org

YesLab: http://yeslab.org

Physicians for Social Responsibility: http://www.psr.org

Center for Story-based Strategy: https://www.storybasedstrategy.org

The Center for Artistic Activism: https://artisticactivism.org

International league of conservation photographers: https://conservationphotographers.org

Environmental defense fund: https://www.edf.org

Earth charter: http://earthcharter.org

Conservation international: http://www.conservation.org

Indigenous environmental network: http://www.ienearth.org

Doctors without borders: http://www.doctorswithoutborders.org

Center for biological diversity: http://www.biologicaldiversity.org

Earth first!: http://www.earthfirst.org

Beautiful trouble: http://beautifultrouble.org

Sea Shepherd Conservation society: http://www.seashepherd.org

Leonardo Dicaprio foundation: http://leonardodicaprio.org

Adbusters: http://www.adbusters.org

The Millennium Alliance for Humanity and the Biosphere: https://mahb.stanford.edu

The Ecological Citizen: http://www.ecologicalcitizen.net

The Ecocentric Alliance: http://ecocentricalliance.org

Planetary Health Alliance: https://planetaryhealthalliance.org

Global Alliance for the Rights of Nature: http://therightsofnature.org

One Health: https://www.onehealthcommission.org

InVivo Network for Planetary Health: https://www.invivonetwork.com

The International Dark Sky Association: http://darksky.org

Mission LifeForce: https://www.missionlifeforce.org

Women's Earth Alliance: http://womensearthalliance.org

350.org: https://350.org

Corporate Accountability: https://www.corporateaccountability.org

NOTES

CHAPTER 1: PREDICAMENT

1 See *Beyond Hope: Letting Go of a World in Collapse* by Deb Ozarko

2 https://www.ncbi.nlm.nih.gov/pubmed/25889196

3 https://e360.yale.edu/digest/antarctic-ice-loss-has-tripled-since-2012

4 http://www.bbc.com/news/world-42982959

5 http://www.nationalacademies.org/hmd/Reports/2011/Reliev-ing-Pain-in-America-A-Blueprint-for-Transforming-Prevention-Care-Educa-tion-Research.aspx

6 https://www.nytimes.com/2014/08/22/health/vicodin-prescrip-tion-drug-abuse-hydrocodone.html

7 https://www.cdc.gov/media/releases/2016/p1216-continuing-opioid-epidemic.html

8 https://www.npr.org/sections/health-shots/2018/05/01/606588504/americans-are-a-lonely-lot-and-young-people-bear-the-heaviest-burden

9 https://www.edelman.com/post/america-in-crisis

10 See also https://www.nytimes.com/2018/05/28/opinion/fear-mistrust-in-pub-lic-space.html

11 http://www.who.int/mediacentre/news/releases/2017/world-health-day/en/

12 https://www.theguardian.com/news/2018/jun/04/what-is-depression-and-why-is-it-rising

13 Centers for Disease Control "Suicide rising across the US" https://www.cdc.gov/vitalsigns/suicide/)

14 https://www.psychologytoday.com/blog/theory-knowledge/201402/the-col-lege-student-mental-health-crisis

http://www.nytimes.com/2016/09/19/opinion/drinking-to-blackout.html

15 https://www.npr.org/sections/health-shots/2018/06/07/617897261/cdc-u-s-suicide-rates-have-climbed-dramatically

16 See https://www.nytimes.com/interactive/2018/08/01/magazine/climate-change-losing-earth.html

17 https://media.csuchico.edu/media/0_2ljujwjg

18 https://www.newscientist.com/article/2176006-global-warming-may-be-come-unstoppable-even-if-we-stick-to-paris-target/

19 http://www.slate.com/blogs/future_tense/2014/03/30/ipcc_2014_u_n_climate_change_report_warns_of_dire_consequences.html New U.N. Report: Climate Change Risks Destabilizing Human Society

"The Intergovernmental Panel on Climate Change's report—which was seven years in the making … linked the changing climate with the destabilization of nation states. It is also increasingly confident of serious effects on food crops, water supplies, and human health, plus global species loss … The entire 44 page summary was agreed to line-by-line by scientists and political representatives from more than 110 governments… "

CHAPTER 2: ANCESTRY

20 https://www.newscientist.com/article/2177334-life-may-have-begun-on-earth-100-million-years-earlier-than-we-thought/

21 https://en.wikiquote.org/wiki/Rachel_Carson#Quotes

22 Most notably *The Old Way: A Story of the First People* by Elizabeth Marshall Thomas

23https://www.npr.org/sections/thetwo-way/2018/04/19/604031141/new-study-says-ancient-humans-hunted-big-mammals-to-extinction

24 https://www.firstpeople.us/articles/Black-Elk-Speaks/Black-Elk-Speaks-At-First-Cure.html

25 See *The Art Is Long* by Frank Forencich

26 https://en.wikipedia.org/wiki/Vimalakirti

27 *The Earth Has a Soul: C.G. Jung on Nature, Technology and Modern Life*, edited by Meredith Sabini, p. 155

28 https://www.chausa.org/docs/default-source/health-progress/a-new-era-pdf.pdf

29 *Confessions of an Eco-Warrior* by Dave Foreman

30 https://www.newscientist.com/article/mg23931940-100-the-me-illusion-how-your-brain-conjures-up-your-sense-of-self/

31 See *Wild Law: A Manifesto for Earth Justice* by Cormac Cullinan and Thomas Berry

32 Attributed to Poka Laenui, one of the leading voices for Hawaiian independence, a radio host, attorney, and an international advocate of indigenous

peoples recognized for his work at the United Nations.

http://mooaupuni.org/wp-content/uploads/2015/01/DIE-OLA.pdf

33 https://jphysiolanthropol.biomedcentral.com/articles/10.1186/s40101-018-0176-8

34 http://www.mdpi.com/2078-1547/8/2/19

35 See also https://www.motherjones.com/politics/2018/06/the-messy-universe-inside-plants-looks-a-lot-like-the-messy-universe-inside-people/

36 https://www.wnycstudios.org/story/from-tree-to-shining-tree/

CHAPTER 3: BODY

37 *Connected: The Surprising Power of Our Social Networks and How They Shape Our Lives* by Nicholas Christakis and James Fowler

38 https://news.yale.edu/2008/10/23/hot-coffee-we-see-warm-heart-yale-researchers-find

http://science.sciencemag.org/content/328/5986/1712

39 https://www.nytimes.com/2018/06/11/books/review/strange-order-of-things-antonio-damasio.html

40 https://seeingthemeaning.wordpress.com/theory/theories-of-cognition/

41 https://jamanetwork.com/journals/jamapsychiatry/article-abstract/2680311

42 https://www.politico.com/agenda/story/2017/09/13/food-nutrients-carbon-dioxide-000511

43 https://www.nytimes.com/2018/02/20/well/eat/counting-calories-weight-loss-diet-dieting-low-carb-low-fat.html

https://jamanetwork.com/journals/jama/article-abstract/2673150

44 https://www.newscientist.com/article/2168584-eating-all-your-meals-before-3pm-could-be-good-for-your-health/

45 See *The Old Way: A Story of the First People* by Elizabeth Marshall Thomas

46 https://www.amazingscience.news/2017/09/humans-jellyfish-are-the-same-they-both-need-sleep/

47 http://advances.sciencemag.org/content/2/6/e1600377https://www.ncbi.nlm.nih.gov/pubmed/27386582

48 https://www.nytimes.com/2018/08/21/health/sleep-productivity-economy.html

49 https://www.newscientist.com/article/2177638-one-bad-nights-sleep-can-make-you-put-on-fat-and-lose-muscle-mass/

50 https://www.ncbi.nlm.nih.gov/pubmed/28810072

51 https://physoc.onlinelibrary.wiley.com/doi/10.14814/phy2.13692

52 https://www.newscientist.com/article/mg23931873-300-weve-started-to-un-cover-the-true-purpose-of-dreams

53http://www.ted.com/talks/jeff_iliff_one_more_reason_to_get_a_good_night_s_sleep

54 https://www.medicalnewstoday.com/articles/319425.php

55 See *Original Wisdom* by Robert Wolff

CHAPTER 4: HABITAT

56 See https://www.utne.com/community/ecopornexposed#axzz2VGjjIUPW

57 http://connection.ebscohost.com/c/articles/55442889/whos-oddball

58 See *Affluence Without Abundance: The Disappearing World of the Bushmen* by James Suzman

59 Woodcock & Custovic, 1998

60 https://www.nytimes.com/2018/02/19/science/migration-animals-west.html

61 In 1998, the philosophers and cognitive scientists Andy Clark and David J. Chalmers wrote the landmark paper "The Extended Mind." The mind, they argued, has no reason to stop at the outermost layer of skin.

http://consc.net/papers/extended.html

https://www.theatlantic.com/science/archive/2017/10/extended-embodied-cognition/542808/

62 http://www.matthewckeller.com/Keller_PsySci_2005.pdf

63 https://www.npr.org/sections/health-shots/2018/07/16/628521596/heat-making-you-lethargic-research-shows-it-can-slow-your-brain-too

64 http://discovermagazine.com/2005/aug/desert-people

65 https://www.politico.com/agenda/story/2017/09/13/food-nutrients-carbon-dioxide-000511

66 https://www.theatlantic.com/science/archive/2017/12/data-from-11-million-infants-suggests-fracking-harms-human-health/548315/

https://www.rollingstone.com/politics/news/fracking-health-risk-asthma-birth-defects-cancer-w517809

67 https://www.npr.org/2018/08/27/642321572/scientists-link-air-pollution-exposure-to-cognitive-decline

68 https://www.theatlantic.com/health/archive/2018/07/a-frightening-new-reason-to-worry-about-air-pollution/564428/

69 https://www.theguardian.com/environment/2018/jul/23/rising-temperatures-linked-to-increased-suicide-rates

70 See http://journals.sagepub.com/doi/abs/10.1177/0013916509341244

71 https://www.sciencedirect.com/science/article/pii/S0013935118303323

72 http://www.mdpi.com/1660-4601/15/6/1248http://mdpi.com/1660-4601/15/6/1248

73 https://www.ncbi.nlm.nih.gov/pubmed/6143402

74 "Pretty, J. "The greening of healthcare." New Scientist. 2007; 32

75 See also http://science.sciencemag.org/content/333/6043/776

"The Internet has become a primary form of external or transactive memory, where information is stored collectively outside ourselves."

76 See *The Art of Tracking: The Origin of Science* by Louis Liebenberg

77 https://www.scientificamerican.com/article/how-awe-stops-the-clock/

78 https://www.nytimes.com/2015/05/24/opinion/sunday/why-do-we-experience-awe.html

https://www.newscientist.com/article/mg23531360-400-awesome-awe-the-emotion-that-gives-us-superpowers/

https://www.youtube.com/watch?v=ysAJQycTw-0

https://www.youtube.com/watch?v=uW8h3JIMmVQ

https://www.youtube.com/watch?v=ysAJQycTw-0

CHAPTER 5: TRIBE

79 See *Becoming Attached: First Relationships and How They Shape Our Capacity to Love* by Robert Karen

80 See the New School for Social Research: http://www.newschool.edu/nssr/centers-special-programs/?id=104444

See also http://www.nytimes.com/2017/01/07/opinion/sunday/yes-its-your-parents-fault.html

81 https://link.springer.com/article/10.1007/s10919-013-0168-7

82 https://www.nytimes.com/2018/04/16/science/friendship-brain-health.html

83 "Dancing really DOES breaks the ice: Children who dance together feel more connected" DailyMail.com June 16, 2016 https://www.dailymail.co.uk/science-

tech/article-3645221/Dancing-really-DOES-breaks-ice-Children-dance-feel-connected.html

84 https://www.theguardian.com/lifeandstyle/2018/jul/16/a-bad-marriage-is-as-unhealthy-as-smoking-or-drinking-say-scientists

85 http://www.scn.ucla.edu/pdf/RT424X_C07-1.pdf

86 https://www.sciencedirect.com/science/article/abs/pii/S0031938416305583

87 https://www.newscientist.com/article/2170073-dentists-can-smell-your-fear-and-it-may-put-your-teeth-at-risk

88 https://www.sciencedaily.com/releases/2018/03/180308143212.htm

89http://onlinelibrary.wiley.com/doi/10.1002/oby.22098/full

90 https://www.ted.com/talks/ tanfo_waldinger_what_makes_a_good_life_lessons_from_the_longest_study_on_happiness

91See Michael Marmot's *The Status Syndrome: How Social Standing Affects Our Health and Longevity*

92 https://www.ncbi.nlm.nih.gov/pubmed/26214169

93 https://www.sciencedirect.com/science/article/pii/S0747563214003227

94 https://www.theguardian.com/commentisfree/2016/oct/12/neoliberalism-creating-loneliness-wrenching-society-apart

CHAPTER 6: ACTION

95 https://en.wikipedia.org/wiki/Artivism

96 More at Culture2 Inc: http://www.culture2inc.com/who-we-are/

97 https://www.newscientist.com/article/mg21628932-100-why-words-are-as-painful-as-sticks-and-stones/

98 http://www.pnas.org/content/early/2010/07/26/1009164107

99 https://www.politico.com/magazine/story/2018/05/27/nfl-national-anthem-protest-colin-kaepernick-trump-administration-218546

100 See the documentary The Reluctant Radical

CHAPTER 7: LIFE

101 https://www.newscientist.com/article/2167003-trees-may-have-a-heartbeat-that-is-so-slow-we-never-noticed-it/

102 https://www.newscientist.com/article/2178556-your-brain-power-varies-throughout-the-year-peaking-in-autumn/

103 https://www.nytimes.com/2018/07/24/well/when-we-eat-or-dont-eat-may-be-critical-for-health.html

104 https://www.newscientist.com/article/2152754-daytime-injuries-heal-twice-as-fast-as-wounds-sustained-at-night/

105 *The Inflamed Mind: A Radical New Approach to Depression* by Edward Bullmore, p. 149

106 https://www.nytimes.com/2018/07/05/well/airline-crew-have-higher-cancer-rates.html

107 See *The Power of Full Engagement* by James E. Loehr and Tony Schwartz

108 http://www.colorado.edu/today/2017/02/01/cant-get-sleep-wilderness-weekend-can-help

109 https://en.wikipedia.org/wiki/Competitive_eating#IFOCE

110 *Bozo Sapiens: Why to Err is Human* by Michael Kaplan and Ellen Kaplan

111 https://daneverettbooks.com/wp-content/uploads/2016/07/HarpersMagazine-2016-08-0086105.pdf

112 https://www.youtube.com/watch?v=oGab38pKscw

https://www.huffingtonpost.com/2013/12/15/psychology-materialism_n_4425982.html

http://www.apa.org/monitor/jun04/discontents.aspx

http://www.apa.org/pubs/books/4317024.aspx

CHAPTER 8: STRESS

113 *Behave: The Biology of Humans at Our Best and Worst* by Robert Sapolsky, p. 132

114 http://journals.sagepub.com/doi/10.1177/0146167212439213

115 For a complete review of the stress research, see Robert Sapolsky's book *Why Zebras Don't Get Ulcers* and his audio series Stress and the Body by The Great Courses

116 *Why Zebras Don't Get Ulcers* by Robert Sapolsky

117 https://www.newscientist.com/article/mg23331100-500-a-meaning-to-life-how-a-sense-of-purpose-can-keep-you-healthy/

118 See also http://www.pnas.org/content/110/33/13684.abstract. This 2013 study led by Barbara Frederickson found that hedonic (pleasure-seeking) orientations were associated with increased expression of pro-inflammatory genes, while eudaimonic (meaning-seeking) orientations were associated with

decreased expression of pro-inflammatory genes.

119See http://www.happinessandwellbeing.org/june-gruber/

120 *The Upside of Stress: Why Stress Is Good for You, and How to Get Good at It* by Kelly McGonigal

CHAPTER 9: MEDICINE

121 https://www.newyorker.com/magazine/2015/05/11/overkill-atul-gawande

122"https://www.nytimes.com/2007/01/02/health/02essa.html

123 https://www.newscientist.com/article/mg19125615-800-time-to-resist-the-illness-industry/

124 "https://www.nytimes.com/2006/05/21/weekinreview/21kolata.html

125 See also http://www.preventingoverdiagnosis.net

126 http://www.mdpi.com/2078-1547/9/1/10/htm

127 https://en.wikipedia.org/wiki/Kludge

"In the Oxford English Dictionary (2nd ed., 1989), the kludge entry cites one source for this word's earliest recorded usage, definition and etymology: Jackson W. Granholm's 1962 'How to Design a Kludge' article, which appeared in the American computer magazine Datamation: kludge: 'An ill-assorted collection of poorly-matching parts, forming a distressing whole' …"

128 https://www.newscientist.com/article/mg23030690-300-in-sync-how-to-take-control-of-your-many-body-clocks/

129 For example, George Engel's biopsychosocial model

130 http://science.sciencemag.org/content/196/4286/129

131http://www.annfammed.org/content/2/6/576.full

132 https://www.cabi.org/cabreviews/FullTextPDF/2017/20173134856.pdf

133 http://www.mdpi.com/2078-1547/9/2/31

134 See "The Canmore Declaration" https://thecanmoredeclaration.weebly.com

135 https://www.nytimes.com/2018/05/28/upshot/it-saves-lives-it-can-save-money-so-why-arent-we-spending-more-on-public-health.html

CHAPTER 10: STORY

136 https://www.nature.com/articles/s41467-017-02036-8

137 http://psycnet.apa.org/doiLanding?doi=10.1037%2Fa0031201

138 https://www.medscape.com/viewarticle/855924

139 https://www.nytimes.com/2018/02/12/upshot/heart-stents-are-useless-for-most-stable-patients-theyre-still-widely-used.html

140 https://www.nytimes.com/2018/02/22/well/move/how-our-beliefs-can-shape-our-waistlines.html

141 https://www.ncbi.nlm.nih.gov/pubmed/28726475

142 http://www.pewresearch.org/fact-tank/2015/05/13/a-closer-look-at-americas-rapidly-growing-religious-nones/

143 *The Myth Gap: What Happens When Evidence and Arguments Aren't Enough* by Alex Evans

144 *Half-Earth: Our Planet's Fight for Life* by E.O. Wilson

145 https://e360.yale.edu/features/should-rivers-have-rights-a-growing-movement-says-its-about-time

146 https://celdf.org/2018/07/press-release-india-court-declares-legal-rights-of-entire-animal-kingdom/

147 *Resonate: Present Visual Stories That Transform Audiences* by Nancy Duarte

148 *Houston, We Have a Narrative: Why Science Needs Story* by Randy Olson

Made in the
USA
Lexington, KY